Slow Living

Slow Living

Wendy Parkins and Geoffrey Craig

Oxford • New York

First published in 2006 by
Berg
Editorial offices:
1st Floor, Angel Court, 81 St Clements Street, Oxford, OX4 1AW, UK
175 Fifth Avenue, New York, NY 10010, USA

Berg is the imprint of Oxford International Publishers Ltd.

Library of Congress Cataloguing-in-Publication Data
Parkins, Wendy.
    Slow living / Wendy Parkins and Geoffrey Craig.
        p. cm.
    Includes bibliographical references and index.
    ISBN-13: 978-1-84520-160-9 (pbk.)
    ISBN-10: 1-84520-160-4 (pbk.)
    ISBN-13: 978-1-84520-159-3 (cloth)
    ISBN-10: 1-84520-159-0 (cloth)
    1. Quality of life. 2. Pleasure. I. Craig, Geoffrey.
II. Title.
    HN18.3.P37 2006
    306.4'81—dc22   2005029981

British Library Cataloguing-in-Publication Data
A catalogue record for this book is available from the British Library.

ISBN-13 978 1 84520 159 3 (Cloth)
ISBN-10 1 84520 159 0 (Cloth)

ISBN-13 978 1 84520 160 9 (Paper)
ISBN-10 1 84520 160 4 (Paper)

Typeset by Avocet Typeset, Chilton, Aylesbury, Bucks
Printed in the United Kingdom by Biddles Ltd, King's Lynn

www.bergpublishers.com

To Madeleine and Gabriel,
for teaching us to slow down.

Contents

Preface and Acknowledgements

In order to write a book on slow living, we logged on to the Slow Food website, emailed people in Europe and the rest of the world we had never met, and transplanted our family, flying from the most remote capital city on earth (Perth, supposedly) to the centre of Western civilization (Rome, supposedly), which took less than twenty hours. During our sabbatical in Italy, we experienced the speeds of autostradas and the longeurs of bureaucracy, the quick espresso and the long lunch. Contradictions? Maybe, maybe not, because slow living, we would argue, is not a counter-cultural retreat from everyday life. Slow living is not a return to the past, the good old days (pre-McDonalds Arcadia), neither is it a form of laziness, nor a slow-motion version of life, nor possible only in romantic locations like Tuscany. Rather, for us, slow living is a process whereby everyday life – in all its pace and complexity, *frisson* and routine – is approached with care and attention, as subjects attempt to negotiate the different temporalities that they daily experience. It is above all an attempt to live in the present in a meaningful, sustainable, thoughtful *and pleasurable* way. Slow living may be particularly evident in certain kinds of practices in everyday life – like walking or cooking, although neither of these are necessarily always done slowly – but it may also be generalized to a wider approach to life. Those who advocate slow practices often suggest that one slow habit leads to another; slowness becomes a preferred mode for the heightened awareness or relaxation it can impart.

This is not, however, a self-help book but rather a speculative consideration of what slow living is, what it may offer, and why it has become evident in a range of everyday practices and broader social impulses. While we explore different facets of slow living, we do not offer a prescription or a check-list of activities that constitute living slowly that everyone should adopt. Rather, we are interested here in exploring and unpacking the concept of slow living across a range of domains – from work and the city to food and politics – because we believe there is a positive potential in slowness as a means of critiquing or challenging dominant narratives or values that characterize contemporary modernity for so many. We argue that slow living assumes a greater importance as the global culture of ever-increasing speed and risk encounters the stubbornness of human and natural limits. We believe, in short, 'the times' are ripe for a serious consideration of slowness.

In our exploration of slow living, we will pay particular attention to the Slow

Food movement, originating in Italy in the 1980s but now with a steadily growing international membership and related media profile.[1] Our approach to Slow Food will not be to offer a detailed quantitative analysis of the movement and organization but to mainly draw on the ideas, writings and philosophies of Slow Food in order to evaluate critically the values and potentials, as well as the tensions and contradictions, bound up with the notion of slow living. That said, our concept of slow living also extends beyond the parameters of Slow Food and is a generalized response to the demands and pressures of 'fast life' of modern western subjects. Slow Food has emerged as an effective means of mobilizing the desire of many to reclaim time and pleasure in their everyday lives, particularly through the significations of food, and it is the *desire* for slowness as much as its achievement that resonates in the concept of slow living. One of the primary attractions of the Slow Food movement emanates from its articulation of the contexts of everyday life with the global food system. The movement has been influential in the formation of our idea of the 'global everyday' where – building upon existing theorizations of global culture and everyday life – we outline the fundamental linkages between everyday practices and values and the global contexts in which we live.

The writing of this book has of course in some ways been an academic exercise. Like Thomas Hylland Eriksen in his fascinating book *The Tyranny of the Moment* (2001), our interest in slowness has been partly motivated by an increasing frustration with the faster pace and growing raft of distractions that characterize contemporary academic life. We have experienced a persistent, if grim, sense of irony that it has always been difficult to find the time to think and write about slowness. In other ways, however, this project has also been more than just an academic exercise for us. As members of Slow Food, we have been personally involved in the challenges and dilemmas as well as the convivial social networks and ethical consumption that the movement offers. In a sense, our research and writing here has been only part of a more general quest to take what opportunities we have to reclaim our time and to build more fulfilling and attentive lives. If the increasing media attention to issues like the difficulties of work/family balance, the growing popularity of yoga and meditation, or the trend towards 'downshifting' is anything to go by, it would seem that we are not alone in looking for alternatives to the frenetic pace of global culture and we hope our work will prompt further analysis of the virtues of slowness and also encourage others to take the slow route.

In thinking through the diverse possibilities of slow living, we are keenly aware of the range of academic disciplines or approaches we traverse in this book, as we consider the implications for our uses and understanding of time, space, food and public life. In the different aspects of slow living we discuss, we have drawn on a range of theories and theorists to elucidate our discussion, within what we see more broadly as a cultural studies' approach to the topic. Again, our intention has been to sketch a broad range of questions and possibilities rather than to provide an exhaustive account of each field we include and we hope the reader will find such an approach suggestive rather than reductive. When we commenced this project – to our knowledge, the first book-length study of Slow Food – there was almost no academic scrutiny of the movement but now it is attracting interest across a range of disciplines, with divergent and sometimes passionate evaluations of its strengths and weaknesses. Slow Food is itself rapidly evolving and responding to new challenges and we believe that the movement needs to be increasingly cognizant of debates, both academic and otherwise, in order to further interrogate its own purposes and activities in the complexities of the global everyday. Our assessment of Slow Food is not uncritical: having experienced the difficulties of applying notions of slowness and ethical consumption at the local level of involvement, we are also aware of the broader, more entrenched problems of sustainability and ethical development in the contexts of global capital. We remain convinced, however, that movements like Slow Food have great potential to 're-make' everyday life in socially transformative ways.

If our exploration of slow living has taken us into a range of disciplinary fields, it has also introduced us to a range of people who have generously bestowed upon us their time, expertise and hospitality, as well as helping us with the many exigencies of everyday life in Italy, Australia and now in New Zealand. Meeting and spending time with these people has been one of the great pleasures of this project.

From our time in Italy we would like to thank Sophie Herron for her invaluable and friendly assistance in Bra and also for help with translation. At Slow Food headquarters we would like to thank Alessandra Abbona, Silvio Barbero, Renato Sardo, Sebastiano Sardo, Cinzia Scaffidi, Franca Chiarle, Anya Fernald and Vittorio Manganelli.

Our warmest thank you to the members of the Bologna Slow Food *condotta* for welcoming the *stranieri* who landed in their city. We would like to especially thank Roberto Ferranti, Renata Ferranti and Elena Bruni who embody the spirit of generosity and hospitality of Slow Food, and who gave us valuable assistance in organizing visits to restaurants, farms and producers in the region. We would also like to thank those farmers, producers, and cooks we visited who gave us their time and insights into their work (and allowed us to eat it, too!). In Orvieto, we thank Mayor Stefano Cimicchi and Massimo Borri, and in Greve-in-Chianti, we thank Mayor Paolo Saturnini and Alessandra Molletti.

Our stay in Italy was made possible by a Senior Visiting Fellowship at the Institute of Advanced Study at the University of Bologna, and for this we especially thank Professor Roberto Scazzieri from Bologna and Professor Roger Griffin from Oxford Brookes University. We would also like to thank the friendly staff at the university's Villa Gandolfi Pallavicini who helped us with everyday life in Italy: 'Signor Ferrante', Antoinetta Uzunova, and Alex Uzunova (for her wonderful babysitting!). We also appreciated the friendliness and collegiality of the other resident scholars at the Villa.

We would like to thank Elena Aniére for her assistance with contacts and her great work while leader of Slow Food Perth and her ongoing assistance now that she is based in Bra. We would also like to thank Ann Meyer, the leader of Slow Food in Western Australia, for her constant encouragement and enthusiasm, Barbara Storey from Barossa Slow, and other Australian convivium leaders that we interviewed there. We also appreciate the feedback of Slow Food Presidia workers around the world who responded to our questions.

At Murdoch University, we thank Associate Professor Gail Phillips, Professor David Hill and Associate Professor Bev Thiele for their support facilitating research leave and grant applications. We jointly received a 2003 REGS research grant from Murdoch University. We would also like to thank our other colleagues, students and friends from Murdoch University and the Centre for Everyday Life, who have put up with us going on about slowness for such a long time! More recently, at the University of Otago in New Zealand we thank Professor Lyn Tribble for her support and understanding in the final preparation of the manuscript.

On the home front, we thank Sian Bennett and Yvonne Kenyon, Graham Rixon from Penrhos College and Hazel Collier from Unicredit. We would also like to thank Mark, Rosemary and Becky Dennison for quite literally giving us the coats off their backs and the shoes off their feet!

An earlier version of parts of Chapter 2 appeared in *Time and Society*, Vol. 13, no. 2/3 (2004), as 'Out of Time: fast subjects and slow living' (pp. 363–82).

Finally, we would like to give a special thank you to Madeleine for her tolerance during *la vita lenta* in Italy, and for being such a tremendous big sister to Gabriel. Despite the attractions of gelato and pizza, it is never easy for kids to be uprooted from their own everyday lives for the sake of their parents' research project. We hope that their memories of the porticoes and *Pace* flags of Bologna remind them that everyday life doesn't have to be routine.

−1−

Slow Living in the Global Everyday

A revolution takes place when and only when ... people can no longer lead their everyday lives.

Henri Lefebvre (1991: 32)

A new relationship between the individual, the local and the global is emerging, and it is here, not in the public realm of governance, that there is a re-evaluation of what an ethics of living might be. ... The individual practice of identity making, of negotiating relationships and defending oneself against the social forces of capital, racism and sexism, is not simply an aesthetic of lifestyle, but the necessary emotional work of everyday life.

Jonathan Rutherford (2000: 66)

The very idea of slow living is provocative. A faster pace of existence, and an increasing 'busy-ness' in the time we have, is a central feature of global culture. While debate continues over whether overall work hours have increased or not in recent decades, complicated by factors such as profession, class and gender (see e.g. Schor 1991; Hochschild 1997; Robinson and Godbey 1997; Green 2001), perceptions of acceleration in daily life are common. Some argue that this perception has in part been created by the dispersion of work hours being concentrated into fewer households (Green 2001), while others single out the increased workforce participation of women, particularly in professional or management roles, as leading to significant 'speedups' in home life to accommodate longer hours spent at work (Runté and Mills 2004: 244). 'Hurry sickness', as a response to the 'acceleration of just about everything', has become a recognizable late modern malaise, even though such perceived stress may be due to increased flexibility or responsibility at work as much as longer hours or faster processes (Gleick 1999; Green 2001). As speed is seemingly equated with efficiency and professionalism, however, slowness can become a way of signalling an alternative set of values or a refusal to privilege the workplace over other domains of life. To declare the value of slowness in our work, in our personal life, in public life, is to promote a position counter to the dominant value-system of 'the times'.

Positioned in this way, slow living is not only provocative but is also receiving much public attention. Newspaper articles and popular books about work pressures, 'anti-careerism' and 'downshifting' proliferate, outlining the increasing difficulty people encounter in finding time in everyday life, while extolling the virtues of free time and family life. In one article, a banking executive proudly declared that he always finds some time for his family despite an eighty-hour working week (Boreham, Ellicott and Jimenez 2001: 5). The popular novel, *I Don't Know How She Does It* (Pearson 2002), opens with the City executive heroine 'distressing' mince pies at two in the morning for her daughter's Christmas concert but ends with her living slowly and happily in Derbyshire. As these two examples suggest, slow living is a relative concept that represents a response to the contexts of flux and speed that characterize much contemporary existence and which people negotiate in a variety of ways through the attribution of a positive value to certain kinds and uses of time (although it is hard to imagine how the bank executive's eighty-hour week leaves space for anything other than 'fast life'). Within the Western world, perceptions of the growing prevalence of 'fast living' prompts us to consider not only the values and possibilities of slowness but also the broader contexts of change that have made our quality of life and an ethics of living more pressing concerns. In this introductory chapter, we will explore the concept of slow living – what we understand it to mean, and how it emerges in a specific social context as a response to globalization and its perceived impact on everyday life. We will outline why everyday life has taken on a new importance, both in public discourse and social practice, and we will then situate our understanding of the political and ethical possibilities of everyday life in relation to concepts such as 'life politics', 'micropolitics' and 'enchanted modernity' in order to foreground how slow living may constitute an oppositional mode within contemporary global culture and everyday life – or what we call the global everyday.

Slow Living

We can currently see a *desire* for slow living being manifested in a range of social phenomena. The so-called 'wellness revolution', for example, places emphasis on bodily well-being and is linked to the increasing popularity of 'slow' practices such as yoga and meditation (Ostrow 2003; Stein 2003). The return to creative practices, such as knitting or gardening, may also signal an intention to lead slower, more 'grounded' lives. The widespread nature of this desire for slow living also coalesces in a range of social movements, such as Voluntary Simplicity and Slow Food. While Slow Food will be our chief example throughout this book, the Voluntary Simplicity movement is perhaps equally deserving of examination as a response to the speed and stress of contemporary life. Mainly – but not exclusively – based in North America, the Voluntary Simplicity movement comprises of a number of non-profit organizations, local 'simplicity circles', websites and a plethora of publications that advocate 'simplifying daily life, reducing waste of time, money and resources' (www.mindfulcanada.com). Many – but, again, not all – of these groups are linked with churches or a sense of 'traditional American values' but the primary aim in all cases is to challenge or critique consumer culture by changing the practices of everyday life and establishing 'intentional communities' (www.mindfulcanada.com).[1]

Simple living, or the simple life, shares some characteristics with slow living but there are also significant distinctions between the two that should be clarified at the outset. While simplicity has always represented 'a shifting cluster of ideas, sentiments, and activities' it has also consistently valued frugality and hard work, expressed a preference for the rural over the urban, and been suspicious of the claims of modernity (Shi 1985: 3–4). Such ascetic frugality is not consistent with all forms of slow living; Slow Food, for instance, places an emphasis on material pleasure while the Slow Cities movement begins from the assumption that (some) forms of urban life offer vibrancy, community and beauty. An investment in the pleasures of everyday life which slow living stresses is also, we will argue, a conscious negotiation of life in the present, rather than a nostalgic retreat to an imagined community or pastoral golden age. So without wanting to overstate differences which may interrelate closely in some people's daily lives, the adjective 'slow' rather than 'simple' to qualify 'living' may signal a greater degree of imbrication in contemporary everyday life – given that slowness can only be judged in relation to speed – while simple living may signal a greater disengagement from, even an outright rejection of, contemporary culture.

A fundamental concern in slow living is *time*. At its heart, slow living is a conscious attempt to change the current temporal order to one which offers *more* time, time to attend to everyday life. In the literature of both Voluntary Simplicity and Slow Food, much emphasis is placed on time – how we have 'lost' it, how we need to 'reclaim' or 'make' it – bearing out the observation that everyday life is to a large extent concerned with 'the temporal order of doing' (Tyrell quoted in Beck and Beck-Gernsheim 2002: 6). But slow living should not be thought of simply as a slow-motion version of postmodern life; it does not offer or make possible a parallel temporality for slow subjects to inhabit in isolation from the rest of global culture. Rather, its patterns and practices, like others in contemporary culture, are non-synchronous, albeit deliberately and consciously. As will be explored in more detail in our chapter on time and speed, slow living involves the negotiation of different temporalities, deriving from a commitment to occupy time more attentively. 'Having time' for something means investing it with significance through attention and deliberation. To live slowly in this sense, then, means engaging in 'mindful' rather than 'mindless' practices which make us consider the pleasure or at least the purpose of each task to which we give our time. Such qualities of mindfulness and attention also, we will argue, have an ethical dimension through the implication of an acknowledgement of otherness – other people, other places, other times – which the distractedness of fast life may often preclude.[2]

'Care', 'attention' and 'mindfulness' are terms which recur in descriptions of slow living practices, whether in relation to cooking, walking, meditating, gardening or just doing *nothing* (e.g. see Parkins 2004b). While we will mention throughout this book a range of practices which we would describe as slow living, we need to stress at the outset that slow living has no singular or prescribed content but may be variously embodied by subjects or practices depending on the context in which 'slow' is being configured against forms of 'fast life'. There is no prescriptive checklist of activities which comprise slow living, nor would a 'slow subject' necessarily engage in all of the practices which we mention. Slow living is, however, best exemplified in all those practices that invest the everyday with meaning and pleasure through a mindful use of time. In an interview with Roland Barthes entitled 'Dare to be Lazy', Barthes lamented his own inability to be idle and asked, 'Have you every noticed that everyone always talks about the right to leisure activities but never about a right to idleness? I even wonder if there is such a thing as *doing nothing* in the modern Western world' (1985: 341, original emphasis). Barthes' distinction between an idleness of doing nothing and the modern propensity to 'cut up time' in leisure activities captures something of the quality of slow living as we describe it here. While practices of slow living may result in productive outcomes (a loaf of home-baked bread, say) it is the process, which from an instrumentalist perspective may well look and feel like 'doing nothing', which is both desired and experienced.[3]

Slow living is not synonomous with 'cocooning' which we understand as a withdrawal from engagement with a hostile world to the shelter of personal space and private life. Since the mid-1990s – and exacerbated by responses to 9/11 – there have been observable sociocultural trends involving a 'turn towards the interior' or 'defended inwardness' (Cullens 1999: 219). We will argue that there is no necessary or inevitable connection between placing a value on 'the simple pleasures of moment-by-moment experience' (Cullens 1999: 219) and political disengagement or gated communities, but rather that slow living may articulate – and be articulated with – global concerns and political affiliations with social justice and environmental campaigns. There is, however, one important aspect of withdrawal in slow living: an emphasis on contemplation and attention requires a kind of withdrawal – of body, of consciousness – from certain kinds of spaces or places (figured as fast or noisy, the two often conflated so that a slow space is also a quiet one) at least for a period of time, for rest or refreshment. Such withdrawal, as a form of bodily practice, can be seen in disciplines like the Alexander Technique, meditation or other body therapies which 'constitute and value the present moment' (Thrift 2000: 41). Such practices, Nigel Thrift has argued, produce 'a set of resources which enable us to separate out and value a present-orientated still-ness, thus promoting a "politics" based in intensified attention to the present and unqualified affectivity' (2000: 42).

In another context, Alberto Melucci (1998) has also argued that the cultivation of attention to the present has positive potential beyond the individual subject to mobilize new forms of political investment and revivify everyday life. In a con-temporary context marked by speed and globalization, Melucci argues, subjects are faced with an imbalance between what he calls the 'inner time' of the subject and 'social time'. Such temporal disparities, in a context where identities are not fixed, require subjects to negotiate 'continuity through change', or 'metamor-phosis':

> The unity and continuity of individual experience cannot be found in a fixed identifi-cation with a definite model, group or culture. It must instead be based on an inner capacity to 'change form', to redefine itself repeatedly in the present, to reverse deci-sions and choice. But it also means cherishing the present as a unique, unrepeatable experience within which I realize myself.
>
> We can only preserve our unity by being able to 'open and close', to participate in and withdraw from the flow of messages. ... Yet in this alternation between noise and silence we need an inner wholeness that must survive through change. To live the dis-continuity and variability of time and space we must find a way to unify experience other than by our 'rational' self. Fragmentation and discontinuity ... demand the wisdom of more immediate perception, intuitive awareness and imagination. (1998: 185)

What this requires is learning a 'new consciousness practice', involving the body and emotions as well as perception and thought (1998: 186), through which sub-jects can both fully inhabit the present and their own *presence* within it: 'The capacity to be present is not a spontaneous capacity of human experience but a paradoxical quality: it is an immediate experience that needs a deep reflexive atti-tude, something to be built, learned and adjusted through one's life processes, events and relations' (Melucci 1998: 182). In short, Melucci argues it is important to find ways in which 'presence can become a resource' not only for the psychic health of subjects but for the resolution of social conflicts 'where deep individual experience transforms itself into a social energy for change' (1998: 180).

Everyday Life

Our conception of slow living, then, is indebted to such articulations of presence and attentiveness in the negotiation of everyday temporalities. But what is the sig-nificance of the everyday in this context? Why do we begin with an assumption of the value of the domain of everyday life? In positioning this book within cultural studies, we are both inheriting and aligning ourselves with a rich and problematic tradition of examining the everyday which has emerged in this field, although we also draw on the extensive literature on the everyday from other disciplines and traditions.[4] Our examination of slow living in the global everyday is our attempt 'to keep open the dilemma of the everyday' (Langbauer 1992: 63; see also Morris 1988: 23), a project also consonant with Ben Highmore's delineation of the importance of everyday life for cultural studies:

> The question the everyday makes vivid for cultural theory is the question of how to attend to the social. ... The everyday makes the particularity of lived culture inescapable. ... Perhaps, then, the everyday is the name that cultural theory might give to a form of attention that attempts to animate the heterogeneity of social life, the name for finding meaning in an impossible diversity. (2002: 174–5, emphasis added)

In focusing our attention on slow living, we can only begin to sketch, from that heterogeneity, how the practices of time, space, pleasure and politics associated with slow living are both enacted in the everyday at the same time as they put the category of the everyday under question.

Despite being such a significant and widely used concept, however, the definition of the everyday or everyday life is often elusive or unstated. It seems to be 'everywhere', as the routine, 'the taken-for-granted' which then becomes invisible (Felski 1999–2000: 15, 31; Chaney 2002: 10). Beyond the problem of defining the facticity of the everyday, however, theorists also dispute the significance and potential of the realm of the mundane. Rita Felski, for instance, has persuasively argued that the focus on the everyday by radical intellectuals over the twentieth century (such as Lefebvre, Debord and the Situationists) rested on the construction of the quotidian as 'an imagined reservoir of utopian energies and unruly impulses' (2002: 609). In this radical tradition, 'To affirm the everyday is thus simultaneously to negate it' because it was only in overcoming the 'very everydayness of the everyday' that its true potential could be realized (Felski 2002: 610). Michael Gardiner, by contrast, with reference to some of the same theorists that Felski examines, argues the virtues of an approach which problematizes everyday life, 'expos[ing] its contradictions and teas[ing] out its hidden potentialities' (2000: 6).

It seems to us that it is possible to recognize the 'unruly' elements of everyday life which point to its 'irreducibly imaginative and symbolic dimension' (Gardiner 2000: 16) without either condemning the immanence of the everyday or excoriating habit as inherently inauthentic (Felski 2002: 608, 615, 611). Seeing the everyday as a messy or 'dilemmatic' site (Honig 1996) is not an attempt to master it, nor to imagine it is possible (or even desirable) to expose all our everyday assumptions to critical interrogation (see Heller 1984). It is an attempt to attend to its ethical and affective potential.[5] The difference between this approach to the creativity of everyday life and the 'aesthetic transcendence' tradition Felski critiques is a twofold one. Firstly, it begins from the assumption that because everyday life is always already a sphere of intersubjective interaction it has an irreducibly ethical dimension (Gardiner 2000: 209, n.1). Secondly, it also assumes that this irrational, creative messiness is part of the ordinary practice of everyday life by *ordinary* practitioners and not limited to the 'boldly disruptive *bricoleur* of everyday life' who Felski sees as the 'idealized alter-ego of the critical theorist' (2002: 612).

Our examination of slow living, therefore, begins from two assumptions about everyday life: that it has a creative and ethical potential; and that it must be reflexively negotiated and managed by contemporary subjects. This latter assumption is indebted to the concept of 'individualization' as delineated by Ulrich Beck and Elisabeth Beck-Gernsheim, who describe the pressure for individuals to construct their own 'biographies' in contexts where traditional ways of life and identities are increasingly under question (see Beck 1997: 95).[6] Differing from earlier manifestations of individualism, 'individualization':

> is a social condition which is not arrived at by a free decision of individuals. ... [It] is a compulsion, albeit a paradoxical one, to create, to stage manage, not only one's own biography but the bonds and networks surrounding it and to do this amid changing preferences and at successive stages of life, while constantly adapting to the conditions of the labour market, the education system, the welfare state and so on.
>
> One of the decisive features of individualization processes, then, is that they not only permit but they also demand an active contribution by individuals. As the range of options widens and the necessity of deciding between them grows, so too does the need for individually performed actions, for adjustment, coordination, integration. If they are not to fail, individuals must be able to plan for the long term and adapt to change; they must organize and improvise, set goals, recognize obstacles, accept defeats and attempt new starts. They need initiative, tenacity, flexibility and tolerance of frustration. (Beck and Beck-Gernsheim 2002: 4)[7]

Individualization, then, has significant consequences for everyday life and places new emphasis on both an ethics and a politics centred on 'the quality of life' (Beck and Beck-Gernsheim 2002: 212), even as it may also account for a withdrawal from public engagement by some constituencies within post-traditional societies (Bauman 2002: xviii–xix).

Individualization becomes more pronounced in a context where globalization has triggered processes of detraditionalization, due to a perceived acceleration of daily life and the adaptability such changes require. Paradoxically, however, such a context can also contribute to a revalorization of tradition as individuals seek means of coping with the stresses and flux of contemporary existence. The aesthetics of 'past times', commodified in the shops of the same name, have enjoyed a revival, as have traditional domestic practices, such as quilting (Parkins 2004b). The appeal of a social movement such as Slow Food or the resurgence of farmers' markets derive partly from an appreciation of the knowledges, customs, tastes and pleasures of previous times, and a desire for their continued currency. Such 'rediscoveries' of traditions – or their selective deployment – become part of the plurality of life options that are available to individuals in constructing their own life narratives and negotiating their own risks (Beck and Beck-Gernsheim 2002: 25–7). While such practices are often seen as nostalgic escapes from the exigencies of the present, we will argue in subsequent chapters that the reclamation of tradition may also form part of a sustained engagement with contemporary problems of everyday life and constitute revitalized networks of community and exchange *in* the present.

Such processes of individualization which throw into question the assumptions and practices of everyday life have seen the category of the everyday take on a new currency, both in popular culture and political discourse (Chaney 2002: 55). From the extraordinary proliferation of lifestyle television in the past decade to recent political debates about the urgency to find a 'work/family balance', the everyday is no longer the background against which important public issues are considered, it is *itself* the issue. This new interest in the 'quality of life' can, paradoxically, be an active engagement with social disparities even as it is a 'desire for the immaterial – rest, free time, friendship, fun, creative work' (Rutherford 2000: 65). Such desires are, however, not equally realizable by all. As Melucci has argued, we need to think of social inequality not simply in material terms but 'more in terms of unequal access to the new resources of individuation' (1996a: 500). It is in the conflicts and discrepancies between individual aspirations or constructions of meaning in everyday life and the differential distribution of new forms of control, rationalization and exclusion that new social movements are produced (Melucci 1996a: 505; see also Chaney 2002: 140). In our study of slow living we will explore some of the ways in which these new forms of being-in-the-world, or new ethics of living, are shaped from the everyday, from its messiness and fragility. If the unpredictability of daily life leads to the possibility for creative and reflexive negotiations, then there are also utopian possibilities within the everyday, in the sense of 'a longing for a different, and better way of living, a reconciliation of thought and life, desire and the real, in a manner that critiques the status quo without projecting a full-blown image of what a future society should look like' (Gardiner 2000: 17).

Global Culture

It follows from our discussion so far that the forms, practices and values of contemporary everyday life are not segregated from broader social contexts. The particular dynamics of contemporary everyday life, captured in the processes of individualization, highlight an indissoluble nexus between individual lived experience and a culture that assumes an increasingly global orientation. Contemporary forms and practices of slow living arise from, and in response to, processes of globalization, we would argue, not simply the immediate pressures of daily life. Practices and organizations associated with slowness, such as Slow Food, moreover, are also often identified with an opposition to globalization, variously understood, so we need to explore some of the aspects of globalization that are implicated with slow living. Our argument is not simply that the complexity of globalization produces the dislocations and dissonances that make slow living seem an appealing alternative but that forms of slow living necessarily emerge from the very particular character of global culture. The complexity of globalization derives from the fact that it is not a singular, monolithic force but a multifaceted phenomenon – manifested in the economy, technology, politics, media and culture. Although by definition globalization has pervasive effects around the world, it is more often than not an uneven process, building on already existing inequalities and opportunities. The term 'global culture' may suggest an integrated global order but it is better understood as 'a complex, overlapping, disjunctive order' (Appadurai 1991: 296).

Processes of globalization have provoked a variety of well-known concerns, such as the increasing economic power of transnational corporations and forms of cultural imperialism, but they can also – paradoxically – facilitate positive change, such as the forging of networks of solidarity across national boundaries through new social movements that critique the deleterious effects of globalization. Such social movements are often centrally concerned with the quality of everyday life in the context of what Beck calls second modernity (2000; Beck et al. 2003).[8] In this account, modernity has not been superseded in contemporary existence but has become 'increasingly problematic' as the certainties of traditional life trajectories have been replaced with a more indeterminate existence, characterized by risks and opportunities (2003: 2). Second modernity 'can be seen as a vast field of social experiment where, under the pressure of globalization, various types of post-traditional social bonds and post-national imagined communities are being tried out in competition with each other' (Beck et al. 2003: 16). In such post-traditional societies, traditional practices, structures and values are 'dis-embedded', subjected to scrutiny, challenge and re-evaluation (Giddens 1994: 96–7).

Our conceptualization of slow living is based on a questioning of the conventional wisdoms regarding the temporal and spatial contexts of global culture. It is commonly observed that globalization ushers in an acceleration in the pace of life, accompanied by a compression and even a dissolution of geographical distance. Global culture is often characterized by the new technologies of communication and transport that instantaneously distribute information around the world and significantly increase the mobility of people, goods, services and information across national boundaries in a phenomenon famously denoted as 'time-space compression' (Harvey 1989). Considered in this context, slow living in the global everyday may be rendered as a quaint and ineffective diversion from the realities of globalization but we argue that conventional accounts positing a singular acceleration in the pace of life and a collapse in the physical contexts of space offer only a limited and monolithic historical narrative (see May and Thrift 2001). As will be discussed in subsequent chapters, the global everyday is not characterized by singular experiences of speed and geographical dislocation but by the negotiation of an increasingly complex coexistence of different temporalities and spatial contexts. In global culture,

> the picture is less of any simple acceleration in the pace of life or the experience of spatial 'collapse' than of a far more complex restructuring in the nature and experience of time and space ... With these changes space is seen to both expand and to contract, time horizons to both foreshorten but also to extend, time itself to both speed up but also slow down and even to move in different directions. (May and Thrift 2001: 10)

Slow living in the global everyday, then, is not an escapist pastime but is both the result of, and a response to, the radically uneven and heterogeneous production of space and time in post-traditional societies.

Slow living in the global everyday also needs to be contextualized within a consideration of how globalization is articulated with the local, given that the very character of globalization threatens to erase the local. Whether strolling through a shopping mall or an airport, one can see evidence that the uniqueness of the local is increasingly undermined by global forces. Globalization represents a shift from a territorial framework to a deterritorialized perspective, to a form of 'supra-territorialization' that is increasingly removed from the reference of physical, geographical space (Scholte 1997). Subjects who are thoroughly implicated in global culture are often defined by their mobility and their freedom from the 'constraints' of local, fixed space, acquiring social capital through such mobility when 'Being local in a globalized world is a sign of social deprivation and degradation' (Bauman 1998: 2). In fact, however, globalization can be seen to be characterized by two seemingly contradictory movements: a power shift away from the national to transnational institutions *and* to more local bodies (Brodie 2000: 115). As in the popular slogan, 'Think Globally, Act Locally', the local can be seen as a site of resistance in global culture (Hall 1996: 619), even as subjects are assumed to have a sense of global responsibility.

The positing of the local as a site of resistance *from* the global does not, however, imply that the local can be isolated or sealed off from the global and its effects. The local may not be annihilated by global forces but it is defined through its particular encounters with globalization, as Robertson's term the 'glocal' (1995) attempts to capture. The mutual imbrication of local and global practices and contexts means that the local can have no meaningful existence outside of these globalized contexts and indeed that globalization in some sense involves the 'invention of locality' (Robertson 1995; see also Beck 2002: 17). If we see slow living, then, as a response to globalization, this is not to define it as merely a defensive retreat to the local but rather as part of a reconfiguring of local social relations and identities in new reflexive ways which 'utilize, criticize and even contribute to globalization, while developing new senses of locality and community' (Purdue Dürrschmidt, Jowers and O'Doherty 1997: 645).

As this reconfiguring of identities and relations within a dialectical understanding of the global and local implies, such a process has profound ramifications for contemporary subjectivity. Globalization establishes a fundamental linkage not only of global forces with everyday life but also of everyday decisions with global outcomes and consequences. Any decision to purchase food or clothing, for example, can be made with awareness of global consequences, whether they are the working conditions of someone in another country or the degradation of the environment due to certain farming practices (Giddens 1994: 57–8; see also Young 2003). Globalization, as Giddens has expressed it, is an 'in here' matter (as opposed to an 'out there' one) 'which affects, or rather is dialectically related to, even the most intimate aspects of our lives' (1994: 95). Alongside a still-influential national sphere of experience there is also the emergence of a global dimension ushering in 'a new way of doing business and of working, a new kind of identity and politics as well as a new kind of everyday space-time experience and of human sociability', a new figuring of cosmopolitanization or '*internal* globalization' (Beck 2002: 17, 30, original emphasis). This new, dialogic cosmopolitanism – or '*rooted* cosmopolitanism' – both ruptures binaries such as local/global and requires a notion of localism (Beck 2002: 19, original emphasis).

We will argue throughout this book that the impulse towards slow living is partly driven by precisely this kind of cosmopolitanization. Everyday experience is understood to have global implications and effects beyond the personal implications of a slower, more attentive approach to life. Indeed it could be said that attention is directed outward as well as inward in practices of slow living. The person who walks rather than drives may be cognizant of the environmental implications of fossil fuels and freeways as well as the pleasures to be derived from bodily exercise, for instance. The slow subject is therefore different from the sense of cosmopolitan subjectivity as the 'everyday currency of global capitalism' (Stevenson 2002: 261) by which elites are able to enjoy the freedoms afforded by greater physical mobility and communication technologies, 'dabbling rootlessly in a variety of cultures' (Featherstone 2002: 1). Rather, the slow subject may live a kind of 'ethical glocalism' (Tomlinson 1999: 195–6).[9]

The global everyday is now both a mundane reality and a site where the process of living is less self-evident, subject to disturbing new challenges and open to liberatory potentials (Tomlinson 1999: 128). The adoption of practices of slow living by the self-reflexive cosmopolitan subject is one of the ways in which this transformation of locality takes place, as the mundane is reinvested with significance through the enhanced awareness that cultural difference and detraditionalization makes possible. One example of this transformation of locality would be the resurgence and growing popularity of farmers' markets in countries such as the UK and Australia. People meet and buy from local producers at an informal weekly market, preferring both the social experience and quality of produce that such markets may afford, while at the same time eschewing the impersonal approach to shopping available in the supermarket. The farmers' market signals a renewed valuing of the local by subjects aware of, and responding to, the global flows of agriculture. Such negotiation of difference within the glocal has become, then, part of the fabric of everyday life – what could be more mundane than grocery shopping? – but at the same time has also become an opportunity for sociality and constructing community. In this sense, the cosmopolitan subject in global culture, while obviously connected to forms of cultural openness, is defined here less through 'manic mobility or hedonism', and more through the 'necessary emotional work of everyday life' (Rutherford 2002: 66; Stevenson 2002: 261).

Slow Arts of the Self

This new focus on everyday life and its complex relation to global culture – the global everyday – requires a new consideration of the intersubjective and political domains. While the rise of anti-globalization movements has already clearly signalled the importance of global contexts and institutions for contemporary politics, political theorists have also recently examined the more mundane implications of globalization for political life and discourse. The values and practices of slow living need, then, to be situated in relation to this recent work, and contextualized within a contemporary political terrain in which, for instance, the legacy of new social movements has placed issues such as the distribution of time on the political agenda, alongside the more traditional attention to the distribution of goods and services.

One such reformulation of contemporary politics is Anthony Giddens' concept of 'life politics', which differs from a traditional emancipatory politics. As a 'politics of lifestyle', life politics presumes some level of emancipation 'from the fixities of tradition and from conditions of hierarchical domination' and focuses on subjects who are engaged in a dialectical relationship 'in post-traditional contexts, where globalizing influences intrude deeply into the reflexive project of the self, and conversely where processes of self-realization influence global strategies'

(Giddens 1991: 214). Life politics cannot, however, simply be categorized as the politics of the middle-class or the affluent who have 'moved beyond' the concerns of emancipatory politics. Echoing Beck and Melucci, Giddens argues that 'access to means of self-actualization becomes itself one of the dominant focuses of class division and the distribution of inequalities more generally' (1991: 228) and hence the problems and challenges of detraditionalization also apply to the poor and the marginalized. Nor can life politics be limited to the politics of leisure. Work, like the rest of life, has become more problematic, losing many of its established structures, rhythms and traditions. Processes of self-actualization are determined increasingly by individual decisions about employment and labour, as well as consumption and leisure.

The concept of life politics could be seen as solely a politics of the personal or the everyday, and Giddens has noted the debt of the term to earlier movements, like 'the personal is political' emphasis in second-wave feminism or the student movements of the 1960s (1991: 215–16). Like those movements, life politics is applicable to a broader conceptualization of politics, where there is struggle over the values that inform social relations, but it is also relevant to the more specific political domain of the state, given that life politics necessarily tackles issues of rights and obligations (Giddens 1991: 226). Emancipatory politics, addressing issues of inequality, exploitation and oppression, obviously remains central to any radical political project and there is often a nexus between areas of life politics and the values and goals that inform emancipatory politics. But as Highmore has noted of second-wave feminism: 'The very fact that such a social and cultural movement immersed itself in the everyday ... should alert us to the potential of the everyday to generate new political forms' (2002: 28). Now, the most personal decisions about consumption, everyday practices, and leisure uses are deeply implicated by social, political and global considerations to such an extent that they undermine traditional divisions between different spheres of life (Rojek 2001: 123).

Giddens's notion of life politics, then, is useful for an account of the politics of slow living but it is not used uncritically here. Firstly, life politics needs to be disengaged from its alignment with the political project of the 'third way' (Giddens 2000; Neocleous 1999). Secondly, an appreciation of the reflexive subject and the changing political terrain outlined in the concept of life politics needs to be balanced with a greater emphasis on the complex and differentiated nature of the self and the structural constraints that operate on the subject.[10] There are limits to reflexivity not only because of conflictual rules and obligations in society but 'because the conflicts are often within ourselves' (Hoggett 2001: 41; see also Rojek 2001; Davies 2001). Most importantly, however, slow living for us is informed by a very different reading of the account of global risk culture (Beck 1992; Lupton 1999), out of which grows forms of life politics. Most attention has been devoted to delineating how the global culture of risk has been instrumental in the production of the flexible, mobile and efficient subjects of the neo-liberal marketplace but we argue that such a culture also necessarily imbues subjects with a greater understanding of contingency, chaos and suffering as well as the limits of nature, time and human life, potentially giving rise to values of community, peace and slowness. Such contexts, and such subject positions, in short, are the basis out of which grow the politics of slow living.

Another take on these issues, which is not dissimilar to life politics but which perhaps better captures the possibilities of slow living, is the notion of micropolitics as proposed by William E. Connolly. Using Nietzsche and Foucault's proposals for self-artistry as 'resources', Connolly has proposed arts of the self as ethical strategies that do not simply aim at self-expression or self-indulgence (1999: 145–6): 'Such artistry, rather, involves *the selective desanctification of elements within your own identity. ...* The most admirable arts of the self cultivate the capacity for critical responsiveness in a world in which the politics of becoming periodically poses surprises to the self-identifications of established constituencies' (1999: 146, original emphasis). If it is the accelerated tempo of contemporary culture that may work to make us more aware of the contingencies of our subjectivity, then this may also facilitate arts of the self through which we can 'desanctify' parts of our self-understanding (i.e. denaturalize them, recognize them as historically contingent and socially derived). But in order to cultivate a capacity for critical responsiveness, time is required, for reflection and response. And it is out of such self-artistry and the new awareness it can foster that 'new possibilities of being', which have consequences beyond the individual, may arise:

> What is an art of the self from one perspective is micropolitics from another. The films, family memories, social movements, dietary regimens, marches, dream work, medical techniques, gossip, medications, curriculum organization, talk shows, identity performances, material disciplines and rewards, sermons, leadership techniques, and rituals you draw upon tactically to work upon the self are, from another angle, micropolitical practices that regularly impinge upon us individually and associationally. Arts of the self and micropolitics are two sides of the same coin. Micropolitics can function to stabilize an existing set of identities. It can also usher a new identity or right into being. ... (Connolly 1999: 148–9)

Arts of the (slow) self are means, then, not only by which people cultivate a subjectivity based on the affirmation of values like attentiveness as daily pleasures, but they are also opportunities for 'modest shifts' in broader articulations of social organization and public culture. Because such slow arts of the self are always situated and practised within social networks and time cultures, they can throw into greater relief the ethical implications of an accelerated culture. In short, 'Self-artistry affects the ethical sensibility of individuals in their relations to others' (Connolly 1999: 149).

But how might these slow arts of the self lead to a greater ethical and political engagement with the world and with others? In order to answer this question, we need to raise what is arguably both the central value, and most problematic aspect, of slow living: pleasure. Pleasure and politics, joy and ethics, are not terms we are accustomed to see linked, except perhaps as antinomies, but in a number of recent works – as well as in the founding manifesto of the Slow Food movement which begins with 'the right to pleasure' – such linkages are insisted upon.[11] In particular, the argument of Jane Bennett in *The Enchantment of Modern Life: Attachments, Crossings, and Ethics* has been influential on our own conceptualization of the centrality and imbrication of pleasure and ethics in everyday life. Drawing on Epicurean philosophy – in which the 'ethical task is to en-joy life with discipline, to receive it with wonder and to add, by one's actions, to its stock of joy' (2001: 88) – Bennett explores notions of joy, wonder, pleasure and enchantment in contemporary life, in a persuasive critique of the Weberian thesis of disenchanted modernity. Bennett seeks both to question the veracity of the narrative of disenchantment in modernity and also to expose the ethical/political implications of the adoption of this thesis by critical theorists for whom 'the quest for enchantment is always suspect, for it signals only a longing to forget about injustice, sink into naïveté, and escape from politics' (2001: 10). Charting the presence of joy and enchantment in a variety of forms and places in contemporary life, Bennett describes enchantment as 'a mood of lively and intense engagement with the world' in which she sees an ethical potential (2001: 111):

> Enchantment is a feeling of being connected in an affirmative way to existence; it is to be under the momentary impression that the natural and cultural worlds *offer gifts* and, in so doing, remind us that it is good to be alive. This sense of fullness – what the Epicureans talks about in terms of *ataraxy* (contentment with existence) – encourages the finite human animal, in turn, to give away some of its own time and effort on behalf of other creatures. A sensibility attuned to moments of enchantment is no guarantee that this will happen, but it does make it more possible. (2001: 156, original emphasis)

Such cultivation of an enchanted sensibility is, then, closely linked to the practices of everyday life and presupposes the creation of a time and space in those daily patterns which would allow an awareness of enchantment, pleasure or wonder to become possible.

To suggest that an 'enchanted/ethical' subject in Bennett's sense may be a possibility in a global context of risk is a high-stakes argument which begs the question as to who has the option to be enchanted in such a context? Who has the time to live slowly? These are questions we have been frequently asked and which we will address more fully in subsequent chapters. While we have signalled here the inequities and disjunctures which characterize everyday life in the global everyday we have also seen how widespread processes of individualization have become and how the concerns of everyday life occupy a space in the public imaginary in new ways. What Bennett's account of the 'enchanted' subject also stresses, however, is the importance of pleasure in everyday life and the questions about the applicability of slowness are sometimes questions about the possibility of pleasure in everyday life. Given that slow living is almost always motivated by a perceived lack of 'quality of life', pleasure is absolutely central to any examination of this mode of life. The potentials of pleasure will be examined more extensively in Chapter 5, where the immediate and sensuous pleasures of food and the joys of conviviality will be linked to slow living but here we want to suggest that an approach to everyday life combining pleasure and attentiveness may indeed be a means of shifting daily life onto a 'new terrain' in which new ways of being-in-the-world as the basis of a new politics becomes foreseeable.

Such an approach to everyday life is often expressed in the literature of Slow Food, so it is not surprising that this movement forms the chief example and basis of discussion throughout this book. The following chapter details the origins, philosophy and structures of Slow Food to allow readers unfamiliar with the movement the necessary background to follow the more specific and selective aspects of Slow Food which are discussed in the remainder of the book. Chapter 2 also situates Slow Food within the debates concerning new social movements and elaborates why we think it should be seen as a movement rather than just an organization. Our aim throughout is to use the evolving significance of the movement as a springboard for our theorization of the concept of slow living. As will become clear from our discussions, we do not see Slow Food as a complete, consistent or unproblematic exemplum of slow living but rather as offering both positive potential and some concrete examples of what the application of slow living in the global everyday might look like. While our examination of Slow Food involves participant observation and interviews, our primary mode of analysis is textual and discursive, deriving from our location within a cultural studies' approach to the study of culture and contemporary life. Our aim was not to write a 'how-to' guide to slow living, although such guides may have a place, but rather to open up some of the possibilities and implications that an alternative mode of everyday life based on slowness may provide and we believe that a textual-discursive approach was best suited to such a venture.

Given our contention that slow living is a broad-ranging concept, influencing and problematizing domains of everyday, social and political life, the delineation of specific subject areas into separate chapters, while necessary, may in some ways work against the purpose of our argument: separate chapters on 'time' and 'space', for example, could be seen to loosen their inextricable linkage (May and Thrift 2001). Given this, we encourage readers to read 'across' the chapters (if they have the time!) in order to trace the threads of slow living. Chapters 3 and 4 address the temporal and spatial contexts of slow living, respectively. Chapter 3 historicizes contemporary notions of 'slowness' and 'speed', in order to show how 'slow time' can be configured as an alternative temporality, and considers the pleasures and possibilities of an ethics of time. Chapter 4 'locates' slow living, discussing the merits of the space of the 'local' in the contexts of the deterritorialized basis of modern global life. The cities of the Città Slow movement are discussed as specific civic entities that are seeking to implement slowness, and more generally the contexts of 'work' and 'home' as possible sites of slow living are also analysed. Chapter 5 discusses the significance of food and pleasure for slow living, noting how the consumption of food mobilizes issues of aesthetic experience, corporeal enjoyment and authenticity. Examining the notion of the shared table, this chapter also considers the consequences for slow living and Slow Food in particular of notions of hospitality and conviviality for issues of gender, family and ethnicity. Our concluding chapter allows us to foreground the politics of slow living, which has been an implicit focus throughout. In particular, the politics of the 'eco-gastronomic' focus of Slow Food is discussed as a specific instance of new formulations of politics in the global everyday, with its attendant problems of transnational institutions and the North–South divide. We end, however, on an optimistic note for the possibilities for slow living in the global everyday, as a reflexive approach which not only seeks to restore meaning and pleasure to everyday life but to acknowledge and address the ethical dimensions of home and work, self and other, culture and nature.

–2–

Slow Food

Slow Food has always defied easy explanation. The name 'Slow Food', bringing together food and temporality, is unusual for many when they initially encounter the movement, even though 'fast food' has a ubiquitous presence in contemporary culture. Similarly, a social movement that engages in conflicts with transnational corporations while also teaching the gastronomic delights of Parmigiano Reggiano is a movement that does not easily fit conventional political and cultural frames of reference for many people. With a core philosophy where 'slowness' is grounded in understandings of pleasure and taste, conviviality, and the value of local products and cultures, Slow Food has grown and diversified its range of activities so that it has become, as Deborah Madison notes, like 'the blind men patting the elephant to determine its nature' (2001: ix). As Madison explains:

> To the gastronome, Slow Food might have to do with artisanal foods and wines. To the person seeking a tempo of life that is more in step with life's natural rhythms … Slow Food offers a sympathetic response. … Those whose historical quests are more aligned with animals and plants will find that Slow Food … provides a place to actively debate the merits of old breeds, from turkeys to sheep, or oysters to apples, and to become actively involved with their preservation. If your concerns are with the politics of social change, you may find yourself in harmony with Slow Food's commitment to land stewardship and food that's grown by sound and sustainable methods. (2001: ix)

This diversity gives Slow Food an affinity with an extraordinary range of social groups and a complex status as both an international organization – now officially recognized as a non-government organization (NGO) – and a type of movement. While the majority of this chapter will be largely descriptive in character, as we outline the origins, philosophy, structure and current projects of Slow Food and its spin-off Città Slow (Slow Cities), we will also make a case for understanding Slow Food in the context of new social movements. Our concern is not to prove that Slow Food fits a taxonomic model of a new social movement but rather to draw on the extensive literature on new social movements to better explain the complexities and possibilities of Slow Food and hence to refute a simplistic dismissal of the movement as 'just a food and wine club'.

Origins, Philosophy and Structure

Slow Food evolved out of the food and cultural interests of a group of Italian left-wing activists but its formal beginnings can be traced back to the formation of the Arcigola group in 1986.[1] Arcigola's membership grew from 500 to 8,000 in three years due to its publishing projects, organized events and tastings, and its restaurant and wine reviews (Petrini 2001: 7). In 1987, it published a wine guide called *Gambero Rosso* ('Red Shrimp') as an insert in the left-wing newspaper *Il Manifesto* and the wine guide quickly became an internationally authoritative guide for Italian wines (Kummer 2002: 20). In 1989, the proposed opening of a McDonalds in the Piazza di Spagna in Rome caused outrage and protests were organized (including protestors sitting outside McDonalds, slowly eating bowls of pasta). Arising out of these protests a new name was coined: Slow Food. As Slow Food president Carlo Petrini has noted, the term 'slow food' was opposed to 'fast food' but what the movement's new name really conveyed was 'our critical reaction to the symptoms of incipient globalization' (2001: 8). The new name, always written in English, was also an acknowledgement of the international spread and aims of the movement. In the following year, for example, Slow Food Editore (the publishing house of the movement) was established. Slow Food officially became an international movement in December 1989 when delegates from fifteen countries met at the Opéra-Comique in Paris to ratify a Slow Food manifesto (see Appendix 1) and approve the movement's symbol of the snail, a 'small, cosmopolitan, and prudent' creature and an 'amulet against speed' (Kummer 2002: 22).

Informed by their leftist political views, the members of early Slow Food wanted the movement to highlight and celebrate the produce, culture and customs of local communities, beginning with Italy. These local ways of life were identified as under threat due to the population drift to larger urban centres and the undermining of small-scale farming by larger agriculture conglomerates. The early Slow Food movement sought to protect local farmers, restaurants and economies through an appreciation of the value of local produce and the promotion of local *osterie*. The *osteria* has a special place in Italian cuisine and culture that is difficult to appreciate outside those contexts. The *osterie* serve simple and comparatively cheap food based on local produce and are an important site of sociality in local villages and communities. The initial defence of the *osterie* and *trattorie* by the early Slow Food movement was therefore an action based on *class*, but not the class associated with elitism, given that the threatened invasion of McDonalds and other global fast food outlets was not going to compete with or undermine the elite restaurants but local, family-based, (more) working-class eating establishments.

The origins of Slow Food undermine conventional political categories and are situated within a uniquely Italian cultural-political context in which the post-war party system and more traditional forms of civic association have declined (Leitch

2003: 457). Even in Italy, the idea of a leftist gastronomic grouping was something of an oxymoron and, not surprisingly, the group was subject to criticisms from a range of sources (see Parasecoli 2003 on the ascetism of the Italian left; and Blim 2000 on recent fragmentations in Italian left politics). As Petrini has noted: 'the leftist intelligentsia when Arcigola was launched ... looked down on us as a bunch of good-timers interested only in stuffing ourselves, while from the other side, the food and wine specialists affiliated with the Accademia Italiana della Cucina distrusted us left-wing gastronomes as incompetent intruders with an ideological agenda' (2001: 10). The movement challenged, therefore, the idea that interest in good quality food and wine was a bourgeois affectation and it argued that progressive political thought needed to give legitimacy to pleasure and aesthetics.

The early Slow Food movement established a philosophical core that remains central to the organization. The virtues of slowness are obviously a defining feature but such a valuation of slowness extends beyond its connection to food. As Petrini notes of the early Slow Food movement: 'Arcigola embraced slow life, not just slow food' (2001: 13). Slowness in Slow Food was intended to be a means of allowing people to be open to sensory pleasures, the company of others, and an attentiveness to self. As Alberto Capatti, who was central to the formulation of Slow Food philosophy in his role as editor of *Slow*, wrote: 'we are aiming at those who wish to listen to the rhythm of their own lives, and possibly adjust it' (1996: 5). Slow Food is arguably most clearly identified by its valuation and promotion of pleasure, evidenced by the title of its founding manifesto as the 'International Movement in Defense of the Right to Pleasure'. Local chapters of the organization are known as *convivia*, which again stresses the importance of enjoyment, and the 'shared table' is a feature of gatherings, with an emphasis on the investment of time in hospitality and commensality.

While Slow Food retains this foundation, the movement has undergone a significant transformation in recent years, most notably developing from a solely gastronomic organization to a self-proclaimed '*eco*-gastronomic' one. Since its inception Slow Food talked about the connections between the pleasure and taste of food and the environment and food production but more recently a new emphasis on biodiversity and sustainable systems of agriculture has gained a priority in the movement. Slow Food now professes itself to be 'a more complex mixture of pleasure and ecology' (R. Sardo 2003). The transformation of Slow Food from a gastronomic to an eco-gastronomic movement has created an unusual conjunction of interest in quality food and produce with a political focus on the deleterious effects of globalization (see Chapter 6). Slow Food, however, distinguishes itself from the direct actions of the so-called 'anti-globalization' protesters, such as the French farmer and activist, José Bové.[2] As Petrini has said: 'Others may take the fight to the streets; Slow Food has a different idea: to rescue eating establishments, dishes, and products from the flood of standardization'

(2001: 28). Silvio Barbero (Slow Food Italy national secretary) has described the movement as 'against "negative" globalization – we're trying to use globality for positive purposes' (Barbero 2003), such as exploiting the global communicative potentials to promote food and cultural differences (through the Slow Food press office and website) and fostering networks of support and cooperation across national borders (such as the Presidia and *Terra Madre* meetings; see below).

The success of this attempt at positive globality – or, 'the other globalization'[3] – is also demonstrated in the growth of Slow Food membership and organizational structure. Currently, there are over 80,000 members worldwide in over 100 countries, organized into almost 800 *convivia* (www.slowfood.com). The *convivium* is the basic structural unit of Slow Food, the local chapter that serves as the most immediate point of contact between members, their local food culture and networks, and the wider public. A *convivium* is required to be an open group, its activities and events not simply limited to members ('Starting a New Convivium'). Slow Food statutes limit minimum and maximum numbers for a *convivium*, and also recommend that the boundaries of a *convivium* reflect a distinctive or definable region as the basis for forging a distinct identity for each group. The direct participation of private companies in *convivia* is not permitted but otherwise each *convivium* is free to organize its own agenda of activities and to initiate supporting links with local producers. *Convivia* also play an important role in the larger projects of Slow Food (see following section), as sponsors or nominators for local food projects in their own region or in other parts of the world. The largest concentration of membership and *convivia* is in Italy (35,000 members and 360 *convivia*, called *condotte* there) but the movement is not confined to Europe, recording strong growth in recent years in countries like the United States, Australia and Japan.

The head office of Slow Food is still located in Bra, Piedmont, but now employs over 100 people with an annual budget of €13 million (McBride 2003). The tasks of this head office include: providing organizational support to local *convivia* and the national offices outside Italy; initiating and administering the larger-scale campaigns and projects enumerated below; promoting the movement through their Press Office; and organizing the big Slow Food events such as the biennial *Salone del Gusto* (Hall of Taste) in Turin. In addition the publishing wing of the movement, Slow Food Editore, publishes over forty titles, including *Vini d'Italia* (in collaboration with *Gambero Rosso*) and *Osterie d'Italia* (which reviews over 1,500 *osterie* and sells over 100,000 copies annually; Slow Food 2002b); manages the popular and comprehensive website, www.slowfood.com, updated daily (on average, over 3,400 visits to website per day); and publishes the quarterly journal *Slow* in six language editions (Italian, English, French, German, Spanish and Japanese), which serves a crucial role in communicating the core values of the movement and uniting its disparate membership.

Despite the scale and professionalism of the Bra offices, Silvio Barbero stresses the 'grassroots' status of the movement, due to the importance of initiatives under-taken by local chapters (such as nominating and sponsoring Presidia projects) and the centrality of the local *convivia* events to the philosophy of Slow Food (Barbero 2003). According to Barbero, the task of the head office is to provide administrative and logistical support to local *convivia* projects and campaigns and, by the staging of the large-scale events, give the movement a heightened visibility which will assist the recruitment of members at a local level. It should be noted, however, that most major initiatives of Slow Food still emanate directly from the President, Petrini. The best recent example of this is the establishment of the University of Gastronomic Sciences, formally opened in May 2004 near Bra on the World Heritage-listed and now fully restored Agenzia di Pollenza (with a second campus at Collorno in Emilia-Romagna). Largely the brainchild of Petrini, the university was able to attract finan-cial support (from the city authority of Bra and the regional authority of Piedmont, in addition to private donors) to undertake the massive restoration and building project to house the university, a wine bank, hotel and restaurant.

While the scale of this project attests to the ability of Petrini to conceive grand plans and inspire others to join in their implementation, the power and influence of Petrini is at the same time being mitigated to some extent by the increasing internationalization of the movement. There are now national offices of Slow Food in Switzerland, Germany, the USA, France and Japan and the increase in mem-berships outside Italy is increasingly reflected in the size and mix of the Slow Food International Council, to which countries can elect a number of national council-lors indexed to the size of their membership base. Currently, Italy has fourteen councillors, the US six, Germany four, Switzerland three, Australia, France and Japan two each, while the UK, Austria and Canada each have one councillor. The International President's Committee comprises of nine members, of which four are Italian (including Petrini). (Other international positions are also occupied by members from Argentina, Ireland and the Netherlands.) While Petrini's charis-matic profile has been unquestionably the force behind the profile of the movement so far it has not been without criticism (e.g. Chrzan 2004). In the coming years, the organizational base and the democratic statutes that have evolved within Slow Food will see an interesting and significant shift of emphasis, as membership numbers outside Italy begin to surpass those in the movement's country of origin, and it remains to be seen how such developments will impact on the leadership and direction of the movement.

Projects

In October 2004, 140,000 people attended Slow Food's biennial *Salone del Gusto* (Hall of Taste) in Turin where over 500 producers from Italy and around the world showcased their unique products over five days, to exemplify Slow Food's philosophy of the need to value the quality and diversity of traditional, artisanal foodstuffs. At the *Salone* of 2002, 311 Taste Workshops were held where 218 cheeses, 1,040 wines and 415 categories of food were tasted. More than 2,000 journalists are accredited for the event, which thus ensures wide media coverage around the world ('Salone del Gusto' 2003: 4). While gastronomic pleasures are highlighted in events such as *Salone del Gusto*, the *eco*-gastronomy of Slow Food is also emphasized, as food is reconnected with territory and community on a global level. Similar events around the Slow Food world, which are modelled on the Turin event, have begun to appear in recent years, offering opportunities for local, regional or national products to foreground the importance of typicality and the artisanal in local food economies and communities. Italy hosts events such as 'Toscana Slow' (held in June 2003), 'Slow Fish' (June 2004 in Genoa) and 'Cheese' (held every two years in Bra), while in the USA 'Westward Slow'(held July 2004) was a kind of American *Salone del Gusto*, with plans for a similar 'southern hemisphere' event for Australia, following on from the success of 'Barossa Slow' in the South Australian wine region in April 2004. The *Salone del Gusto* and related events are not intended to offer an elitist global smorgasbord for the discerning 'foodie' but are conceived as means of giving a visibility to the distinctiveness and embeddedness of contemporary foodways in the global everyday. As Cinzia Scaffidi, who works on the Slow Food Awards, puts it, 'If there is something important that globalization teaches us I think it is the impossibility [of leading] a perfectly individual life. We are all connected and … so our behaviours, our choices, what we eat and how we have fun – everything we do has a response somewhere else. Everything is linked' (Scaffidi 2003a). Such spectacular events have the capacity to generate significant media interest in the labours of artisanal producers who may not otherwise have attracted the attention of journalists at home, due to their small-scale production or relative isolation from metropolitan food scenes and the associated food press.[4]

Slow Food's more explicit commitment to a broader agenda of global agricultural concerns such as sustainability and biodiversity began in 1996, with the formation of the 'Ark of Taste', a kind of catalogue or database of rare, endangered or unique products from around the world, as a response to what the movement considered an increasing homogenization of food and flavours, and an alarming decline in global biodiversity. (Slow Food estimates 30,000 vegetable varieties have become extinct in the last century, and 33 per cent of livestock varieties have disappeared or are on the brink of doing so [www.slowfoodfoundation.com]). The metaphor of the Ark was intended to signify 'a protective receptacle for quality products that should be saved from the deluge of standardization and world-wide distribution' and signalled a commitment to regionality and the promotion of 'new forms of "slow" production and supply' (Petrini 1997: 8). The Ark was followed by the Slow Food Foundation for Biodiversity in 2002 with the aim to 'organize and fund projects that defend our world's heritage of agricultural diversity and gastronomic traditions' (www. slowfoodfoundation.com). The Foundation, an independent non-profit entity, was established in partnership with the regional authority of Tuscany and a range of public and private donors (including other regional and city authorities in Italy, food and wine producers and consortia, and Slow Food *convivia*) whose contributions range from €2,000 to over €50,000 annually (www.slowfoodfoundation.com). This Foundation currently oversees two chief activities: the Slow Food Awards and the Presidia. The Slow Food Awards are decided by an international jury of over 500 members (including journalists, food and wine professionals, and researchers) who propose nominations from which the President's committee selects the prizewinners, 'people anywhere in the world who defend, promote or enhance the biodiversity of species and produce' (Scaffidi and Kummer 2000: 15). The diversity of the projects which are thus supported and promoted by Slow Food may be seen in the range of the recipients of the Special Jury Prizes at the inaugural awards in 2000, which included the director of the Vegetables Department at the Vavilov Institute in Russia and a beekeeper from Turkey.

The chief concern of the Foundation, however, is the establishment and support of the Presidia (presidium means fortress or garrison), small projects to assist artisan producers, which were initially identified from items catalogued in the Ark of Taste. Indeed, the motivation for the Presidia project was the desire to preserve all the Ark items, beginning with Italy – where they have had considerable success – but now also throughout the world. The goals of the Presidia are: 'to promote artisan products; to stabilize production techniques; to establish stringent production standards and, above all, to guarantee a viable future for traditional foods' (www.slowfoodfoundation.com). Sponsoring projects (costing between €3,000 and €15,000 in the first year of the project) may take a variety of forms, from providing infrastructure to maintain or improve production, establishing local or regional networks or consortia to support it, to training (such as apprenticing young people to preserve a dying skill, or training the producer in business or networking skills necessary to market their produce), payment of salaries to workers and producers, and providing travel to Slow Food events to meet with other artisanal producers.

While envisaged as a means of 'saving' traditional produce, the Presidia also aim to provide support for communities whose livelihood and sustainability has been closely linked with the artisanal produce. As Corby Kummer puts it, 'Ark products must live in the modern world' (2002: 23) and the Presidia projects constitute inventive ways in which Slow Food can articulate the distinctive cultural value of products, together with the importance of recognizing the social capital in the form of producers and communities in which these products are embedded. The Presidia thus implicitly foster slow living through the maintenance and support they offer communities to sustain a unique quality of life in the face of the threats posed by globalization and industrialized agriculture. The Presidia also serve an important function in the life of *convivia*, which may take on the sponsorship of a Presidium project, either in their own region or in the developing world (or sometimes both). Supporting a local project means that the *convivium* members become more integrated into the production of traditional foods in their region, building a network of support and knowledge between producers and consumers which is an important value in the Slow Food conception of authenticity and informed or situated pleasure (see Chapter 5). Similarly, the support of a distant project also exemplifies Slow Food's aim to be an international movement in which producers and consumers are increasingly aware of global concerns and the ethical interconnections between global subjects. The Presidia exemplify what Slow Food calls the 'New Agriculture', which is 'part ecological and part gastronomic', 'a productive philosophy that is based on quality, biodiversity, respect for the environment, animal well-being, landscape and the health and enjoyment of the consumer' (www.slowfoodfoundation.com).

A recent study concluded that a Slow Food Presidium 'acts as a cultural matrix, bringing together territory [*terroir*] and product, typicality and quality', and also acts as a means of identity-formation for the local community ('Evaluating' 2004).[5] The Bocconi study found that the considerable economic success experienced as a result of the Presidia was not limited to increased farming income but also included indirect economic benefits such as tourism to the area through heightened public awareness of, and support for, the artisanal product. The *Robiola di Roccaverano* cheese Presidium, for example, resulted in increased tourism in the area, which 'then led to the opening of an ageing facility and retail outlet and the inclusion of another Piedmontese traditional product, *Filetto Baciato* of Ponzone' ('Evaluating' 2004). The support of one product, therefore, can become a hub in a broader network based on an interlinked culinary and farming heritage. While both Scarpato (2002) and Donati (2004) have signalled a concern for the possible negative consequences that may arise from a Presidium success, such as the impact of increased tourism on local communities especially in the developing world, the significant rise of ecotourism, ethical tourism or 'travel philanthropy' as it is becoming known in the USA (Needham 2004: 9), suggests that the increased social exchange which arises from such encounters may be another instance of the ethical cosmopolitanism which we argue is increasingly shaping people's decisions and consumption in everyday life, whether at home or abroad (see also Petrini 2001: 54–8 and Chapter 6).

The potential of Presidia projects to have broader international consequences has also been demonstrated in the agreement signed in April 2003 between Slow Food and the Brazilian government, in a joint initiative linked to the government's 'Zero Hunger' programme. This programme aims to address the chronic poverty and reliance on food imports suffered in Brazil by recovering and promoting a diversity of small-scale agriculture and production, and reversing the previous trend to large-scale intensive farming for export (e.g. coffee) which concentrated wealth in fewer hands and developed agro-industrial monocultures at the expense of traditional and sustainable farming linked to communities and indigenous groups. The joint protocol signed by Slow Food and the Special State Minister for Food Safety and the Battle against Hunger includes objectives to revive knowledge of traditional cultivation and animal husbandry techniques, to protect animal and vegetable biodiversity, and asserts as a basic human right the 'access to healthy, safe and quality foods for all' (quoted in di Croce and LaValva 2003: 51). In particular, a series of Presidia will support small-scale food production, such as guarana in the Amazonian forest (di Croce and LaValva 2003: 50).

More recently, another initiative that indicates an increasing global awareness within Slow Food was '*Terra Madre*: World Meeting of Food Communities', held in October 2004 to coincide with the *Salone del Gusto*. *Terra Madre* gathered 5,000 small-scale producers and farmers from around the world who each represented a 'food community', 'which means they are part of a chain of production, linked by a common product, ethnic identity, region, history, or approach' ('*Terra Madre*' 2004). The aim was to foster networks of contact and exchanges of everyday knowledges, which are at present so localized they are under threat of being forgotten, in order to constitute what Petrini calls 'virtuous globalization' ('Interview' 2004: 52). The 'new rurality' ('Interview' 2004: 52) advocated by Slow Food is not a Year Zero project to make everyone an agricultural worker but, while certainly seeking to revitalize rural environments and communities, is based on an ethical cosmopolitanism, in which people are aware of the global connections which bind them to distant others, and in which this connection is fundamentally connected to food, whether through growing, distributing or consuming. The Slow Food world-view, according to Petrini, is one 'convinced that efforts to create a better world begin with how one grows one's food and end with how one consumes it' ('Interview' 2004: 51). As a result of this meeting, an ongoing *Terra Madre* forum has been established, with plans to develop the networks of contact between food communities.

Given this commitment to an awareness and exchange of knowledge about how food can be sustainably – and pleasurably – produced and consumed, it is not surprising that another long-term campaign of Slow Food has been taste education, which is carried out in a variety of ways, from the large-scale events like *Salone del Gusto* (which in addition to the main tasting halls also includes Taste Workshops for children) to the edible gardens projects in Slow Food USA, or the Master of Food programme run through *condotte* in Italy, and now the newly opened University of Gastronomic Sciences. At the local *convivia* level, tasting education and workshops are the core activity, as the primary site of conviviality, and the means by which social networks and relations of knowledge and trust (e.g. linking local producers with informed and supportive consumers) are established and sustained.

While the concept of 'taste education' may at first glance merely denote distinction or cultural capital we would argue that a sustained investigation of this aspect of Slow Food's activities reveals the more ambitious aim of returning to the sensory experiences of food, based on pleasure and a commitment to the investment of time in such pleasures. Teaching children, for instance, of the panoply of possible flavours, textures and colours, with an emphasis on the tactile and sensual experience of food – from garden to kitchen to plate – is not about the cultivation of *taste* in the traditional gastronomic sense but of *appetite* – for food, play and knowledge – which Adam Phillips links to inspiration and imagination (1998: 7). Of course the word 'taste' – especially when coupled with 'education' – can never be an innocent term but bears the trace of class-based notions of value and the Slow Food agenda for taste education for children is unapologetically predicated on an explicit valuing of certain foods (fresh and hand-made, for instance) over others (mass-produced, homogenized, artificially flavoured, high in saturated fats and sugars), and, by implication, certain pleasures over others. Taste education for Slow Food – whether directed at children or adults – does not address itself to the correct usage of a fish-knife, nor does it reduce food to nutritional value, but attempts to situate food in what it sees as more authentic, enriched and convivial contexts where the aim is how best to savour and enhance pleasure, rather than gain a momentary 'fix' from food, as Chapter 5 will explore in more detail. As Capatti puts it, the challenge in taste education is to foster the Slow Food 'pleasure principle' of food and conviviality (2002c: 4–5). Whether it succeeds in these aims, and avoids the charge of elitism, remains a continuing challenge for the movement and one which may determine much of its future success and relevance.

To that end, within Italy, taste education has been fostered through collaborative projects between Slow Food and regional school authorities, with support and finance also from the ministries of agriculture, health and education (in ways not dissimilar to the French model of *Semaine du goût,* which Petrini explicitly acknowledges as an influence; 2001: 74). Developing interdisciplinary programmes based on 'sensory literacy', Slow Food has been involved in teacher-training projects since the mid-1990s, and government accredited to train school personnel since 2002 (Venturi 2002: 54–5). In Piedmont, for example, a teacher-training scheme involving around 1,000 participants has been launched, based on taste workshops and training in the region's food and agriculture heritage (Venturi 2002: 56).

At the adult level, Slow Food Italy has developed its Master of Food course, which was developed in collaboration with, and designed for, local *convivia,* as a more structured means for *convivium* members to enhance their own understanding and knowledge of food. While the Master of Food is popular and implemented in

Italian *condotte* – about 500 courses were run in 2002 (S. Sardo 2003) – it has not been adopted outside Italy.[6] There are plans to export the Master of Food to other Slow Food national networks of *convivia* but this may be one area where the Italian traditions of food appreciation, embedded in local contexts and traditions, are distinctive; such food appreciation does not carry the same class connotations it does, for instance, in Anglo-countries where Slow Food may be seen as just an association for food and wine appreciation. While Italian cuisine varies from region to region, an interest, even a passion, for food and wine is by no means limited to the bourgeoisie. Despite its current specificity to the Italian context, however, the Master of Taste remains an area of interest in the spread and development of Slow Food for two main reasons: it has proved to be an effective means for recruitment of members (4,000 new members in 2002 as a direct result of the courses) and, perhaps surprisingly, it appeals to a younger membership base than the traditional *condotte* activities within Italy (S. Sardo 2003). Sebastiano Sardo, who administers the Master of Food from Bra head office, believes that the 'youth appeal' of the Master's courses reflect an increasing 'global perspective' among younger Italians (S. Sardo 2003).

Perhaps Slow Food's most ambitious project to resignify gastronomy is the new *Università di Scienze Gastronomiche*, the University of Gastronomic Sciences, officially opened in May, 2004 in Pollenza, Piedmont. The first intake of 60 students (culled from over 2,000 applications from around the world; McCarthy and Kirby 2004) began study in October 2004 and this private university will offer degree programmes, as well as short-course training, and serve as an interdisciplinary research centre for studies in gastronomy, enology, culture, communication, hospitality and agriculture. The idea for the university sprang from both the popularity of the Master of Taste programme in Slow Food Italy and a perceived gap in current European universities' curricula:

> At present, European universities train agronomists, livestock experts, nutritionists and dieticians on a purely scientific basis, focusing on mathematics and chemistry so that students understand industrial food processes and can analyze food consumption and its impact on public health. To date, no university has approached the study of food from a historical, sensorial and gastronomic perspective, examining the canons of taste from past to present and the foods we eat in terms of their appeal and sheer pleasure. (http://www.unisg.it/eng/index.htm)

While the innovation and 'flagship' quality of the new university makes it a significant contribution to the international profile of Slow Food, the movement's commitment to local campaigns as the key to significant, broad-based reform of eating and foodways remains its most important initiative and this commitment is perhaps best exemplified by the school gardens projects which have emerged in the past few years as a prime initiative, largely due to the rapid growth and increasing influence of Slow Food USA within Slow Food internationally. The importance of this project lies in its potential to be taken up by the movement worldwide and its timely articulation of broad social concerns about children and food. Slow Food USA has implemented a national goal to form an education project such as edible gardens in each of its 130 *convivia* (www.slowfoodusa.org/education/index.html) and at the 2003 International Congress of Slow Food in Naples a motion was carried to expand the school gardens project throughout the movement worldwide, with each *convivium* urged to participate (Slow Food 2003).

The success of this initiative will potentially give the movement a significantly higher profile, as well as providing an interesting test to judge the increasing strength and influence of Slow Food USA in relation to the movement's home base in Italy (the membership is currently doubling in the US every two and a half years; Dimock 2003: 12). For a movement which has always stressed its commitment to 'grassroots' issues and constituencies, school gardens provide extremely fertile ground to propagate the values of Slow Food. The American initiative was largely inspired by the example of the Edible Schoolyard at Martin Luther King Jr Middle School in Berkeley, California, established in 1997 and sponsored by Alice Waters, a high-profile chef and Slow Food vice-president. An acre of asphalt parking area was cleared and planted, and the school's disused cafeteria was refurbished as a kitchen/classroom. Currently, there are school garden projects supported by local *convivia* scattered across the USA. Taste education in Slow Food USA has also been taken in other directions as well, with a collaborative project at Riker's Island prison in New York, involving organic gardening and cooking by the inmates (Mayo 2003: 79). Slow Food Australia has also had a similar beginning with edible gardens, admittedly on a smaller scale than the US example so far. The well-known Australian chef and food writer, Stephanie Alexander, instigated a school garden similar to that at Berkeley in Collingwood, Melbourne, which has been running since 2001 and involves 120 students, aged seven to twelve, with minimal funding support from the Education Department but primarily reliant on a network of volunteers (Alexander 2003: 1–2). As a means of integrating slow principles into everyday life practice, we believe that school garden projects hold great potential. If they can manage to avoid the twin pitfalls of the instrumentalism of traditional nutritional education and the distinction of traditional gastronomy, school gardens can reconnect daily practices of food with larger questions of ethics and pleasure.

Slow Food's taste education commitment – like so many other aspects of the movement – is both embryonic and potentially riven with contradiction: between equity and elitism, pedagogy and pleasure, not to mention theory and practice. We would emphasize, however, that taste education needs to be considered in its broad scope within Slow Food as part of the articulation of a different ethics of living based on slowness, lest it be simply dismissed as food appreciation for the discerning palate. At the 2003 International Congress, Petrini stressed the contradictions in taste education – from school gardens to a gastronomic university – but in doing so, situated both undertakings in a consistent, if ambitious, project which refuses to accept that ecology, equity and pleasure are irreconcilable. In his President's Address, Petrini said: 'Our ideas are modern and, in some respects, revolutionary. Slow Food wants intelligent gastronomic renewal accompanied by deep ecological awareness, rejecting quantity as the only measure of our lives' (2004a: 10).

Città Slow

The success of Slow Food has given birth to the associated Slow Cities or Città Slow movement that attempts to extend the Slow Food philosophy to all aspects of urban living (see Chapter Four for further discussion).[7] Beginning in 1999, with the election of Greve-in-Chianti mayor Paolo Saturnini as president, Città Slow is an autonomous organization but with close links to Slow Food. It is governed by an elected assembly of ten mayors with a president, now Stefano Cimicchi (the mayor of Orvieto), three vice-presidents and a chief operating officer (Knox 2005: 7). In addition to protecting and enhancing traditional food and wines through actions such as the banning of fast food outlets and the promotion of local markets, Slow Cities implement a range of urban planning and transport measures such as the reduction of traffic, the improvement of parks, the restoration of old buildings, and the banning of neon signs, car alarms and mobile phone towers.

Slow Cities are not cosmopolitan metropoloi but are small cities or largish towns. Casalbeltrame in Piedmont is the smallest Città Slow member with about 1,500 people and the larger towns in the movement have populations around 50,000. The size of the Slow Cities aims to facilitate the virtues of urban living while minimizing conventional problems: the intermediate size of slow communities between the conventional mass city and the small rural community means that it is more possible to balance familiarity with others and security of community life with the freedoms of city living. Città Slow is still an evolving organization; it has experienced great growth since its inception and much media attention but it has not yet developed the global profile of Slow Food and has only begun to spread outside of Italy in more recent years: in 2001, all of the twenty-eight certified Slow Cities were Italian and in 2005 the forty-four member towns included Ludlow and Aylsham in Britain, Sokndal and Levanger in Norway, and Hersbruck, Schwarzenbruck, Uberlingen and Waldkirch in Germany. Other towns from a range of countries, including Brazil, Switzerland, Greece and Croatia, are seeking certification (Knox 2005: 7).

Città Slow membership is bestowed on the cities themselves as a result of their acceptance and implementation of a range of public policies, as outlined in the

Città Slow charter, relating to urban planning, technology, the environment, tourism, business, agriculture and public health. The charter declares that Slow Cities will 'abide by a shared code of conduct which stresses the importance of the quality of the fabric of life in their local areas'. Such notions of 'quality of life' are often difficult to delineate but a variety of ethical and political values inform the processes of governance of Slow Cities so that they are not limited to the quaint outlawing of cars from the city centre or the banning of advertising billboards. The charter highlights 'individuality' and 'creativity' at the local level in opposition to the 'proliferation of uniformity' that occurs in global culture. Of course the production of individual difference is always understood in specific relational contexts: the Città Slow community's rejection of the standardization of much global food, goods and everyday practices is itself replaced by an enforced ideal of traditional, albeit locally unique, food, goods and everyday practices. The movement also promotes its democratic basis declaring that the Slow Cities' vision 'is one where the pursuit and dissemination of excellence are seen not as something to be enjoyed by a select few, but as an experience that enriches the lives of all'. Most importantly, the movement seeks to promote the pleasures of the towns, requiring the removal of 'any physical obstructions or cultural obstacles that might prevent full enjoyment of all that the town has to offer' (www.cittaslow.net).

Some Slow Cities are well known tourist destinations, such as Positano and Orvieto, but many are low-key, smallish market towns that have managed to sustain a slow way of living and so the designation 'Slow City' should not be seen as simply a tourism branding exercise. While Città Slow membership can attract increased tourist attention, which paradoxically may make it more difficult to sustain the 'slow' characteristics, membership can also revive such places while retaining their character and ways of life: one local resident of Aylsham says the town was 'teetering' five years ago but now has a new lease of (slow) life (Barkham 2004). Slow Cities do not present themselves as living museums: the organization promotes its towns as living communities that embrace modern technologies and practices provided they enhance the 'quality of life' of residents in a slow-friendly manner. While towns are admitted only after a strict auditing process and are reviewed every three years, slowness is implemented in variable ways and to varying degrees across different towns (Cimicchi 2003). Slow Cities seem to have broad community support although both Cimicchi and Saturnini have acknowledged that there were initial difficulties in their respective towns as residents became accustomed to the requirements of Città Slow membership and the adherence to regulations remains an ongoing issue (Saturnini 2003; Yeomans 2002). Saturnini also stresses that a Slow City designation can have significant infrastructural impact, as in Greve-in-Chianti where building developments have been rejected or scaled back to meet Slow City requirements.

With its identification of pleasure and slowness as desirable aspects of everyday life, Città Slow, like Slow Food, is a promising manifestation of the possibilities of slow living. The appeal of this organization, however, like Slow Food, derives from the Italian context where mid-sized cities of distinctive character already have a positive cultural resonance for many. It remains to be seen, then, how widely and how effectively Città Slow can spread a slow civic ideal beyond Italy and how this model can translate to other urban forms without the same history and traditions to anchor it. Given the increasing interest in sustainable cities and urban renewal, however, we believe that notions of slow living can be made very pertinent to urban contexts and that the model of local government intervention proposed by Città Slow is an effective way to enhance everyday life in the city.

New Social Movements and Slow Food

Given its structure and diverse aims, how are we then to classify Slow Food? As an officially-recognized non-profit NGO (through its affiliation with the FAO – Food and Agriculture Organization of the United Nations – and its participation in events such as the World Social Forum)? An educational organization (through its emerging links with schools)? Or a consumer-rights group (as Chrzan 2004 names it)? Slow Food tends to refer to itself as a movement, and while some have disputed such a nomination (e.g. Chrzan 2004), we think it is valuable to situate Slow Food within the extensive literature about new social movements to best represent how Slow Food not only seeks to intervene in public discourse and policy but also to foster a different approach to everyday life among its supporters and indeed to operate as a symbol of an alternative to 'fast life'.[8] Like other new social movements, Slow Food seeks to 'generate a public debate about matters of public morality and social organization, contesting the norms by which we live our lives' with implications for private or everyday life (Crossley 2003: 295–6). Of the many definitions offered of social movements, it is still perhaps Blumer's which best captures our sense of Slow Food: 'Social movements,' Blumer proposed, 'can be viewed as collective enterprises seeking to establish a new order of life … [which] derive their motive power on one hand from dissatisfaction with the current form of life, and on the other hand, from wishes and hopes for a new system of living' (1969: 99). We begin, therefore from the assumption that Slow Food is, as it names itself to be, a movement, albeit one with a formalized (if still evolving) organizational structure and a sizeable administrative headquarters.[9]

The altered political terrain of the past few decades, marked by diverse responses such as an increased focus on matters of lifestyle and the growing significance of cultural politics, has partly resulted from the growth of non-institutional political formations like new social movements. These developments have led some to talk of a 'movement society' in Western democracies (Rucht and

Neidhardt 2002: 7), or at least to argue that social movements now 'lie perma-nently at the heart of social life' (Touraine 1981: 29). The importance of new social movements, however, goes beyond an acknowledgement of the more public and political focus that issues of culture, identity and lifestyle have assumed. The most important contribution of new social movements could be said to be their ability 'to name the world differently' by redefining or reframing social life (Melucci 1996a: 494). This contribution is seen not only in the *content* of new social move-ments (their public promotion of cultural issues, for instance) but also through their often non-hierarchical, non-permanent and non-standard *form* which arises from – and responds to – the indeterminacies of contemporary public life.

Many social movements today are attentive to the way ethico-political values are manifested in identity formation and everyday life, but they are also motivated by a keen awareness of macro-political issues. The cultural focus of new social move-ments cannot be considered in isolation from their role as political agents, with the capacity to shape and intervene in contemporary global politics. Social move-ments can arise at the local, regional or national level but increasingly they are ori-ented in relation to globalization, giving rise to the designation of 'global social movements' (Cohen and Rai 2000: 6). Social movements can adopt a range of political responses to globalization: some seek change through reform of existing government policies and institutional practices, some may try to insulate the local from global forces, while others implement strategies of transnational resistance (Goodman 2002: xv–xxiv). Increasingly, however, movements have arisen in response to the mobilization of capital on a global scale (Cohen and Rai 2000: 7–8).

Recently, we have also seen the emergence of anti-corporate movements: protests like those in Seattle in 1999 and Prague in 2000 can be seen as attempts to regen-erate democracy and the public sphere and hold accountable those institutions that influence the everyday lives of millions, transnationally, while 'fair trade' schemes and consumer boycotts mobilize everyday consumption choices within public debate over globalization and the power of corporations (Crossley 2003: 298–9). Since at least the early 1990s, there has been evidence of an 'incipient transnational civil society' emerging as networks of activists, non-governmental organizations and other actors connect, whether through cyberspace or international fora, 'in an attempt to intervene in matters of global governance' (McLaughlin 2004: 156). Such anti-corporate, anti-globalization movements have foregrounded what has often been missing from accounts of new social movements and that is a consider-ation of ethnocentricity (Crossley 2003: 300), or the 'transnational turn' (McLaughlin 2004: 161). The internationalism of the anti-corporate movement 'draws attention to the distinctly Western and national bias of new social movement theories and their conception of the "new society"' (Crossley 2003: 302; see also Mohanty 2002: 509).[10] Focusing on the 'post-materialist' issues which are relevant to many in the West may occlude, that is, both the material deprivation faced by the majority of the world and the extent to which First World prosperity and stability may be at the expense of the exploitation and oppression of workers in other parts of the world (Crossley 2003: 300). The changing and expanding agenda of Slow Food in recent years needs to be considered in this context, as the result of an increasing global awareness and a growing preparedness to face more directly some of the implications of North–South divides.[11] Against charges that Slow Food has not yet ended world hunger (Laudan 2004), or that *Terra Madre* was just a 'photo-opportunity' (Chrzan 2004), we need to consider how the forms of global exchange and communication that a movement like Slow Food seeks to mobilize may play an effective part in ongoing public debates about globalization and the power of transnational corporations; how, in short, it may be a participant in an emerging transnational civil society.

Two key questions which recur in recent analyses of new social movements are highly relevant to any examination of Slow Food. These are questions about what's new about them (e.g. Cohen and Rai 2000; Crossley 2003; Edwards 2004), and the place and importance of the middle class in such movements (e.g. Bagguley 1992; Cleveland 2003). Both these questions – and the various answers given by theorists – involve important assumptions about what constitutes politics, or more specifically, a legitimate form of politics in contemporary contexts. If, as Crossley (2003) and Edwards (2004) have argued, the distinction between 'new' and 'old' social movements has been overdrawn by some theorists (e.g. Habermas), it is still fair to say that the movements which have emerged since the 1960s have given a new prominence to questions of identity, culture and everyday life – what Habermas called 'the grammar of forms of life' (1987: 392).[12] While Melucci has also argued that new social movements seek to bring about social change 'by means of changes in language, sexual customs, affective relationships, dress and eating habits' (1988: 249) his formulation stresses their dynamism and inventiveness (as opposed to the defensive, protective implication in Habermas's account), which we think better captures the aims of a movement like Slow Food (see also Melucci 1989, 1996b). As will be further discussed in Chapters 5 and 6, for instance, Slow Food has mobilized a reflexive approach to authenticity and tradition as a response to, and critique of, contemporary 'forms of life' without rejecting contemporaneity outright but using (post)modern forms of promotion and communication alongside face-to-face events to intervene in culture and everyday life.

Given the focus in new social movements on social change in everyday life through an emphasis on cultural politics, such movements have often been seen as an exclusively middle-class domain (e.g. Offe 1985). Assumptions about class interests in new social movements require interrogation, however, not least because there is nothing conclusive about the proportional over-representation of the middle class in new social movements as they are also over-represented in conventional political organizations (Nash 2000: 106). Critiquing class-based analyses of new social movements, Paul Bagguley concludes: 'It seems to be the case that all you need to do is discover the social characteristics of the majority of the social base, identify their interests and/or their values, and you have explained the movement' (1992: 36). With its attention to good food and wine, Slow Food may seem an obvious target for critiques of the political efficacy of a social movement based on supposedly bourgeois habits, tastes and values. Certainly in our experience of discussing Slow Food at academic seminars, the most commonly asked question is something like 'but isn't it *just* a middle-class thing?' (which always seem to imply an unspoken corollary 'and therefore not real politics'). For us, it is interesting to consider that, while the politics of class has rightly been an important site of debate within other social movements (such as feminism or environmentalism), the predominance of middle-class members has not led to such movements being dismissed as '*just* middle-class' but has warranted ongoing interrogation of the aims and practices in such movements. By contrast, the fact that Slow Food has a predominantly middle-class support base is sometimes seen as sufficient grounds for dismissal as a legitimate agent in the politics of everyday life and anti-globalization (e.g. Laudan 2001 and 2004; Gaytán 2004). Given the social resources for political mobilization which the middle class possesses, however, which can feed into 'a whole range of social movements, new, working-class, reactionary and otherwise' (Bagguley 1992: 40), it cannot be simply a matter of drawing a straight line between the class affiliation of membership and the interests and goals of a movement. We cannot assume, that is, a direct correlation between the social base of a movement and the interests it represents (Bagguley 1992: 40). As outlined here, the history of the Slow Food movement has been a narrative of a complex amalgam of social capital and a specifically Italian Leftist orientation at its foundation, developing into a transnational social movement with a middle-class support base and an extensive global network of partnerships and collaborations, from national governments and international NGOs to local chapters and food producers' collectives.

The enormity of such global problems and divides cannot of course be met by one entity and, despite its level of success and proliferation of projects, there remain significant challenges for the Slow Food movement that need to be overcome if it is to develop a diverse but global identity and hence offer a sustained critique of the dominance of 'fast life' in the global everyday. Albert Sonnenfeld (2001) has identified economic, political and strategic challenges for the movement. The economic challenge relates to the issue of pricing and the difficulty of persuading people to pay more for quality produce. For many low-income earners this is an impediment to adopting the principles of Slow Food, even though packaged, processed food at large supermarket chains may well be more expensive than a diet that has greater emphasis on fresh fruit and vegetables. Sonnenfeld also identifies the 'perils of elitism' (2001: xiv) as the political challenge for Slow Food. While the organization gains a growing profile from its particular battles with processes of globalization, it also continues to wrestle with the politics of trying to democratize ideas of 'quality' and 'taste' and hence distinguish itself from the elitism commonly associated with gastronomy organizations.

The strategic challenge for Slow Food is to develop a greater global identity in place of the strong Italian presence that still informs the movement. While Slow Food membership is growing rapidly in a number of countries, Slow Food Italy still constitutes the majority on the governing bodies, in line with the strong membership base in the country. The pleasures of the 'slow life' that underlie the movement can be traced back in many ways to a specifically Italian heritage and now the challenge is to translate this ethos to individual countries. There is some anecdotal evidence that the 'Italianicity' of the movement has been both a strength and a weakness. The leadership and astute media presence provided by Carlo Petrini has translated very well outside Italy, with a positive impact on both press attention and membership whenever he makes public appearances.[13] Presidential initiatives, however, can present serious challenges to membership outside Italy to implement on the scale envisaged by Slow Food headquarters. A good example of this was the *Terra Madre* World Meeting of Food Communities which required national offices to nominate and sponsor local food culture leaders to attend; such a task is much more difficult for membership in Australia and New Zealand to fulfil (due to distance and associated expense) than, for instance, Slow Food Germany. (Slow Food head office was responsible for sponsoring participants from less-affluent regions such as Latin America.) While the connotations of conviviality, cultural authenticity and outstanding food and wine associated with Italy provides a very positive image for Slow Food, there has also been some resistance to membership – despite sympathy with its principles – evident where there are historical antipathies to 'foreign' influence on food and culture, as in the UK or France, or in places where gastronomic interest may be seen as taking food 'too seriously', as in Australia.

Another important challenge for Slow Food – and the one most relevant to our concerns in this book – resides in attempting to implement a slower pace of life in the everyday lives of members. While the movement has been successful in mobilizing supporters, engaging with political authorities over a range of issues, and initiating an educational infrastructure, the implementation of 'slowness' in everyday structures and rhythms remains a goal rather than part of a systematic initiative, apart from the efforts of Città Slow. Many members express a *desire* for slowness and an appreciation of its virtues but they also acknowledge the reality that their everyday lives are lived at odds with such sentiments. There is much in the philosophy of Slow Food to give the idea of slow living prominence and credence but the widespread and everyday realization of those principles, with ensuing fundamental political ramifications, remains an unmet ideal. The 'slow' in Slow Food, that is, is both a significant means of differentiating itself from dominant values and practices in the global everyday and also a perpetual reminder of the complex realities of slowness, as the following chapter will explore.

–3–

Time and Speed

To think about time is to think about one's life, and to come to some clarity about time
is to live somewhat differently.

Brann (1999: 101)

In a recent television advertisement for a high-tech refrigerator which incorporates
a computer screen, a group of elegantly dressed young people are (somewhat inex-
plicably) sipping cocktails grouped round the fridge. On the fridge's screen is the
image of an absent friend who announces to the group, 'Sorry, I haven't got time
to talk right now.' While the advertisement seems to promise a sophisticated
sociality based on technology, it illustrates (apparently unwittingly) the problem of
finding time to talk, despite the invention of internet refrigerators. 'Finding time'
implies that time has been lost – or least misplaced – and yet we seem to do more,
more quickly, and supposedly more efficiently, than ever before, from 'just-in-
time' production to 'speed dating'. But is contemporary life faster? After all, cultural commentators since at least the nineteenth century have been critiquing the
acceleration of life and its concomitant instrumentalist mentality.[1] More recently,
however, a number of studies have attested to a faster pace of life in economically
developed industrialized countries (e.g. Levine and Norenzayan 1999; Levine and
Bartlett 1984).[2]

As many have argued, moreover, the appeal of speed – its valorization if not its
achievement – has become a defining feature of contemporary culture, in which
speed 'intensifiers' like channel-zapping TV remotes, speed dialling and sound
bites are part of everyday experience, not to mention that lift button that makes the
door close a few seconds sooner (Gleick 1999: 9; see also Eriksen 2001: 20;
Castells 1996; Adam 2003).[3] The valorization of speed in part attests to the spread
of work-culture into other domains of life. Speed is 'best practice' in the business
domain, according to best-selling business advice books like *It's Not the Big that
Eat the Small, But the Fast that Eat the Slow* (Jennings and Haughton 2002; sub-
titled: 'How to Use Speed as a Competitive Tool in Business'). Speed is often associated with decisiveness, slowness with weakness or prevarication; a 'slow thinker'
sounds too much like a 'slow learner'. As Simon Gottschalk argued in analyzing
representations of speed in television commercials: 'Under the speed regime, a

new binarism positions *fast* as a signifier of desire, resource, superiority, efficiency, libidinal energy, performance and intelligence. *Slow*, in contrast, becomes a signifier of frustration, lack, inferiority, deficiency, impotence, weakness' (1999: 312).

The assumed correlation between speed and productivity, however, is often belied by the experience of many who increasingly feel that they are actually accomplishing less and deriving less satisfaction from what they do. Even leisure, supposedly 'time out' from paid or unpaid labour and responsibilities, is also subject to 'time intensification', especially for women, who may experience a greater fragmentation and scarcity of leisure time (Deem 1996). Empirical research on time and work has shown that respondents 'did not just want to have "more free time" but rather "enough time for meaningful things"' (Reisch 2001: 374; see also Nowotny 1994: 108–9; Fitzpatrick 2004). As we outlined in the introductory chapter, slow living is a manifestation of this desire for 'time for meaningful things'. To live slowly, to carry out our practices of everyday life at a slower pace, would mean taking more time to complete tasks, and hence less would be done in a day; creating the effect of slowing time as well as movement. In the process, such mindful use of time through 'slow' practices may construct 'slow subjects' who invest the everyday with meaning and value as they negotiate its temporalities. In this chapter we will examine how 'slow' time comes to be seen not only as a rejection of negative qualities associated with speed but as a more ethical and pleasurable mode to inhabit. We will argue that time is increasingly becoming a key indicator of the core values in people's everyday lives: what people devote their time to, rather than what they spend their money on, may be a better indication of their values and priorities – their ethics of living. In response to this, we will explore the possibilities of an ethics of time. While examining the significance of time in practices of slow living, we will give particular attention to the understandings of time found in Slow Food. In these understandings, slowness can become a deliberate subversion and form a basis from which alternative practices of work, leisure, family and relationships may be generated.

The Temporalities of Modernity

Non-EU citizens who intend to reside in Italy are required to register their stay at their local *questura* (police station). Hence, on a cold, drizzly February morning we joined a queue which snaked down a Bologna side street and, four hours later, received a form requiring us to return in six weeks' time and another form to proceed to an office down the street for fingerprinting. We were among the lucky ones; those behind us in the queue were not processed that day and told to return the following week (which we subsequently discovered could lead to a string of lengthy visits to the *questura*). The incredulity with which we reported our experience to our Italian acquaintances was met either by puzzlement (they of course had never had to procure documentation for residency) or, more commonly, by a philosophical attitude towards the duration of such processes. This experience was a salutary reminder that slowness is not always a virtue and that 'slow time' is a culturally variable experience. Bureaucratic inertia aside, however, a temporality based on slowness can potentially lead to a reinterrogation of everyday practices and a fostering of a more contemplative approach to life, as the Society for the Deceleration of Time puts it. Based in Austria, this organization supports slowing down activities wherever possible or practicable, in order to endow time with greater significance and to critique the dominant temporality of the culture (http://zeitverein.uni-klu.ac.at). One could say that the goal of the Society more broadly is to 'think less of what speed makes *possible* and think more about what it makes *impossible*' (Miller and Schwartz 1998: 21, original emphasis).

In order to think about the ethical and other possibilities of slow time, it is first useful to briefly consider some recent theories of time from within the field of the sociology of time (Zerubavel 1981: 140) before considering the complexities of modern temporalities and some of the debates surrounding them. Since at least Durkheim, social scientists have contrasted social time with natural time and described social time under industrial capitalism as machine time or clock time. The dualism of natural/social time, however, fails to capture the complexities of lived time, or the varying temporalities people inhabit or experience (Adam 1995: 43). Instead of a binary between social and natural time, Barbara Adam argues for a distinction between 'temporal' and 'non-temporal' time. Non-temporal time is based on measurement: time is measured and repeatable but also quantifiable and hence may run out. Temporal time, by contrast, is a mode of experience rather than a form of measurement; it is not a sense of time as invariant repetition but as con-stitutive, a becoming of what has *not* been before, which can be experienced rather than measured (1995: 52).

This is a useful way of thinking about time in order to stress that attempts to 'slow down' time are not based on an implied 'natural' temporality against an inau-thentic social one. Rather, a sense of 'slow time' may interrogate the instrumental forms of social time that dominate the global everyday and seek to offer an *alter-native* to speed as the only available temporality. An awareness of seasonality through gardening, for instance, may heighten an understanding of being situated within different temporalities which cannot simply be seen as 'natural' as opposed to social (1995: 54). Gardening is marked by multiple, simultaneous time-horizons (e.g. different times for planting and harvesting; differential growth rates) in which nature and culture are mutually imbricated (e.g. through climate, diet and season) but if gardening is consciously adopted as a practice of slow living it can become a different way of marking and inhabiting time, in which the temporality of the garden offers either respite or contradiction to the dominant temporality we expe-rience.

Another way of thinking about contradictory senses of time in contemporary life is to pose 'instantaneous time' against 'glacial time' (Urry 2000). The advent of 'instantaneous time', as distinct from clock time, is a form of temporality when everything is (potentially) available now, resulting from developments in information and communication technology (Urry 2000: 127–9; see also Agger 2004).[4] While instantaneous time may be a promise or expectation rather than an everyday reality, this understanding of time, John Urry argues, has become linked in the popular imaginary with a sense of the accelerating pace and simultaneity of experience, and a sense of inhabiting a 'throwaway' society marked by features such as an increasing disposability of products, ephemerality in fashion and casualization in the labour market (2000: 129). One response to dissatisfaction with this sense or experience of time has been the mobilization of 'glacial time', a notion of time as 'extremely slow moving and ponderous, de-synchronized from both clock and instantaneous times', context-specific, and 'beyond assessment or monitoring within the present generation' (Urry 2000: 157, 158). A glacial sense of temporality may be deployed in various forms of resistance to the 'placelessness' of instantaneous time, such as ecological or community preservation protest movements, and allows people to appeal to the 'weight of history', as opposed to an ephemerality which they perceive as a threat to the memories and practices within a specific place (2000: 159). Some aspects of slow living may derive from a similar impulse to preserve, bound up with a resistance to instantaneity as an ultimately unsatisfying form of experience. Whether making bread by hand or growing heirloom vegetables, there is a dual impulse towards time and history in such 'slow' practices which connects a mindfulness in the present with a heightened awareness of historicity. More specifically, Slow Food projects such as the 'Ark of Taste' campaign (described in Chapter 2), which seeks to catalogue and preserve endangered species and cuisines, is motivated by a glacial sense of time which opposes the 'throwaway' mentality of a fast (food) culture.

Such conceptualizations of time mobilize alternative accounts of, and responses to, lived experience in the global everyday which do not posit a naive understanding of a natural/social time binary opposition. As the idea of glacial time insists, moreover, time cannot be thought of as an abstraction, divorced from a situated materiality and embodiment. Even as we have divided time and space into separate chapters to enable different points of emphasis and analysis we begin from the assumption of 'a radical unevenness in the nature and quality of social time itself' which results from considering spatiality as constitutive of social time (May and Thrift 2001: 5). Such unevenness can most clearly be seen during the long period of modernization when, at the same time as acceleration came to be seen as the defining experience of modernity, a greater awareness and valuing of slowness also became apparent (Nowotny 1994: 84).

While at the beginning of the twentieth century the Italian Futurists announced, 'Time and Space died yesterday. We already live in the absolute, because we have created eternal, omnipresent speed' (Apollonio 1973: 22), it would be true to say that from at least the turn of the nineteenth century the experience of slowness began to emerge as a positive value in response to newly emerging technologies of speed. Speed *created* slowness, as it were. The example of rail travel may best exemplify this point. In the nineteenth century, as Wolfgang Schivelbusch (1986) has notably argued, the development of the railway not only had economic and geographical consequences but greatly affected people's experience of time-space. Railroad time, for instance, was adopted as general standard time in Britain in 1880 (Schivelbusch 1986: 44). With the speed of rail, however, came a new perspective on earlier modes of transport: horse-riding and walking could be newly appreciated as leisure activities which offered a heightened sensory or aesthetic experience (Schivelbusch 1986: 121; Urry 2000: 54; see also Jarvis 1997). Slower travel could also be healthier: a way of avoiding 'railway shock' or 'bicycle face' (Kern 1983: 111).[5] Slowness, then, became recognized and could be redefined as a desirable or virtuous quality when it became a *choice*, rather than the only option, and when speed could be associated with negative characteristics such as alienation, stress, or desensitization (Nowotny 1994: 14–15). As in Ruskin's repudiation of rail travel, slowness could become the basis of formulating a critique of modernity or modernization.

Many theorizations of modernity and postmodernity have, however, tended to side with the Futurists in focusing on speed as a sine qua non of modernity. Whether describing the history of the last two hundred years as 'a history of acceleration' (Virilio 1986b: 51), or 'time-space compression' (Harvey 1989), or characterizing modernity as a 'maelstrom' of constant change (Berman 1983: 16), many accounts have favoured the 'exponential acceleration' thesis (Ross 1995: 10). While we are arguing here that a temporality of speed dominates contemporary culture, what accounts such as Harvey's and Berman's may occlude is the heterogeneity and complexity of time as experienced by subjects in modernity. The reductive application of the 'time-space compression' theory of postmodernity, for instance, threatens to reduce 'changes in the experience of time to simple feelings of acceleration and dissolution', verging on a technological determinism (May and Thrift 2001: 10). Against such accounts, we would favour those which emphasize the *differential* temporalities of modernity (e.g. Williams 1973; Baudrillard 1987; Osborne 1992; Seremetakis 1994). As Kristin Ross has argued, modernization may offer 'a perfect reconciliation of past and future in an endless present' but is in fact experienced by subjects as uneven (1995: 11; see also Highmore 2002: 174).

The relationship between temporal disparities and social inequalities is an important one to explore in an analysis of slow living, in order to consider the difference between choosing to live slowly and having slowness thrust upon one, through being physically or economically unable to both keep up with the speed of the global everyday and to manage its disparate temporalities (see Nowotny 1994). Some of the reasons for the differential experience of modernity by differently situated subjects were suggestively explored by Ernst Bloch (1977/1932) who developed the notion of 'non-synchronicity' in the 1930s to describe the experience of living 'out of sync' with one's time due to economic stagnation, personal disaffection, regional isolation or a combination of these factors (to which we would now also add differences of gender, sexuality, ethnicity and age, to name a few). In contemporary times, 'non-synchronicity' becomes even more problematic when the pressures of individualization require flexible but self-regulating subjects capable of time management (Beck and Beck-Gernsheim 2002). In a context of 'instantaneous time', moreover, slowness can either signify abject failure or a repudiation of the expectations of the modern temporal subject, especially in work culture.[6]

The ease with which one may 'fail' the expectations of flexibility, mobility and instantaneity and hence suffer social marginalization is poignantly illustrated in the film *Time Out* (2001; dir. Laurent Cantet). The unemployed protagonist, Vincent, is able to keep his job loss a secret from his family because he retains his mobility – represented by his car and mobile phone. The longueurs of this film, as Vincent 'kills' time in chilly parks and motorway cafes while he is believed to be a UN executive in Geneva, symbolizes the problematic status of identity when subjects stop circulating in the economy of acceleration (Nowotny 1994: 96). What *Time Out* narrativizes so effectively are the disparities between fast and slow time in contemporary culture, and the social costs of fast time 'cannibaliz[ing]' slow time (Eriksen 2001: 129). What happens to the 'losers' like Vincent? What time are they in? The unemployed, together with children, women at home and the elderly comprise a significant section of the population who are often outside 'fast time' and may hence be overlooked by the 'fast', resulting in temporal inequalities being translated into social inequalities (Nowotny 1994: 32). Speed has the capacity to significantly distort engagement with, and experience of, others who resist speed (Gottschalk 1999: 315) and while there may be obvious social benefits for the 'fast' (e.g. career advancement, levels of disposable income) there are also losses in the encroachment of work time into all other domains of life, such as the experience of stress and a withdrawal from social interaction.

Given technology such as mobile phones, pagers and laptop computers a worker is technically always 'available' (i.e. able to be contacted by the office or client) (Agger 2004). 'Free time' – 'a not-work time that exists only in relation to the time of markets and employment' (Adam 1995: 96) – may refer to a time when one is not physically in a work *space* but the potential for one's *time* to be invaded by work is almost limitless with the inevitable resulting impact on family and social life. The Taylorizing of family life (Eriksen 2001: 132) – micro-management of the disparate time schedules of family members – frequently results from the private requirements of family life having to be reconciled with the temporal regulations of gainful employment (Eriksen 2001: 132; Nowotny 1994: 113, 107). In the film *Time Out*, Vincent is not only outside 'work time' he is also 'out of sync' with family time as well: his visits home disrupt the busy schedules of his wife and children, he seems aimless in comparison with their purposeful busy-ness. The result of such time pressures may in effect privatize the family still further, as the 'extra' activities undertaken when time was more available (such as community involvement or neighbourhood socializing) are jettisoned to preserve whatever time is left for the family (Hochschild 2003: 204).

The solution to such time pressures, however, is not simply a matter of reorganizing time (and society) to better accommodate the spheres of work, family and community because different sections of society inhabit different time cultures, which may be incompatible (Nowotny 1994: 125). As Jenny Shaw (2001) notes, while there seems to be a growing tendency to equate the good life with the slow life, not everyone wants to live slowly. More women than men tend to complain about the fast pace of life, but young people often seek out places to live, work and socialize where the pace is faster, assuming a link between speed, vitality and excitement (Shaw 2001: 132, 120, 122; see also Deem 1996).[7] Nor can we assume that the private domain may be a space of slowness: the private sphere may in fact offer women fewer opportunities to 'slow down' or take 'time out' because it is the sphere defined by traditional gender expectations of feminine nurture and caregiving responsibilities (Davies 2001: 144–5). While some defences of slow living are based on the assumption that 'Family life is by nature slow' and has been speeded up in late modernity to the detriment of all (e.g. Eriksen 2001: 132), it is hard to envisage a time when the private domain did not impose taxing regimes and careful management of time and resources on all but the most privileged women. From the perspective of the driven pace and flexible deployment of contemporary work culture, the home may look like a tranquil space of slower rhythms and continuities, but to the primary carer of a newborn baby, for instance, the repetitions and relative immobility such care requires may represent a far less ideal temporality. Characterizations of private life as 'slow', then, may derive more from the fact that family time is still often associated with a notion of more 'natural', 'anti-linear' or 'pre-industrial' time than from an experiential perception of slowness in that domain (Shaw 2001: 126).

If debates over work and family are conceptualized in terms of conflicting time demands, then, they are also mapped onto particular places, with the 'family meal table' being both a particular site of conflict and seen as an indicator of diminished family intimacy. The oft-repeated lament about the demise of family meal times identifies the loss of both a time ('dinner time') and place (the dining table), which is taken to represent a 'lack of collective rhythm holding families together' (Crang 2001: 191; see also Murcott 1997; Zerubavel 1981; and Chapter 5). This 'colonization' of the family, and the body itself, through the impact of speed and busy-ness on the practices of meal preparation and consumption is central to the Slow Food movement; it is concerned not only with *what* is eaten but *how* (where, when, by whom). Distinguishing 'slow food' from 'fast food' is in part an attempt to demarcate a *time*, as much as a practice, distinct from work and its associated pace and pressures. As will be discussed further in Chapter 5, a desire to reclaim time for the pleasures of food and sociality, however, is not necessarily the same as 'slowing down' the time of family members as the family meal requires not only a common time-frame in which to partake of it but someone to prepare it, with the regressive potential to reinstate traditional gender identities as a solution to conflicting time demands (for discussion of this in the Italian context, see Counihan 2004).

In recent years, the desire to reclaim time, and 'family time' in particular, has also manifested in the growing phenomenon of 'downshifting' (Schor 1998), defined as making 'a voluntary, long-term, lifestyle change that involves accepting significantly less income and consuming less' (Hamilton and Mail 2003: vii). National surveys have shown that, over the last decade, in the 30–59 age group, 25 per cent in Britain, 23 per cent in Australia and 19 per cent in the USA have down-shifted (Schor 1998: 113; Hamilton 2003: 12; Hamilton and Mail 2003: 26). Contrary to a popular misconception, moreover, downshifting cuts across gender, demographic and income levels (Hamilton and Mail 2003: 26) and does not most commonly result in people leaving cities to live in the countryside (Hamilton 2003: 12). A Newspoll survey on downshifting commissioned by the Australia Institute in 2003 found that more than a third of respondents nominated 'more time with family' as their main reason for downshifting, followed by other reasons such as 'more balance' and more personal fulfilment, echoing similar results in a UK study (Hamilton and Mail 2003: 21; Hamilton 2003: 19). While reduced income and a shift away from consumerism are hallmarks of downshifting, 'For most downshifters the dominant change in their lives involves taking control of their time and devoting it to more satisfying activities' (Breakspear and Hamilton 2004: 17).

The appeal of time sovereignty which downshifting represents shows the extent to which time has become invested with value in everyday life. The extent of the downshifting phenomenon not only marks a noteworthy development in how people are reconfiguring their lives in the global everyday but also signals a kind of re-evaluation of the ethics of living which has implications for contemporary political agendas (Rutherford 2000: 66). Work, family and gender are significant factors in the constitution and perpetuation of temporal disparities and inequities, and in the negotiations or solutions people offer to them in contemporary culture. Attempts to demarcate space or activities as slow may be seen as evidence of the new status of time – its usage, its value, its quantity – in public and popular discourse, as the currency of the term 'quality time' represents (see Deem 1996; Shaw 2001). Increasingly, we might say, the public–private divide is experienced in *temporal terms*, as people struggle to allocate time and space to valued relationships and practices (Shaw 2001: 126). Despite the emergence of downshifting as a significant social phenomenon in countries such as Australia, the UK and the USA, however, it is not possible to argue that the desire for 'slower' living is a universal one nor that slow living should be implemented across the board. While people may frame their desires to live differently in temporal terms, endowing time itself with a variety of significations to represent these desires, a politics of temporality would need to be based not only on the recognition of the multiplicity and unevennesses of social time but the relation between social and temporal inequities. It would, in short, require an *ethics* of time, which the following section will explore.[8]

An Ethics of Time

Is there an ethics of time? If the temporal organization of a society reflects its privileged values (Tabboni 2001: 5) and temporal differences increase social inequities (Nowotny 1994: 42), could deceleration to a different temporality improve the quality of life and the equity of society, prevent the slow being eaten by the fast? The dominance of machine time and its associated instrumentalist emphasis on productivity under industrial capitalism has seen the application of such time management processes not only to business and industry but to areas such as education and household management.[9] In the early twentieth century, the Taylorists Frank and Lilian Gilbreth saw the applicability of the principles of the productive use of time, even its shortest intervals, to a wider context beyond the workplace. In their 1916 book *Fatigue Study*, the Gilbreths proposed the importance of 'Happiness Minutes' for workers, recognizing that breaks in routine and non-work practices were good for efficiency (Kern 1983: 117). In recent years, the Gilbreths' ideas have had a late modern application by corporations, which have begun to institute forms of 'Happiness Minutes' for employees above and beyond the legal provisions for employment regulation, from providing free snacks to free yoga and adult education classes to boost staff morale and retention rates (Hochschild 1997: 239; Der Hovanesian 2003: 56; Florida 2003: 123–8; see also Chapter 4). Some might argue that contemporary ideas about slow living could be considered a postmodern extension of 'Happiness Minutes': a reconfiguring of time for the purpose of maximizing productivity within a capitalist paradigm. But slow living at its best envisages more than just a redistribution of time and an increase in leisure. It points towards an alternative understanding of time itself, similar to Adam's 'temporal' form of time, where time is 'neither finite nor usable as a quantitative measure' (1995: 52). As an alternative to machine time, this conception of time sees it as embodied and embedded in all our social practices and the materiality of the body and its environment (Adam 1995: 54, 44), so that living differently – slowly – would necessarily begin with a different approach to time, which would include both time for the self and time for the other: an ethics of time.

An ethics of time would begin with a sense of the irreducibility or alterity of time. On some levels, there is no substitute for time: contra Franklin's 'time is money', it cannot always be traded for something else. This 'stubbornness of time' implies a different currency of reciprocity, of 'time for time' (Nowotny 1994: 130). The concept of time poverty, or a declared 'need for more time', registers an inability to respond to the stubbornness of time. Reisch has described the dissatisfaction of time-poor subjects in late modern culture this way: 'This is the dilemma: obtaining non-material satisfaction calls for attention, demands involvement, requires time. Hence, having too many things makes time for non-material pleasure shrink and thus, paradoxically, an overabundance of options can easily diminish full satisfaction. Time poverty degrades the utility of the wealth of goods' (2001: 378).[10] Western patterns of consumption conflict, then, with 'wealth in time' defined as: having the *right amount* of time to carry out activities; having time at the *right time* according to both personal and social rhythms; and *synchronizing* with the rhythms of broader public temporalities in society (Reisch 2001: 377–8).

In the movements promoting slow living, alongside the metaphors and significations of time which are used to distinguish a desired form of temporality from the pace of the global everyday, there is also an awareness of this alterity of time and a desire to pay attention to this, to distinguish it from what Bourdieu calls 'time-as-thing' in which even 'free time' cannot 'readily escape from the logic of investment in "things to do"' (2000: 206; 209). In the novel *About a Boy*, Nick Hornby has appositely described this common perception of free time as 'units' to be filled, or crossed off, in the life of Will, a man of independent means who has never worked a day in his life:

> His way of coping with the days was to think of activities as units of time, each unit consisting of about thirty minutes. Whole hours, he found, were more intimidating, and most things one could do in a day took half an hour. Reading the paper, having a bath, tidying the flat, watching *Home and Away* and *Countdown*, doing a quick crossword on the toilet, eating breakfast and lunch, going to the local shops … That was nine units of a twenty-unit day (the evenings didn't count) filled by just the basic necessities. In fact, he had reached a stage where he wondered how his friends could juggle life and a job. (1998: 71–2, ellipsis in original)

Will's occupation of time, which mimics the segmentation of a typical workday, is fundamentally at odds with a notion of the irreducibility of time, in which the 'temporality of everyday life means that humans experience not only the passing of time, but also the necessity to wait until one temporal process has run its course in order for another to begin' (Weigert 1981: 227). In contemporary life, waiting is usually an unpleasant experience. It is a *waste* of time, a failure to fully utilize our resources which triggers impatience. Being kept waiting can signify our diminished status, our lack of importance compared to the person or institution on whom we wait. Waiting on technology in the age of 'instantaneous time' is also a common frustration in everyday life. 'Microwave time', for instance, can be a tantalizing period of time which cannot be usefully deployed on another task while we stand transfixed before the digital clock as it counts down a relatively short period of time – two minutes or even thirty seconds of our life we will never have again. (Unless, that is, we can synchronize it with the time we are waiting for an internet download and thus achieve a triumph of postmodern efficiency). Waiting – as a gap or marker between different activities – can, however, be reconfigured as a different temporal experience. Rather than seeing waiting as 'an interstitial and static experience of time' (Vannini 2002: 194), it might be both 'an open possibility for change' and an opportunity to wait for the other, in the Levinasian sense (1986, 1998; see also Schneider 1997: 96). Such a resignification turns on its head our commonsense temporality in which 'We feel that everything that requires time requires too much time. *Time itself is viewed as delay*' (Schneider 1997: 92, emphasis added).[11] The recultivation of our approach to time which is at the heart of movements promoting slow living does not derive from a belief that deferred gratification is 'better' than instant gratification but rather an acknowledgement of the irreducibility, the otherness, of time. Acknowledging the alterity of time in turn opens us to the possibility of acknowledging the alterity of the other and their claims on our time.

The temporality of waiting as an example of time's irreducibility is echoed repeatedly in a popular genre of writing which narrates experiences of slow time, usually in exotic locales, especially rural France or Italy. In best-selling books like *Under the Tuscan Sun* (Mayes 1996), the author-narrators recount their experiences of purchasing and renovating country houses in romantic villages which apparently offer a qualitatively different life experience based on a slower pace.[12] In this literature, the virtues of slow living are embodied in the practices of rustic life in which the appropriate time must be devoted to each task and attention given to its performance, especially in relation to food preparation (Parkins 2004a). But the class and power implications of the temporality of waiting are not sufficiently acknowledged in these accounts of Tuscan life. Who is waiting? Who is *responsible* for waiting? Or to put it another way, who has the *time* to wait? The local peasant whose limited material resources make waiting unavoidable or the privileged outsider on holiday from their real (pace of) life? It is time for the self rather than time for/with the other which is celebrated in these accounts, precluding an ethical investment of time. And yet in the Tuscan literature in which time is used both carefully and intensively, there is also an attempt to imagine an alternative temporality, to think outside the culture of speed and to refigure waiting as a positive experience of temporality rather than a punishment. It is this alternative temporality in another place which is no doubt the appeal to 'time-poor' subjects who can scarcely afford the few hours taken to read a book which equates slowness with a sense of balance.[13]

While rosy accounts of personal epiphanies in Tuscan farmhouses privilege 'self time', then, they also raise – sometimes inadvertently – important questions about how self-expression may be reconciled with an ethics of time. If fast subjects who reap the rewards of speed have an obligation to those who are left behind for their lack of speed, how can this obligation be reconciled with the oft-repeated desire for more time for oneself? Or are they irretrievably at odds? If an ethics of time, put simply, means people having time for each other then is a desire for 'own time' incommensurable with a desire for greater social equity or for 'social life' itself, in Levinas's terms (1989: 55)?[14] Part of the solution to this tension may lie in cultivating a combination of wonder and generosity in everyday life. As others have argued (Irigaray 1993; Bennett 2001; La Caze 2002), wonder, as a sense of 'surprise at the extraordinary' can have an ethical dimension because it implies accepting the object of wonder in its alterity (La Caze 2002: 2, 6). Such a response, however, presupposes a certain temporality in which wonder becomes possible: distractions such as noise, haste, multitasking, or demands on our attention from multiple sources may preclude the possibility of us being moved to such a response and hence diminish our experience in/of everyday life. Wonder, as openness to otherness, gives us the possibility to respond differently, it opens alternative possibilities to us. On its own, however, wonder is not enough. It could be used to imagine the object of wonder as exotic, for instance, so that instead of openness it merely reconfirms a prior judgement of the other (Young 1997a: 56). It may also by implication unnecessarily denigrate the everyday because 'objects worthy of wonder stand out against the undifferentiated background of those everyday and familiar things that we can easily categorize' (La Caze 2002: 3), thus returning the everyday to an irredeemable space of repetition and routine. Generosity is needed in addition to wonder because it is generosity that strengthens a regard for others together with an appropriate judgement of our own worth (La Caze 2002: 12, 11).[15] It is generosity that may predispose us to evaluate everyday encounters positively. La Caze explains the interrelation necessary between generosity and wonder:

> Generosity can provide the limit that prevents wonder from falling over into exoticism … because generosity is a fundamental sense in which we are all of worth, regardless of the differences that may exist. Generosity involves a proper judgement that needs to follow wonder.
>
> Conversely, wonder can prevent the presumption that others will think and act as we do and desire the same kinds of things as we do such that we could make decisions and

judgements on their behalf. It helps us to recognize the limitations on our own power. Wonder also allows for openness to difference and change in the other. The two passions of wonder and generosity have to work together in a complex way to provide the basis of an ethics of respect for difference. (2002: 14)

In a temporality of speed, we would contend, there is no time for wonder or generosity, no time to attend to the enchantment in daily life and no time to extend to ourselves or others a sense of worth which an investment of time can signify. In order to make wonder and generosity more than momentary reactions, a practice of slow living can make it easier to cultivate such qualities to become an attitude (in the dual sense of both a habit and a virtue; La Caze 2002: 14). The daily practices which allow us to cultivate an attitude of wonder and generosity will vary according to our contexts and inclinations but require time, for reflection and attention, which reminds us of our connections to nature and others.

While we suggest that a fostering of wonder and generosity makes an ethics of time more possible, we also need to acknowledge that the increased velocity of cultural life no longer makes it possible – if in fact it ever did – to assume that slow living is an ethical imperative or is good for everybody. In a fast world where the contingencies of identities are made more readily apparent, however, practices of self-artistry and micro-politics may take on a new significance (Connolly 1999: 85). The existence of different time cultures and time *desires* is not simply a problem to be resolved, then, but a reality to be recognized and accommodated as a means of enhancing diversity in social and ecological, private and public systems of life (Reisch 2001: 378). An ethics of time can never have the goal of a singular, shared temporality for all. It is not a case of imposing slowness on everyone, or turning back the clock, but rather allowing an alternative to speed to be possible, to be thinkable, to be do-able; to allow *spaces* for slowness (to employ a spatial rather than temporal metaphor) in both personal and public domains; to allow time for the other (and time *as* the other).[16] The Victorian custom of the Sabbath, in which social prescription compelled people to do nothing except to reflect deeply or read sober religious texts, is not the prototype for slow(er) living in the twenty-first century. It is a case, rather, of seeing in a new valuation of certain temporalities the possibilities for life-enhancement, social engagement and political participation (and these are not seen as mutually exclusive options) that slow time can create. As Christiane Müller-Wichman puts it: 'We need time for everyday culture. We need time for the chance to be a public person. And we need time for leisure. We do not need leisure time instead of a job, instead of a family, instead of politics. We need it as surplus time' (quoted in Nowotny 1994: 102).

Sloworld

We are arguing, then, that a desire for more time for *oneself* is not necessarily incompatible with time for *others*, as the micro-political dimension of these practices can lead to a wider recognition and application of such practices, which in turn creates a temporality more conducive to ethical relations with others. But slow living is not simply an individual response to the temporal pressures and disparities of the global everyday; it also has a number of collective manifestations. Like the car-free days in some cities, larger movements can be generated which seek to 'protect' rather than impose slowness and, moreover offer 'selective slowness' as a way of enhancing social and public life (Miller and Schwarz 1998: 21). Since the 1980s a number of organizations have appeared which represent time as signifying those things missing (or lost) from everyday life: meaning, authenticity, security or identity. Such organizations critique current social practices through deploying a semiotically rich concept of time (and speed) and offer a version of the 'good life' grounded in a different, slower temporality. For example, The Society for the Deceleration of Time, observing that 'We are living in an age where time is accelerating' and 'Speed has become the yardstick by which we measure the value of our activities', urges the value of deceleration in order to foster a more contemplative approach to life (http://zeitverein.uni-klu.ac.at). The stated aim of this society is as follows:

> Every member should, regardless of what kind of activity he or she engages in, prolong the time taken for that activity whenever it makes sense to do so. In this members are assured of the solidarity of the Society as a whole. They should stand up for the right to pause for reflection in situations where mindless activism and vested interests produce solutions that are expedient rather than genuine. (http://zeitverein.uni-klu.ac.at)[17]

In a similar vein in the USA, a 'Take Back Your Time Day' campaign was launched on 24 October 2003 and repeated in 2004, sponsoring a large range of events and activities across the country which encouraged people to take the day off work as part of a 'national initiative to challenge the epidemic of overwork, over-scheduling and time famine that now threatens our health, our families and relationships, our communities and our environment' (http://www.simpleliving.net/timeday; see also Eriksen 2001 on a similar campaign in Norway). An awareness of temporality and the time taken to live requires – and presupposes – an investment in the meaning-making practices of everyday life. The movement most associated with the reinvestment of time in everyday life through slowness is Slow Food. We will not focus here specifically on food or food practices (the subject of Chapter 5) but consider how the adjectives 'fast'/'slow' are endowed with such semiotic weight in articulating slowness as a critical response to global culture in the discourse of Slow Food.

Slow Food has always taken a broad approach to the conjunction of slowness with food. As one Slow Food writer put it: 'There can be no slow-food without slow-life, meaning that we cannot influence food culture without changing our culture as a whole. ... Once we tackle the problem from this perspective, we realize that what we are faced with is not a "taste" problem, but a "political" one' (Portinari 1997: 23). In opposing itself to 'fast food', the 'slow' in Slow Food is, then, not only intended to signify an opposition to speed and all it stands for (alienation, dislocation, insecurity) but the presence of positive values associated with pleasure, authenticity, connectedness, tranquillity and deliberation. This section – the name of which is taken from a regular section in *Slow* on major Slow Food events and news from around the world – will explore the meanings and discourse of slowness and the understandings of time as they are proposed and debated within Slow Food, drawing on the *Slow* quarterly, the manifestos of the movement and interviews with Slow Food officers to articulate this discourse. That is, we focus on the development of an official Slow Food discourse on slowness, as distinct from the everyday practices of slow living carried out by Slow Food members. We adopt this approach not because we are uninterested in the daily applications or otherwise of the idea(l)s of Slow Food but in order to tease out the complexities and potential conflicts in constructing slowness as a discourse of critique and resistance. What will emerge is not a singular meaning of slowness as a positive term of value as some have claimed (e.g. Chrzan 2004: 121) but an overdetermined signifier which is constantly interrogated and redeployed within the movement in response to factors such as a diversification of aims and projects and the increasing heterogeneity of membership. While this diverse and evolving discourse of slowness within Slow Food makes it difficult to offer a definitive analysis it also makes it a promising case study for exploring the possibilities of cultivating a critically reflective capacity through everyday arts of the self.

As described in Chapter 2, from its inception the Slow Food movement associated slowness with pleasure, and therefore speed with the absence of pleasure. When it was launched as the International Movement for the Defense of and the Right to Pleasure in Paris on 9 November 1989, Slow Food adopted a manifesto (reproduced in the Appendix) endorsed by delegates from fifteen countries, defining the movement against 'Fast Life' (which like the term 'Slow Food' always appears in English in Slow Food texts) in which speed enslaves and infects humanity, and endangers the natural environment. The manifesto, however, is a genre with a particular history, as both a product of, and a critical response to, modernity. Recent discussion of Slow Food manifestos, and its founding one in particular, have failed to engage with the *genre* of the manifesto – its conventions and history – and have thus insufficiently acknowledged the complexities and tensions in Slow Food's deployment of this genre (see Gaytán 2004: 104–6 and Chrzan 2004: 120–1). We will here analyse the early manifestos in some detail in order to show that Slow Food's usage of the manifesto form is neither due to ignorance of its earlier political deployments (cf. Laudan 2004: 138) nor to overly simplistic conceptualizations of resistance (cf. Chrzan 2004: 121). As Janet Lyon has argued, the manifesto was the genre of choice for political and aesthetic movements across the spectrum, whether celebrating or denouncing the modern: from the French Revolution to the suffragettes and the Futurists, the manifesto was the means by which movements articulated their own identity by rhetorical denunciation of their enemies. This task required a binarist conception of the world, in which the manifesto writers positioned themselves as the vanguard of truth, justice or art against the might of the powerful, the ignorance of the many or the complacency of the establishment (or all of the above) (Lyon 1999: 2–3, 24). 'Throughout its historical transformations,' Lyon argues,

> the manifesto has shaped passionate political address as a genre at once intelligible and intransigent … [T]o write a manifesto is to announce one's participation, however discursive, in a history of struggle against oppressive forces. The form must be understood therefore as more than 'plain talk': the manifesto is a complex, convention-laden, ideologically inflected genre. (1999: 10)

In the founding manifesto of Slow Food may be seen the three characteristic conventions of the manifesto which Lyon identifies. Firstly, the manifesto deploys a selective and condensed version of history which has led to the present moment of crisis (1999: 14), as its opening statement makes clear: 'Our century, which began and has developed under the insignia of industrial civilization, first invented the machine and then took it as its life model. We are enslaved by speed and have all succumbed to the same insidious virus: Fast Life'. The condemnation of speed as the product of the machine age is more usually associated with a critique of modernity offered by conservatives who lament a lost organic community, destroyed by the machine (e.g. see F. R. Leavis and Denys Thompson in *Culture and Environment*).[18] What is unusual about this view, in the case of Slow Food, is that it was a movement conceived and founded by a distinctly leftist coterie (Petrini 2001: 149). Rather than a conservative yearning to return to the good old days of real food and conviviality, it was an attempt to rebrand traditional, local food as the *true* revolution, and fast, global food as the passé, the outmoded, the failed. This view of fast food was more recently restated by Capatti in a *Slow* editorial: 'Fast food is foundering under its own weight, like a ship in shallow water, and competition is hammering at its rusty bulkheads in a new way of interpreting and cooking time. Old recipes are being recovered. … The world of eating is moving backwards: the past lies ahead and modern food fads have been left behind' (2001: 6). Such a reinvention, an inversion even, of temporality – where the 'new' is dying and the old is reborn – allows Slow Food to present itself in the tradition of a leftist vanguard as the authentic radicals, offering 'true progress' and liberation through a revolution which reconstructs temporality as well as food. Such a strategy has been effective in invigorating and inspiring a movement, and perhaps accounts in part for its broader appeal than a simply gastronomic association could inspire, as evidenced by the recent growth of Slow Food membership and profile in countries such as the United States and Australia, where an interest in food culture has a 'hipness' that traditional European cuisine alone would not foster.

The second characteristic of the genre present in the founding Slow Food manifesto is the enumeration of grievances or demands, constructing a 'struggle between the empowered and the disempowered, or between the corrupt and the sanctified, or between usurpers and rightful heirs' (Lyon 1999: 15). This struggle is encoded through a homonym of values constructed around the binary of slow/fast. These opposing values are listed below, showing how the binarist logic of the manifesto genre is employed (with the italicized terms being direct quotations from the manifesto, paired with their implied opposite):

fast	slow
enslaving	liberating
virus	health/antidote
multitude	individual
inauthentic	*real culture*
false progress	*true progress*
absence of taste	*taste*
homogenized globalization	*international exchange*
worse future	*better future*

Given this Manichaean vision, only the opposite of speed and 'Fast Life', that is slowness, can provide hope for a 'better future'. This corresponds to the third characteristic of the manifesto, its use of declarative rhetoric which directly challenges the enemy while uniting its audience in a call to action (Lyon 1999: 15): 'To be worthy of the name, Homo Sapiens should rid himself [*sic*] of speed' the manifesto declaims, 'A firm defense of quiet material pleasure is the only way to oppose the universal folly of *Fast Life*. ... Our defense should begin at the table with *Slow Food*' (emphasis in original). The 'call to action' here is a call to sit at the table rather than rush to the barricades, to sit down for slowness rather than dash around for speed. In place of Fast Life, Slow Food offers the pleasures of the table: taste, flavours, regionalism, locatedness, but also 'international exchange'. To make this alternative future of slowness a possibility, an 'international movement' of 'qualified supporters' is needed but the negative terms in which the multitude has already been represented in the manifesto make this a somewhat problematic undertaking (how many can sit at the table?). By positing the (implied) inviolate individual (able to resist the virus of speed) against the 'contagion of the multitude', and the pleasures of the (private?) table against the 'universal folly of Fast Life', the manifesto obscures how the intersubjectivity of Slow Food may be figured positively (see also Sonnenfeld 2001: xiv). Similarly, the notion of expertise implied here places a question mark over the inclusion of amateur pleasure-seekers at the Slow Food table. If, for the initial signatories, the enemy was a clear and easy target – fast life, fast food – future support for their objectives seemed simultaneously obvious and indeterminate, as they sought to create 'a provisional community whose power is located in a potentially infinite constituency' (Lyon 1999: 26).

It could be argued that the manifesto is by its nature not only a genre lacking in rhetorical subtlety but also anti-democratic, denouncing the status quo from an implied position of truth/superiority to those who need to be exposed or enlightened; it is not a dialogue or an exchange among equals. The vanguard has always had an uneasy relationship with the cohort it seeks to inspire to revolution and the manifesto form mirrors the problematic status of collective representation in modernity (Lyon 1999: 8). Sometimes, in the case of movements like Vorticism or Futurism, the rhetorical strategies of the manifesto genre neatly matched the anti-democratic orientation or incipient fascism of the movements themselves; in other cases, the fit between the desire for social inclusion or equity and the genre was not apparent (as in the case of suffragettes and socialists). For Slow Food, the leftist discourse in which its founders were steeped may well account for the repeated use of this form (Slow Food manifestos even extend to topics such as biotechnologies and raw-milk cheeses!). The problematic associations between slowness and the realm of the individual or the private, which are constructed here, however, raise from the outset the question of how the pleasures of slowness are to be made available equitably, through an international movement itself opposed to globalization. More recently, Petrini and others within the movement have begun to speak of processes of 'virtuous globalization' ('Interview' 2004: 51), in which they situate the activities and aims of Slow Food within a more nuanced conceptualization of the global dimensions of the movement and its collective identity.

While the founding manifesto offers only a broadbrush defence of slowness, 'In Praise of Slowness' expands on the values and qualities sought by the movement.[19] Although it ends with a somewhat muted call for action characteristic of the manifesto genre, it is more a meditation on slowness, as its title implies, which focuses on the snail, the symbol of the Slow Food movement (and the subject of seven articles in the first issue of *Slow)*, through drawing on a seventeenth-century book devoted to snails. The snail, it is contended, being 'of slow motion, ... educate[s] us that being fast makes man [*sic*] inconsiderate and foolish'. The snail is not only an embodiment of slowness, in the sense of an absence of haste, but of the more abstract qualities of slowness, or slow subjectivity, which are here enumerated as 'prudence and solemnity, the wit of the philosopher and the moderation of the authoritative governor'. These anthropomorphic qualities of 'a creature so unaffected by the temptations of the modern world' seem more those of the ascetic than the pleasure-seeker but, the manifesto maintains, the snail offers a counter to 'those who are too impatient to feel and taste, too greedy to remember what they had just devoured'. So it is a *considered* form of material pleasure which Slow Food values and sees represented in the snail, in contrast to a fast-food approach to consumption which reduces 'food to consumption, ... taste to hamburger, ... thought to meatball'.

It is, however, not only the pace with which the snail engages with the world which makes it a fitting symbol for the Slow Food movement; it is also its 'prehistoric' appearance which enables the snail to express the 'desire to reverse the passing of time', to represent an alternative to the endless rush into the future which the obsession with speed activates. As an embodiment of 'glacial time' (Urry 2000: 157–9), the snail is a reminder of different temporalities which coexist alongside fast-food restaurants, and so a reminder also, as the manifesto expresses it, of the 'contradiction' between temporalities which Slow Food seeks to address and reconcile. While this manifesto reiterates the negative consequences of speed expressed in the founding manifesto, it also tentatively begins to expand on the possibilities of what this 'new way of life' represented by slowness might entail. If the first tenet is a rejection of fast food, as the symbol of speed and instrumentalism bound up with globalization, the second is a form of cosmopolitanism, apparently embodied by the snail. The snail 'is readily at home everywhere. Cosmopolitan and thoughtful, it prefers nature to civilization, which it takes upon itself, with its own shell'. The potential contradiction between globalization, as the *bête noire* of Slow Food, and cosmopolitanism as one of its virtues is reconciled here through recourse to a symbol from nature. The snail's successful negotiation of nature/civilization in its own body and its willingness to engage openly with the world suggests some of the desired aspects of slow subjectivity which may develop if we '[come] out of our shells'. Here, then, cosmopolitanism is constructed as a *slow* virtue, an ethical encounter and engagement with the world, rather than a 'rootless dabbling' in other cultures (Featherstone 2002).

This clarification and expansion on slow living was taken up in the second issue of *Slow*, which took the theme of 'rest', represented in a cover image of a sleeping woman. Again, the editorial from this issue, 'In Praise of Rest,' by Capatti, is now located in the manifesto section of the Slow Food website, signalling its continuing relevance as an articulation of the values of the movement (1996: 5–7). 'In Praise of Rest' is more programmatic than Petrini's meditation on slowness, more closely conforming to Lyon's characteristics of the manifesto genre, as Capatti directly addresses the reader who wants to learn how to live slowly, as well as addressing critics of the movement. Rest is very carefully delineated and distinguished from laziness and boredom in this manifesto/editorial:

Our praise of rest is not intended for the lazy or for sleepyheads, for the weary or neurotic. They simply would not appreciate it. Instead we are aiming at those who wish to listen to the rhythm of their own lives, and possibly adjust it. Such is the second point of the *Slow* programme, which advises you to go slowly (No. 1), take your time, have a break (No. 2) and find a friend who can provide food and hospitality (No. 3). (1996: 5)

The struggle between 'the corrupt and the sanctified' Lyon identified is expressed here as the difference between the lazy (those who cannot grasp the ideals of slowness) and the slow (those who seek to practise them). In a familiar rhetorical manoeuvre, Capatti first raises the objections of the lazy/unenlightened in order to rebut them: 'You *Slow* people, you are trying to live on another planet, we are often told. You *Slow* people, you have shaped an imaginary shell for yourselves so that you can withdraw into it whenever necessary, retreating into the meanders of Utopia. Now this may well be true' (1996: 5). Furthermore, Capatti concedes, 'lying on a sofa ... is not enough to extricate oneself from this maze of contradictions' which an attempt to live slowly may create: 'Instead, we should *reflect* on the principles underlying our supposedly utopian world' (1996: 5, emphasis added). So what may look like a withdrawal from the world – like the sleeping woman on the cover – is in fact 'a certain degree of detachment', as Capatti puts it, a stepping back from the fast world as a temporary respite from speed in order to evaluate and reconsider the practices of everyday life.

What begins to emerge, then, alongside the Manichaean logic that divides the lazy, unenlightened and fast from the restful, contemplative and slow, is an emphasis on reflection and deliberation as the key to slowness. The more time one has available to reflect and evaluate, the greater the possibility for either more fully committing to one's tasks or, more likely, changing one's practices, habits and ideas. The repetition of words like 'careful', 'reflective', 'mindful', 'considered' and 'attentive' in Slow Food discourse underlines the centrality of these values and distinguishes them from the simple unconsciousness or inertia of sleep. Such reflection sounds a somewhat sober occupation – not like the rowdier pleasures of a shared table of good food and wine one might imagine as the mainstay of Slow Food – but in Slow Food discourse pleasure reflected upon is pleasure enhanced. And if reflection (questions like 'Why do I do this? How can I do it differently?') reveals that there is not sufficient pleasure in the activity under consideration, it may well lead to the creation of pleasure, through choosing different activities.

Posing such questions to the self may also provide an example of how, following Connolly, one might move from practices of self-artistry to micropolitics. Capatti's manifesto-editorial still has the implicit goal of 'a better world', indeed it recognizes the practice of thinking/conceptualizing a better world as *itself* one of life's pleasures. Neither simply a duty nor an ethical obligation, developing a politics of transformation is *pleasurable*, an idea not often expressed (or even thought) in the usually unimaginative domain of politics as we know it but perhaps reserved for utopian literature. In a sense, 'In Praise of Rest' seeks to break down the distinction between utopian discourse and politics, private pleasure and public praxis, insisting on the preservation of a space outside these binaries where 'the imaginary projection of ethics' might be fleshed out (1996: 6):

> Nothing is more relaxing and pleasant than fantasizing about a better world, clearly outlining its customs and enjoying a feeling of togetherness, whether drinking or playing, relaxing or reading. But to make this possible, a certain degree of detachment is required, a moment of calm, better use of idle time ... even a bed in which to dream before arising and reaching out to other people. (1996: 7, ellipsis in original)

Through the apparently simple concept of rest, then, relations and tensions between the individual and the social, the private and the political, can be articulated and considered. If we begin with the question 'What should we "do" to rest well?' as Folco Portinari argues in an article in the same issue of *Slow*, we are quickly led from the individual to the social, as the implications of how we practise 'rest time' are bound up with work time and the complexities and disparities of the time cultures in which we are situated (1996: 8). Portinari, like Capatti, connects reflection and slowness so that just as rest is more than recovery from fatigue, so slow living, it is implied, is more than moving slowly (1996: 11).

But even at this early stage of Slow Food discourse, the adjective 'slow' as the primary value of the movement comes under question and deconstruction to some extent.[20] In a section on fast food in the second issue of *Slow*, the historian Massimo Montanari disputes the valency of the binary fast/slow to encapsulate the concerns of the Slow Food movement:

> In my opinion, the contrast between a 'slow' and 'fast' culture – which is the *raison d'etre* of this magazine and its underlying movement – has very little to do with the concepts of slowness and haste. In some apparently 'slow' situations, slowness means exhaustion, uneasiness and even suffering (surely you must have been to at least one terribly boring wedding reception?). Vice versa, 'fast' situations are not always disagreeable. ... Contrasting 'slow' and 'fast' is not the point. We badly need other adjectives. (1996b: 56)

Instead, Montanari proposes 'care' (caring for, as well as caring about) as a core value rather than solely relying on the quality of slowness to mark a different approach to both food and life more generally:

> I think that the point is: are we ready to prepare, serve and taste food with great care? In my opinion, it is just a matter of care: caring for the selection of ingredients and the resulting taste, caring for food methods ..., caring for the sensory messages conveyed

by what we eat, for presentation, for the choice of people sharing the food with us, etc. An endless series of *caring for* which, in my opinion, can be applied to any circumstance with equal dignity: a meal at home or at the restaurant, a drink at the pub or a sandwich in a snack bar. ... When assessing the quality of these experiences, what makes the difference is not how long they last: it all depends on whether we are willing and have the possibility of experiencing these events with care. This requires a *structurally* 'slow' culture, the capacity to understand and assess, a critical disposition which may – or may not – be there at any one moment. ... (1996b: 56, original emphasis)

Again, it is the capacity for reflection which is insisted upon as central to slowness. The need to protect slowness – as a set of practices denoting care and attention – at a cultural, not just a personal level, Montanari implies, means that 'slowness' transcends the private domain of choices (about time usage, food preparation and consumption) and requires institutional support for its continued existence, and for the improvement of society as a result.

What is also articulated in Montanari's plea for a care-ful culture, however, is a view of everyday life in which habit and inattentiveness dominate (supposedly epitomized by the uniformity and ubiquity of fast food). This view of the everyday raises the question whether slowness – as a mode of attention, reflection and care in everyday practices – is an intellectual exercise in the aestheticization of everyday life (Featherstone 1992)? Or is it an ambitious attempt to reconcile the aesthetic, the political, the corporeal *and* the everyday, by its insistence on the centrality of pleasure and the body? Historically, the development of academic/aesthetic interest in the everyday associated the everyday with a mode of perception where habit was represented as 'the enemy of an authentic life' (Felski 2002: 607). Beginning with the work of Viktor Shklovsky and modernists from Dada to Brecht, and reemerging in the work of Henri Lefebvre and Guy Debord, the solution to this habitual mode of unconsciousness was the necessity for aesthetic experience to jolt us out of everyday inattentiveness through a heightened sense of perception (Felski 2002: 608). Through techniques like defamiliarization, it was believed that the everyday could be transformed (Felski 2002: 609).

Some parallels may be seen between this approach to everyday life and that found in the examples of Slow Food discourse cited so far which outline an avant-gardist position, a mission even, for Slow Food, in its denunciations of the life-denying habits of speed and the stultifying effects of fast-food consumption. The attention given to time in the discourse and practices of slow living may also be seen as attempts to 'redeem the quotidian' through transforming the temporality of everyday perception (Felski 2002: 610). Such a redemption may indeed be seen as a kind of aesthetic, if by this is understood 'a loose ensemble of techniques, performances, and intensities of experience that can revive and even revolutionize the everyday by registering its rich and mysterious particularities' (Felski 2002: 609).[21] But it would also be true to say that 'redeeming the quotidian' does not in this case mean the same as purging it; it is rather a kind of remaking which seeks to restore pleasure, agency and a sense of history to everyday life.

So, as Montanari's article in particular stresses, there is a clear aesthetic dimension to slow living, an investment in material practices of everyday life which offer pleasure and enrichment to the slow subject. The speculative nature of these discussions of slowness and the tentative projections of the broader implications of slowness are not surprising in the early texts of the movement which attempt to stake out a terrain for slowness for the membership. More than fifteen years after the movement was launched, however, when membership has expanded substantially and the projects of Slow Food have evolved considerably, how is slow living envisaged now? Interviewing staff at the international head office of Slow Food in Bra, Piedmont, it soon became apparent that slow living was not an everyday practice for employees of the organization who were predominantly young and childless and who worked long hours, as well as regularly attending Slow Food events throughout Italy and beyond. Staff members espoused slow living as both an ideal and a significant challenge for the movement but also saw it as a case where members may need to find their own way, rather than a case for intervention from the top down (Barbero 2003; Abbona 2003). Given that Bra is itself a designated Slow City, however, the daily experience of these employees is already being shaped by the provision of opportunities for slowness, so that their everyday lives are a prime example of the disparate temporalities which characterize the global everyday. As one employee of Slow Food noted, the work culture of the organization would inevitably change when employees started to experience the conflicting time demands which family and work seem to provoke. Even for Slow Food employees, it seems, slow living is an evolving negotiation between lived experience and the larger structures in which the everyday is located.

The politics of slowness, the ethics of time, and the practices of slow living currently remain, therefore, sites of potential in Slow Food rather than a working prototype of a 'slow culture'. If the temporal dimension of social inequities are experienced as everyday problems such inequities cannot easily be reversed or disentangled.[22] Some have adopted a pessimistic outlook in response to the complexities of the time/speed problems described here. Nowotny, for instance, argues that literal attempts to slow people down (motorway speed limits, cycleways) are 'pathetic and defensive', concluding: 'The braking experiments will undoubtedly be continued and in part even institutionalized – but is not a well-functioning braking device part of every decently constructed machine?' (1994: 150). Nowotny's bleak view of the integration of slowness as merely a constitutive part of the machine of speed may itself be already obsolete now, a decade after it was proposed, and the following chapter's examination of the spaces of slowness, in particular through the processes of 'institutionalization' associated with the Città Slow movement, will present a more positive evaluation of the implementation of slowing-down strategies. Contra Nowotny, we argue that the deployment of notions and practices of slowness mark attempts to make the present not only habitable but pleasurable and suggest that thinking about time makes it possible to live somewhat differently (Brann 1999: 101; May and Thrift 2001: 37).

—4—

Space and Place

Slowness in this formulation becomes a metaphor for a politics of place: a philosophy complexly concerned with the defence of local cultural heritage, regional landscapes and idiosyncratic material cultures of production, as well as international biodiversity and cosmopolitanism.

Leitch (2003: 454)

Slow living is manifested in complex negotiations within and across different kinds of spaces. The previous chapter demonstrated the complexity of time, arguing that while there has been an overall acceleration in the pace of life, granting slowness an increased value and desirability, it is the unevenness and heterogeneity of *timespace* (May and Thrift 2001) that makes slow living possible. Similarly, our discussion here will unpack the complexity of spaces in global culture, noting the increased value of the specificity of place at a time when space seems less 'grounded' and more 'virtual', subject to either 'deterritorialization' or even 'annihilation' (Marx 1993/1939–41), while also noting the heterogeneity and different experiences of spaces in global culture. Indeed, it is the coexistence of a valuation of the particularities of place together with a participation in more problematized, fluid spatial contexts that primarily define the spatial negotiations that occur not only in slow living but also more generally in modern life. This returns us to the relationship between the local and the global that was outlined in Chapter 1. The local and the global are mutually imbricated in contemporary subjectivity, as described in Beck's (2002) concept of cosmopolitanization where global issues and perspectives are part of the everyday consciousness of individuals. The spaces of slow living are often grounded in locational and cultural specificity in opposition to global capitalism's production of homogenized spaces but the spaces of slow living are themselves necessarily produced and defined through their global contexts. To rephrase Beck, we might declare that for slow living there is no localism without cosmopolitanism.

Slow living is not a counter-cultural movement: it does not propose the establishment of alternative spaces but the transformation of the spaces we currently inhabit. There is no single space where slow living occurs: it involves a variety of spaces and is practised by a range of subjects. In this sense, slow living represents a more generalized response to the changing spatial and temporal contexts of global culture. At the heart of slow living is a certain 'mindful' consciousness where activities, practices and encounters are invested with care and attention and such a consciousness requires particular spatial contexts as much as it requires a slow temporality. As we noted in Chapter 1, slow living is not synonymous with a form of social withdrawal represented in 'cocooning' but the kind of attention and deliberation practised in slow living is best served by delineated spatial contexts where there is some degree of consolidation and certainty. In this sense, while slow living is something of an 'empty' category, conducted in no particular places, it is nonetheless always a 'situated' phenomenon and as such always gives emphasis to its spatial contexts. The 'slowness' of slow living, then, requires a 'spatial consciousness', an awareness of location or an appreciation of the specificity of place.

Given our focus on slow *living*, it follows that for us, space is a profoundly social phenomenon. As Lawrence Grossberg has asked: 'what cultural practice is there that does not mobilize space?' (2000: 13). We understand 'spatiality' in dialectical terms, where 'the social and spatial are inextricably realized one in the other', where 'society and space are simultaneously realized by thinking, feeling, doing individuals', where there are also 'many different conditions in which such realizations are experienced by thinking, feeling, doing subjects' (Keith and Pile 1993: 6). To so argue is not so much to declare space a 'social construct' but to conceptualize 'the spatial as a *dimension* of all social life' (Simonsen 1996: 505, original emphasis). The social nature of spatiality emphasizes that while spaces are agents of definition, they are not 'closed' and 'containing' entities but come into being through their organization of social relations, an organization which is always constituted through the management of difference. As Grossberg argues: 'Places are not figures of containment for it is precisely around such places that maps of meaning, desire, and pleasure, that relations of identity and difference, can be articulated in ways that open out' (2000: 21).

Slow living may not necessarily be limited to particular places, but there are, nonetheless, certain kinds of spaces that best facilitate slow living and the value of these spaces arises from a consideration of their contexts in the deterritorialized, global culture in which we live. The pressures of fast living are perhaps felt most strongly in the spaces of home and work and the changing dynamics of these spaces will be firstly analysed here. We will then discuss the nature of deterritorialization and consider how this process determines an orientation towards the site of the local. We will argue that the local, defined through its more specific engagement with the natural environment and social relations, can be judged as the most appropriate site where slow living can occur. We will then consider the spaces of slow living through a more specific discussion of Slow Food and the Città Slow organization, and their varying mobilizations of *terroir* and tradition.

Home and Work

The routine and unremarkable nature of everyday life has often been highlighted in cultural studies' theory and yet for us slow living, and the centrality of everyday life for slow living, grows out of an emerging *crisis* in everyday life. The pressures of speed – flexibility, efficiency, multitasking – make the living of everyday lives more arduous; everyday life becomes a 'dilemma' that requires attention and there is a corresponding increased consciousness and valuing of those positive features of everyday life that seem to be receding from us. While we believe that practices of slow living do address such dilemmas of contemporary everyday existence, we also posit everyday life as a heterogeneous, non-containable site that offers not so much specific answers but more an ethical and affective potential that can be variously mobilized in the life trajectories of subjects.

As much as slow living is about an approach to everyday life, it is axiomatic that it is concerned with how we inhabit the space of the home: the site where so many everyday bodily practices, personal relations, food preparation and consumption take *place*. Indeed, 'home is … an active practising of place' (Felski 1999–2000: 24). Yet the question of how we can use the space of home in slow living is not so easy to delineate, given the difficulty of defining what we mean by home, while subsequently unpacking and critiquing both the positive and negative connotations of the concept. Understandings of home must attend to the boundaries of the site, its physical and organizational features, the social relations that occur within the space, and its emotional and imaginary resonances. The home has an intimate material reality: a particular physical place, grounded in a specific location and layout, together with individual objects and commodities. Yet the home is also much more than such a prosaic context. Bachelard (1994) highlighted that the home is also a poetic space, a space of the imagination, a site of sensory richness that provokes memory and desire. In a sense 'there *is* no place like "home"' because everyone variously 'construct[s] its image in memory and imagination' (Chapman 2001: 144, original emphasis).

Domestic space provides a site that ideally helps to facilitate identity formation, our relations with others, and many of the pleasures of everyday life. As a pre-eminent site of everyday life, the home is often where we can be most 'ourselves'; writings on the home are often informed by a 'foundational assumption about domestic space as both material product and metaphor of individuality' (Cullens 1999: 212). The home can be a space that provides the fundamental needs of everyday life such as familiarity, intimacy, security and comfort (Heller 1984: 239). On the other hand, home is also all too often a site of conflict and violence, especially for women and children, and for this reason can never be idealized as a 'solution' to the problems of contemporary culture. It has also been subjected to critique both within the discourse of modernity – which often celebrates an unfettered mobility (Felski 1999–2000: 23) – and in criticism of the commodification of contemporary existence, manifested in the ubiquity of magazines and lifestyle television programmes devoted to the home, interior design, and gardening. Such commodification is often offered as evidence of a general retreat from engagement with public space and political life: in this sense, the 'sacralization of everyday life and [domestic] space [are presented] as the last logical application of modernism's promise of transformation, once that promise is personally perceived as having reached a dead end or played itself out in the realms of art, public policy, and politics' (Cullens 1999: 220).

Conscious of the profound multi-accentuality of 'the home', we believe it is nonetheless possible to mobilize a positive potential in domestic space in the conceptualization of the spatial contexts of slow living. Here we follow the work of Iris Young who, while agreeing with many feminist critiques of the home, argues that, from the 'deeply ambivalent values' (1997b: 134) of house and home, it is also possible to 'retain an idea of home as supporting the individual subjectivity of the person, where the subject is understood as fluid, partial, shifting, and in relations of reciprocal support with others' (1997b: 141). The home facilitates the materialization of identity through two levels, where 'my belongings are arranged in space as an extension of my bodily habits and as support for my routines, and … many of the things in the home, as well as the space itself, carry sedimented personal meaning as retainers of personal narrative' (Young 1997b: 149–50). Home always negotiates change and constancy and thus is productive of both identity and agency: 'Home as the materialization of identity does not fix identity, but anchors it in physical being that makes a continuity between past and present. Without such anchoring of ourselves in things, we are, literally, lost' (Young 1997b: 151). Our attempt to retrieve a more positive – but not naive – portrayal of the home is also based upon recognition of the paradoxical quality of both the boundedness of the space of the home and its connectedness to other spaces. In one sense, while conscious that places are always constituted through the interactions of geography and social relations, the home is an important site in slow living because it can represent a demarcated sphere of existence that can facilitate a particular quality of time. That is, the home can represent a relatively fixed site in the flux of everyday experience and in this sense it is a space that can enable the kind of care and attentiveness that we have posited as central to slow living.

The space of the home, however, also generates meaning through its status as a relational phenomenon. The home, arguably more so than any other social space, has been subject to mythic portrayals of its reassuring boundedness but as Doreen Massey reminds us: 'The identity of a place does not derive from some internalized history. It derives, in large part, precisely from the specificity of its interactions with "the outside"' (1994b: 169). Of course, the renewed interest in the home in contemporary times is prompted by precisely this relationship: greater attention to the physical organization of the home, energy devoted to the purchase and display of material possessions, the devotion of greater time to home cooking and home-based leisure activities – all encapsulated in the phenomenon of 'cocooning' – is designed to insulate people from the perceived ravages of public life. Similarly, the trend of longer working hours and the more permeable boundaries between work and home have generated coping strategies, such as the idea of 'quality time'. Such examples attest to the fact that 'all too often, home is regarded as a place upon which society impacts, rather than a place that impacts on society' (Chapman 2001: 136). By contrast, our understanding of home in slow living is defined fundamentally through its articulation with broader social contexts and through the desire for it to impact upon society: 'This concept of home does not oppose the personal and the political, but instead describes conditions that make the political possible' (Young 1997b: 159). Practices grounded in the home space, that is, can be means of engagement with the world rather than a retreat from it. Growing vegetables or collecting rainwater, for instance, may be prompted by concerns about the social and environmental impact of domestic consumption and a desire to make sustainability part of everyday life.

Implementing such practices, however, requires not only space (ie. a garden) but time and, contrary to some proclamations in previous decades, the twenty-first century has not ushered forth an age of leisure. Rather, everyday life has become more problematic for many simply because more people are required to work longer hours, at a greater pace, and under greater stress.[1] These work requirements of late capitalism have also initiated structural changes with increased 'busyness' fuelling growth in service jobs: more of the working poor 'have McJobs than even a decade ago because people's lives are so accelerated that they don't have time to cook, clean, babysit, or mow their lawns' (Agger 2004: 75). Work has intensified and lengthened for many because it has been disengaged from space and place: the delineation between work and home has become increasingly blurred and for some the very existences of 'work' and 'home' have vanished as cost-cutting has led to unemployment and destitution. The development of communications technologies in particular has meant that the spatial boundaries between work and home have been dissolved: for some, this has allowed greater freedom to negotiate the demands of work and home life but for others it has only contributed to a work culture where one is perpetually 'on-call'.

The changing structures and demands of work, their interactions with other spheres of everyday life, and the multiplicity of responses to those changing structures and circumstances, are part of the landscape of second modernity. Work has become increasingly problematic, not only with regards to the growing demands on workers by global capital, but more fundamentally through proliferating *conceptualizations* of work. The varying responses to contemporary work demands, whether options of part-time employment or 'downshifting', represent the kinds of reflexive biographical construction accounted for in Beck and Beck-Gernsheim's (2002) understanding of individualization. Such individual decisions represent a kind of experimental life that is nonetheless informed by encounters with social structures and networks that yield a diverse range of opportunities and risks. Slow living is located within these contexts as individuals seek to manage the structures of their everyday lives and enjoy the experiences of work, leisure and home life. As we have previously stated, slow living is not a simple matter of 'slowing down' but rather it is more fundamentally an issue of *agency*. It represents an attempt to exercise agency over the pace of everyday existence and the movements across, and investments in, the respective domains of everyday life. Central to a politics of slow living would be an explicit thematization of the class basis of workers who are variously able to exercise such agency over the patterns of their work life. Work is recognized as a valuable part of everyday life but slow living rejects a work culture that overwhelms everyday life and operates with such speed and fury that it denies people the opportunity to mindfully consider the pleasures and purposes of each task. Such a declaration may be dismissed as a utopian quest by some but we point to and seek to exploit the utopian impulses in everyday life that are manifested in the difficult choices a range of individuals *are making* about how they are to live in the global everyday.[2]

The issue of *place* becomes central in the negotiations people make about work and everyday life. People are increasingly making choices about where they work and live according to the quality of the time of a place, associating a better quality of life with a change in location (Shaw 2001: 120). The idea of the quality of time in a particular place, commodified in the tourism industry, posits the stresses of 'normal' fast life against the 'healing quality' of time spent on holidays and short breaks. Indeed, one British Household Panel Survey found that most people consider that the main purpose of holidays is simply to preserve family unity (Shaw 2001: 127). Research has shown how the pace of life differs around the world (Levine 1997) but increasingly we are seeing instances of internal migration where people move places within a country to secure a better quality of life. One of the most popular television programmes in Australia in recent years was *Seachange*, a story about a corporate lawyer in Melbourne who escapes to a sleepy, seaside town to take up a position as the town's magistrate, and the programme's name has now become a term for a significant contemporary cultural phenomenon in Australia. Sometimes a change of place involves a 'dropping-out' – a rejection of mainstream, consumer culture – but increasingly professional people are seeking a 'seachange' in order to gain a slower lifestyle while still remaining connected to work contexts through the uses of communication technologies that overcome the tyranny of distance.

Perhaps to prevent employees seeking such changes, corporate culture in recent years has instituted changes in the temporal and spatial contexts of workplaces: the increasingly longer working day has prompted some corporations to transform workplaces into more 'comfortable', 'fun' and 'homely' spaces, introducing cafes and food bars as well as 'family-friendly' features, such as child-care facilities, even extending to the development of 'company towns' (Hochschild 2003: 198). Such spatial transformations of workplaces, manifested most famously in the workplaces of computer companies such as Microsoft and Apple, are a particular feature of the so-called 'creative class' of professionals 'whose economic function is to create new ideas, new technology and/or new creative content' (Florida 2003: 8) but they also increasingly extend to more traditional businesses. Underlying such workplace transformations is a drive to keep people at work: 'The message and function are clear: No need to go wandering off; stay right here at work' (Florida 2003: 123), or, as Hochschild notes, 'the Faustian bargain' between the corporation and workers has become: 'We'll bring civic life to you at work. You work long hours' (2003: 211).[3] The ever-growing demands of capitalism are beginning to attempt to reverse the traditional 'emotional cultures' (Hochschild 2003: 203) of work and home: about 20 per cent of workers at one company of 26,000 employees described work as a 'haven' from the pressures of home life (2003: 209). Paradoxically, for a corporate culture that is usually driven by speed and constant change, the creation of such workplaces is also testament to the requirements of an extended temporality, if not actual 'slowness', in the creative processes of many such corporations. Not only are workspaces organized around the dynamics of 'traffic flow' rather than a hierarchical organization but there are usually central, common areas that encourage staff to mingle, interact and just plain 'hang out' (Florida 2003: 123). While much is often made of the high levels of dedication of such workers, manifested in their long working hours, more casual and less strictly disciplined workday schedules are also a feature of such workplaces in recognition of the spontaneity and serendipity that so often initiates creativity.

Generally, however, the stresses of fast living are particularly felt in the contexts of increasing demands on workers in the form of longer hours, demands for ever-increasing productivity levels, and less job security with more 'flexible' employment policies. Around the world, labour organizations advocate reduced work hours, arguing that this would provide people with more time to engage in volunteer activities and public life as well as having significant environmental benefits due to less material input and waste associated with the consumer society ('Reduce Work' 2002). Even within work culture, though, slowness can sometimes be a choice, and one which is more available in some cultural contexts than others. Much has been made, for instance, of the contrast between the labour policies in some European countries and that of the United States and Britain. What might be called the 'slow economics' (Foroohar 2001: 22) of countries like France has been demonstrated to have an economic viability, although it continues to be challenged by global economic forces ('Europe finds' 2004: 22). The French, with their 35–hour workweek, are more productive on an hourly basis than US and British workers, and research has shown that the shorter working week has facilitated greater labour-market flexibility (Foroohar 2001: 22). The growth in 'part-time' and 'temp' employment is also a labour-market trend that can be chosen by some to facilitate slow living. Indeed, a 1999 EU survey found that 77 per cent of temp workers chose their mode of employment in order to give themselves more personal time (Foroohar 2001: 23–4). Slow living, then, is not antithetical to work nor is it opposed to some trends in employment practices, providing those practices enable a better balance between work and personal time. It is not only work, of course, that has been radically transformed through the disengagement of space and place and in the next section we will consider the process of deterritorialization more generally and discuss how slow living can be located in such contexts.

Deterritorialization, the Local and Place

On a grey and bitterly cold early Saturday morning at Dunedin's weekly farmers' market we struggle with our bags of shopping as we make our way awkwardly through the crowded pathway. As we do we cannot but think of the new, shiny supermarket that has opened this week down the road from where we live. Its well-lit, warm interior beckons and it prompts us to wonder why we are here rather than there. As we do, we pause for a moment and take in the scene around us: the bustling stalls selling local fruit and vegetables, people tasting the organic pork sausages, the smell of coffee in the air, as well as much talk and laughter. We know we are putting up with the cold because we are committed to local food systems but we are also here because we enjoy the the *sensory* nature and the *sociality* of this space. There is a quality to this kind of space that distinguishes it from many other everyday experiences of space, including the new supermarket. Such an observation firstly reminds us that places are not just particular physical sites but they are also constituted as settings of interaction. Secondly, the material specificity of the farmers' market is appealing because it is different from, and challenges, conventional experiences of space in the global everyday: culture, traditionally thought of as bound to locality, is now derived from more abstract, deterritorialized contexts and relations. What implications does such a deterritorialized existence have for any conceptualization of the spaces of slow living? We will argue in this section that the concept of 'place' retains a significance in the global everyday and that deterritorialization paradoxically can contribute to a revitalization of the site of 'the local'.

Modernity has initiated fundamental changes in the relationship between space and place:

> In premodern societies, space and place largely coincided, since the spatial dimensions of social life are, for most of the population ... dominated by 'presence' – by localized

activities. The advent of modernity increasingly tears space away from place by fostering relations between 'absent' others, locationally distant from any given situation of face-to-face interaction. In conditions of modernity ... locales are thoroughly penetrated by and shaped in terms of social influences quite distant from them. (Giddens 1990: 18–19)

This process has been exacerbated in recent decades by forces of globalization, whereby contemporary culture, social relations and identity formation are increasingly disengaged from specific, local contexts and identities. A variety of terms, such as 'deterritorialization', 'delocalization' and 'displacement', have been employed to describe this general feature of present-day life. Manuel Castells has famously noted how the 'space of flows' is becoming 'the dominant spatial manifestation of power and function in our societies' (1996: 378). Certainly, we now live in a world where our experiences are increasingly mediated through the global reach of news media, telecommunications and the Internet, and for many connection to place has been loosened by greater degrees of mobility. The homogenizing effects of global capitalism are also manifested in the proliferation of standardized, impersonal and ahistorical spaces, such as airport departure lounges, motel chain rooms and supermarkets, which have been characterized as 'non-places' (Augé 1995). Such non-places are contrasted with examples of 'anthropological place' that have distinct individual identities, grounded in cultural memory and identity, forged through traditions and social customs. Ultimately, it could be speculated that the process of deterritorialization culminates in an understanding of the planet as a 'single place', a singular 'global' space.[4]

Observations about the global transformation of space and place can also be overstated and a more sober perspective can draw attention to variable experiences of such processes of change and a more nuanced understanding of the impact of deterritorialization on specific local places. Massey, for example, asks us to consider the 'power-geometry of time-space compression' (1994b: 149) and the way that different social groups have differentiated degrees of mobility with varying degrees of control over such movements:

From jet-setters, to pensioners holed up in lonely bed-sits, to Pacific Islanders whose air and sea links have been cut, to international migrants risking life and livelihood of the chance of a better life ... all in some way or another are likely to be affected by the shifting relations of time-space, but in each case the effect is different; each is placed in a different way in relations to the shifting scene. (1994b: 164)

A focus on the processes of deterritorialization does not involve a denial of the persistence of the local as a site of lived experience. Life lived locally, even for more cosmopolitan souls, still occupies the majority of an individual's time and space. The fundamental transformation of culture that occurs in contexts of globalization is not so much captured in the 'trope of travel' as in the way deterritorialization accounts for 'the transformation of localities themselves' (Tomlinson 1999: 29). This may well involve the penetration of local places by global forces and at least a disruption of the knowledges, values and practices that distinguish a specific locality but the material realities of physical embodiment and the ongoing need for situated political, social and economic relations mean that the local persists as a significant site in global culture. As noted in Chapter 1, we then arrive at the complex constitution of everyday life in global culture that sees '"roots and routes" as always coexistent in culture, and both as subject to transformation in global modernity' (Tomlinson 1999: 29).

Paradoxically, this understanding of deterritorialization, based on the interaction between global forces and local spatial contexts, can be the basis for a renewal of local territory. We must not understate the corrosive impact of global forces on the specificity of local places and the proliferation of homogenized 'non-places' but equally we must give full consideration to the ways that deterritorialization facilitates a cosmopolitan disposition that in turn offers the possibilities of 'reterritorialization'.[5] Globalization instigates a paradoxical process whereby a trend towards increasing global unicity in turn provides the means by which expressions of difference are more keenly identified. Deterritorialization does engender a greater sense of the world as a 'single place' but this world is primarily experienced not as a homogeneous, undifferentiated site or a simple unity of a global community but as a *consciousness* or *relational context* that informs subjectivity and spatial relations. This consciousness more broadly is the 'dialogic imagination' that is for Beck (2002) the defining characteristic of the cosmopolitan perspective which involves the 'pluralization of borders', including the border between the global and the local. Globalization, in this sense, is not an exogenous force that annihilates whatever specificity it encounters but a *reflexive framework* through which the specificity of actions and places are understood and attributed with value. Of course, encounters with a more global world can lead to hostile reactions, as we see in ethnic, nationalist and religious fundamentalist movements, but equally the development of a cosmopolitan disposition can have more positive ramifications including an 'awareness of the wider world as significant for us in our locality, the sense of connection with other cultures and even, perhaps, an increasing openness to cultural difference' (Tomlinson 1999: 200). The effect of this global reflexive framework is to produce a pluralistic valuation of the local: global culture can replicate localities (e.g. shopping malls) but it can also provide people with a more acute realization and appreciation of the specificity of their place, and the specificity of other places. Such a reflexive concept of locality offers a way of thinking about – and valuing – the local beyond a simple defensive refusal of contemporary global contexts.

The local, however, retains a degree of ambiguity despite the critical attention it has received, most notably through the many theorizations and discussions of globalization. We can ask of the local: 'Is it an opposition to the national and the global, a community, a discursive field, a level of government, the city?' (Brodie 2000: 117). The local can be both a descriptive and normative term and it can refer to both a specific geographical site and a particular organization of human relations. It can be mobilized by either progressive or conservative forces and subject to a variety of evaluations. The local is valued for its specificity, but should not be conflated with the concrete which would implicitly render global contexts as more abstract and thus deny the equally 'concrete reality' of global culture and economic forces (Massey 1994b: 129).

There is a strong sense of the fragility of the local in contemporary times, transformed and complicated as it is by the powers of the nation-state in local subject formation, the extent of diasporic flows and the mediated basis of modern existence. In this context, locality is 'primarily relational and contextual rather than … scalar or spatial' and locality can be contrasted as a category with the term neighbourhood which refers to 'the actually existing social forms in which locality, as a dimension or value, is variably realized' (Appadurai 1996: 178–9). The production of locality, then, is always the result of a dialectical relationship: neighbourhoods are themselves contexts within which various kinds of human action occur and they also require and produce 'outside' contexts against which their own design and logic is given shape and development. In this sense, no local community however apparently stable or isolated, can be regarded as outside history (Appadurai 1996: 185) and the ability of a local community to establish its own identity, practices and values is profoundly affected by the 'locality-producing capabilities of larger-scale social formations (nation-states, kingdoms, missionary empires, and trading cartels) to determine the general shape of all the neighbourhoods within the reach of their powers' (Appadurai 1996: 187). In many ways, the construction of locality occurs increasingly as a 'structure of feeling' in the contexts of 'the erosion, dispersal, and implosion of neighbourhoods as coherent social formations' (Appadurai 1996: 199). Such an account of the production of locality importantly establishes the ground, however real or virtual, upon which local community formation occurs, as well as its relational basis, where the specificities of place and identity are always constituted through their struggle with larger social formations. The local, then, is not a closed entity but is defined through the particular articulations that are established through that site. The local may well have a specific, grounded locale but it is also attributed with meaning through the complex composite of flows of people, goods and services and representations that occur from, to and between it.

At the heart of the spatial dynamics of slow living is not only an awareness of the complex constitution of the local but also a more comprehensive appreciation of the character of specific *places*. 'The local' and 'the global' are 'scales, processes, or even levels of analysis' but an emphasis on place refers in a more intimate way to the experience of a particular location with a specific sense of boundaries, ground and links to everyday practices (Escobar 2001: 152). An emphasis on place highlights an awareness of unique geographical and lived features and the individual and social attachments that are produced through engagements with a particular place. To speak of *place* in slow living highlights the importance of the individual specificity of lived experience and a revived appreciation, within the contexts of the global everyday, of the importance of gathering, dwelling and belonging. An emphasis on such fundamental spatial contexts becomes the basis not only of individual subjectivity but also – in an age of deterritorialization – of emergent political struggles. Our understanding of the centrality of place to slow living is informed by a belief that the effect of many theorizations of globalization and deterritorialization has been to understate the significance of place. As Arturo Escobar (2001) has noted, 'culture sits in places' even if it is not limited to them. 'Place' here is not posited as a closed concept of unproblematic simplicity in contrast to the dominating, abstract and global production of 'space' but rather place is here seen as fundamental to the spatial dynamics of the global everyday and the production of culture: 'We are, in short, placelings' (Escobar 2001: 143).

For most of us, our place is a complex urban location, itself constituted by different spaces and our movements across those terrains. In such circumstances, slow living is about installing the *possibility* of slowing down, the importance of creating, and being able to access, 'slow spaces' in our everyday contexts.[6] As such, slow living is based upon recognition of the complex contemporary experience of time and space that is articulated in the understanding of *timespace* (May and Thrift 2001), while also battling to preserve that heterogeneity of *timespace* experience through a promotion of slowness. Valuing spaces where slow living can occur is to posit such spaces in the context of the flux of modern living (Ambroise 1997). This recognition of the value of 'slowness' is therefore necessarily context specific, acknowledging that speed can be valuable in facilitating the possibility of slowness. Illustrating what this means in an urban context, Sofi Ambroise uses the analogy of transport:

> We may believe that all city-dwellers have the right to enjoy slowness, but this does certainly not imply waiting in long traffic jams, or for trams that never come. On the contrary, and paradoxically, it means having access to qualitatively *slow* spaces and time by means of transport that links up any two points with the maximum speed. (1997: 84, original emphasis)

Town planning, Ambroise argues, must construct the spatial contexts and networks necessary for the 'good life' that involve multiplicities of 'slowness' and 'speed' so that we can 'go and see a friend off at the airport without wasting half the day, leave our bikes at the station when we catch a train, and not despair when we miss the bus because we know that the next one will be along soon' (Ambroise 1997: 85). Such urban 'slow places' can take many different forms: they may be refuges for the busy professional classes or they could be used as sites of resistance, as found in Simpson's study of an alternative music store (2000). Spaces of slow living in urban contexts, then, arise from and highlight fundamental public spatial requirements that are at least undermined by the contexts of 'fast life': the need to disengage – however momentarily – from the flow of urban life for individual orientation, attention and contemplation; and a fundamental 'need to gather' (Simpson 2000: 712) to facilitate group identity and community formation.

The specificity of place has also been influential in the political struggles of social movements and indigenous and activist groups against the destructive deterritorializing forces of global capital. Such struggles are based upon a valuation of place while also fostering engagement with global organizations (such as transnational feminist alliances and international human rights and environmental groups). Indigenous groups whose continued existence was perceived to be precarious have in some cases been revitalized through global networks (Kearney 1995: 560). In such cases we see the meaning of the local as constituted through forms of mobility and flow and articulations with other spaces. Escobar, for example, notes that black communities of the Colombian Pacific are involved in a 'triple localizing strategy for the defense of their territories':

> ... a place-based localizing strategy for the defense of local models of nature and cultural practices; a further strategy of localization through an active and creative engagement with translocal forces, such as similar identity or environmental movements or various global coalitions against globalization and free trade; and a shifting political strategy linking identity, territory and culture at local, regional, national, and transnational levels. (2001: 163)

The importance of the specificity of place in slow living, particularly given our focus on Slow Food, is also exemplified in the recent rapid growth of farmers' markets and food circles. While such food markets have historically been a manifestation of 'the local', their resurgence in recent years attests to a complex response to the global food system, including its abstract deterritorialized spatial relations. Such alternative forms of food production, distribution and consumption are able to arise because of the *limitations* that global food corporations experience in negotiating the spatial relations of the global everyday. A greater awareness of the social and environmental problems associated with 'food miles', the struggle of global food corporations to respond quickly and effectively to emerging 'niche' markets, and to cultivate relationships of trust with consumers, have opened up spaces for alternative food networks in the global everyday (Hendrickson and Heffernan 2002).

The emergence of such alternative food networks are based upon the mobilization of particular values associated with 'the local'. The value of the local firstly derives from its very character: its physical environment (land, climate, flora and fauna). The local, for example, is the site from which the seasonality of produce can be understood and appreciated. Of course, the global food system benefits from *overcoming* such spatial and temporal 'limitations' but an increasing number of people seek reconnection with such seasonal patterns. The local can also be promoted because it facilitates expressions of difference. It is the site where we encounter the variety and richness of particular cultural products, identities and rituals. The global food system has benefited from the proliferation of choice and availability of a wide range of products but trends toward greater homogenization of food products have resulted in the reinvigoration of local difference. Of course, the production of difference is also always relational (Heldke 2003): the 'difference' of the local valued by an organization such as Slow Food is its cultural specificity in contrast to global forces of standardization. As we will see later in this chapter, the local itself must manage relations of difference in the constitution of its identity.

The local can also be privileged because it is a site where the agency of individuals can be exercised. To declare the importance of slowness and to act upon it is a powerful expression of agency in a world that so strongly propels us in different directions. The local may in some ways be privileged as a site of agency because of the constancy of tradition, because of its established ground, its certainty of routine and convention, but alternatively, as we have already noted, the local is also always a fragile entity and the agency of subjects can also be undermined by powerful outside forces. The assertion that the local facilitates expressions of agency is also, to some degree, problematic (see Chapter 6). As in all discussion of agency, we need to ask 'for whom' does this apply? The local can stifle and deny the individual exercise of agency and we must ask what kinds of subjects are able to choose slowness in contexts of a fast-paced culture, how freely are they able to move between different temporal orders, and also what kinds of subjects have no option but to participate slowly and locally? That said, the increasing popularity of farmers' markets and food circles emanates from the proximity and interaction that its spatial contexts provide which in turn give people a greater sense of autonomy and more fulfilling relationships. In their study, Hendrickson and Heffernan note that the 'localness' of the Kansas City Food Circle is best captured in the 'personalized' (2002: 364) nature of the space as food production is reembedded within a community, and trust is generated between producers and consumers: 'Trust ... is a subjective relationship negotiated between people, and can [be] broken into the concepts of responsibility and community. Producers feel a responsibility to produce healthy, wholesome food that will be eaten by people whom they know. Eaters feel a responsibility towards producers who are members of their community' (2002: 362–3).

We must resist, then, the understandable temptation in a global culture of deterritorialization to give the specificity of place a security that stems from a belief that places have a fixed, self-contained identity. Instead, the identity of the local is always the result of a process of articulation through both the shifting interrelations between one place and another, and the dynamics of social relations that occur in that place.[7] Such an understanding, however, does not devalue specificity of place or culture (Massey 1994a: 117). Rather, specificity of place acknowledges the particularity of social relations in a location and how people interpret them, which in turn produces new social processes and effects.

Terroir and tradition

In his account of the beginnings of the Slow Food movement, Carlo Petrini recalls visits in the early 1980s to the French regions of Burgundy, Bordeaux, Alsace and Champagne where he marvelled at the 'sense of place' that the territories evoked. Petrini concluded the particular identity of the regions was a complex amalgam of factors that extended beyond particular types of produce and businesses. The status of such regions emanated from 'a certain idea of production combined with a communication strategy that makes it possible to "sell" the world a complex image combining history, landscape, wine, cuisine, and a style of welcome' (Petrini 2001: 38). Armed with such an idea, Petrini and the newborn Arcigola movement considered their own Langhe region in Italy and set about '"building" a territory' (Petrini 2001: 39) that recognized and highlighted the region's agricultural traditions, its quality produce and landscape.

Such a story attests to the complex constitution of places, combining natural features and resources with human practices, traditions and contemporary uses, as well as the discourses and images that provide meaning to places, attributing them value in a global economy and locating them in political struggles. In Petrini's project a valuation of geographical specificity coexists with a consciousness informed by a global perspective. On the one hand, he values the concept of territory, or to use the French term *terroir*, that combines the natural and human features that give an agricultural locality its unique character. *Terroir* refers to the specificity of place that stems from its traditions, the uniqueness of local food cultures and regional produce, that resides in the landscape, soil and climate, as well as the types of food grown, the farming techniques, and the cultural contexts that inform food preparation and consumption.[8] On the other hand, Petrini recognizes the significance of the broader contexts within which the specificity of places is defined. He highlights the importance of promotional strategies that communicate the values of territory to others and he understands that the increasing cultural, political and economic value of the specificity of the visited French regions and his own Langhe region occur in global contexts. Petrini's project, then, exemplifies the relational nature and value of places. There is a reclamation and celebration of the physical and social particularities of place but it is not a romantic and naive valorization of place where some 'essential' identity that is fixed in the past is insulated from historical change. The task of '"building" a territory' is a recognition that it is the contemporary constitution of meanings of the territory that is at stake, however much it is based upon a valuation of its past. The identity and valuation of the place resides in its differentiation from other places and spaces and this necessarily requires communication and promotion. The promotion of the *terroir* of the place is not a cynical marketing and tourism exercise but it is nonetheless explicitly – if reflexively – used in an economic and political struggle against homogenizing global forces.[9]

Petrini's project highlights how the relations between the past, present and future can be mobilized in the conceptualization of place in a way that builds upon the fundamental relationship between space and time that has already been described. Of specific interest here is a consideration of the historical sense of temporality, how the valuation of the particularity of a place often gives emphasis to its history and traditions and how that is used subsequently in contemporary political struggle (see Terrio 2000). The knowledges and values that are associated with the physical and human features of a region only occur over time; the concept of *terroir* is not only about the specificity of place but the accumulated history of the place through the human practices and social relations associated with it (Tomasik 2001: 525). In this sense, then 'it may be useful to think of places, not as areas on maps, but as constantly shifting articulations of social relations through time; and to think of particular attempts to characterize them as attempts to define, and claim coherence and a particular meaning for, specific envelopes of space-*time*' (Massey 1995: 188, original emphasis).

An important feature in the conceptualization of place in slow living is a fore-grounding of the value of traditional ways of life and the historicity of place. As Massey (1995) notes, it is that very postmodern experience of the dislocation of the present from the past that drives us beyond the fast food outlets to the English pubs in London, or the cafes in Paris. There, at last, we can feel that we experience the distinctive and 'real' characters of the respective cities. Similarly, the cities of the Città Slow movement could be presented as capturing some sense of an 'authentic' Italy, where traditional foods, cultural practices and customs can be observed, experienced and enjoyed. This essentialist way of thinking about a place, of course, ignores the fact that places are 'always already hybrid' (Massey 1995: 183). The 'authenticity' of Slow Cities, for example, is variously and cumulatively the expression of Italian national, regional and more local 'uniqueness', each of which are themselves the products of historical connections, influences and assimilations. An essentialist understanding of place can work against any progressive politics because it closes down contestations about place between rival claimants.

It is not necessary, however, to conflate the local with tradition and hence exclude it as a site for radical politics. Rather, local struggles can be 'place-*based*' rather than 'place-*bound*' (Massey 1995: 184, original emphasis). Tradition can be something more than nostalgia for a past that can now be only maintained or lost; it can also be a site of political struggle. Such interpretations of a tradition are, of course, not just a reading of the past but they also serve to 'legitimate a particular understanding of the present [and] are put to use in a battle over what is to come' (Massey 1995: 185).

This particular understanding of the historical temporality of place is important in any conceptualization of the spaces where slow living occurs. The promotion of slowness, and all the traditional practices and ways of life associated with it, may seem initially to be a simple rejection of the pace, pressures and lifestyles of modern living and a subsequent refusal to engage with the difficult 'realities' of contemporary global life. Slow living, however, is not an escape from global culture into an ossified past but rather it is part of contemporary arguments about how we are to live now and in the future. The idea of slow living represents a contemporary interpretation of the past of places and communities and a mobilization of their traditions, principles and values in order to critique the present and provide alternatives for the future.

Città Slow

The places of slow living are arguably found most evocatively in the towns of the Slow Cities or Città Slow movement. While slow living cannot be limited to specific kinds of spaces, the Città Slow towns represent civic entities, managed by municipal governments with broad community support, that are organized around slow living. Just as Slow Food derives its conceptual significance through its binary opposite, the Città Slow organization attracts interest through the unusual conjunction of slowness with cities, the spaces most often associated with the fast life. However, as we noted in Chapter 2, the cities of Città Slow are, in fact, towns, limited to a maximum population of 50,000. This is an important defining feature of Slow Cities that not only acknowledges the benefits of the structures and scales of past urban existence but also points towards the needs of future town planning, as outlined by Città Slow President and Orvieto mayor, Stefano Cimicchi:

> We want [Città Slow] to become a player at European level to make sure that the Constitution currently being drawn up takes into account the reality of small towns and cities. Scholars, town planners and sociologists have recognized that the most human dimension to live in is that of the small agglomerates of no more than 50,000 inhabitants. The model for the ideal city is the late-medieval and Renaissance one, with the piazza functioning as a center of social aggregation. Europe has to remember its roots

and acknowledge the historical role its cities have played in the construction of its identity. (Abbona and Nano 2003)

The towns of the Città Slow movement, then, seek to exploit spaces and flows of urban existence, such as town squares and streetscapes, that facilitate slow living and community development, while at the same time eschewing those features of modern urban places that limit the possibilities of slowness. While the Città Slow movement distinguishes itself from global metropoloi, it is in dialogue with the administrators of large cities about ways to implement slowness across the spectrum of civic structures. At the 2002 Città Slow Awards, for example, an award for the implementation of slow principles in the urban design of large cities was given to Paris mayor Bertrand Delanoë (Slow Food 2002a). Of course, some of the features of Slow Cities, particularly the exclusion of traffic, are also general town planning devices to improve the quality of life in a range of urban centres. All modern cities now deploy measures to at least slow or 'calm' traffic. Many European cities now hold car-free days annually; Paris and Rome have initiated different city events where traffic is banned; and London began a road toll for all cars entering the city centre on week-days in 2003, cutting overall traffic by 20 per cent (Honoré 2004: 107). More recently, Naples has banned Vespas from the narrow streets of its central city, allowing pedestrians greater freedom as well as reducing urban noise.

As with the early Arcigola supporters and their task of '"building" a territory', the Slow Cities movement adapts the features and characteristics of the past of places in the contemporary construction of the towns. As Greve-in-Chianti mayor and founding Città Slow President Paolo Saturnini told us: 'the movement is not against change, it is against the wrong way to change. The wrong way is to cancel the past' (Saturnini 2003). That is, any suggestion that the structures and rhythms of Slow Cities emanate solely and unproblematically from the cumulative force of history overlooks the fact that the Città Slow towns are explicitly bureaucratic creations and are constituted through elaborate mechanisms of modern governance. While there is public support for the Città Slow movement within the respective towns and cities, membership of the movement is bestowed on the cities themselves as a result of their acceptance and implementation of a range of public policies, as outlined in the Città Slow charter. The features of Slow Cities are the result of public policies relating to urban planning, technology, the environment, tourism, business, agriculture and public health.

The emphasis on the generation of a particular 'quality of life' in Città Slow suggests how completely Slow Cities are governed; there seems to be an extensive policing and promotion of public practices and private activities that standardize and homogenize the identity of the Slow City community. The governance of Slow

Cities seems to be inspired by the same kind of utopian dream which Nikolas Rose attributes to the cities of the first half of the twentieth century: 'the perfect rational city planned in such a way as to maximize the efficiency, tranquility, order and happiness of its inhabitants while minimizing crime, disorder, vice, squalor, ill health and the like' (Rose 2000: 95). On the other hand, Slow Cities are also representative of contemporary cities, where there is a 'pluralization of the problematizations of life that take an urban form, and a pluralization of the ways in which programmes have been designed to address them' (Rose 2000: 95). One noteworthy feature of such cities is an emphasis on health, no longer conceptualized as the segregation and management of disease but rather as a 'network of living practices of well-being' (Rose 2000: 100). Health has ceased to be a specific and limited field defined in opposition to disease or disability but pertains to the quality of everyday life: what we eat, how we counter stress, and how we conduct relationships. The physical and psychological health of the individual is also considered in the contexts of their immediate working and home environments as well as the more general environment of the city, captured in concerns about traffic, pollution and urban design. Positano, for example, has installed a sophisticated sewage treatment system to improve the quality of life of its inhabitants and preserve the surrounding marine environment (Yeomans 2002: 218). Although health is not mentioned explicitly in the Città Slow charter, the movement is very much prompted by this conceptualization of urban health; the Slow Cities movement offers itself as an antidote to the psychological stresses of fast living, the ill effects of poor urban design, and recognizes that the health of individuals must be grounded in appropriate everyday practices.[10]

Contrary to initial expectations, the slow spaces of Città Slow are dynamic sites of enterprise. As with other forms of contemporary cities, the Slow Cities distinguish themselves through the construction of a particular 'kind of ethico-economic character of enterprise' (Rose 2000: 104–5).[11] A process of economic regeneration is accompanied by a localized form of citizenship where the promotion of trust, allegiance and obligation is a necessary ingredient in the formation of the new city of enterprise (Rose 2000). The promotion of Slow Cities is an effective exercise in civic 'branding' and an explicit device designed to enhance the tourism industry in each of the cities and towns. Saturnini acknowledges the risk that Città Slow may be perceived as purely a marketing exercise but also stresses the stringency of qualification and review procedures which prevent cities committing to the movement for short-term marketing benefits: several towns have withdrawn from initial interest in the movement after they realized the costs of required municipal changes, together with the strictures associated with membership renewal every three years. In this sense, slowness can also bring economic costs: while there has been much preservation of the older buildings in Greve-in-Chianti, a number of new building developments have either been rejected or scaled back considerably and large supermarkets have been excluded in order to ensure the survival of the local retail outlets (Saturnini 2003). For many Città Slow towns, however, the benefits outweigh the costs. Indeed, more so than other contemporary forms of tourism, the greater influx of tourists not only benefits accommodation and food businesses directly but they also provide impetus to the broader economy of the town. A central component of the attraction of Slow Cities for tourists is the *nature* of the *economy itself*: the direct connection with producers of foodstuffs and other goods and the accessing of a unique range of local and regional produce.

Finally, given its fundamental importance to slow living, Slow Cities are also spaces of pleasure. The contemporary city often works to commodify the civilized or transgressive pleasures of its past and Slow Cities, as tourism ventures, do commodify the pleasures of good food and wine and other civilized pleasures of urban living. Part of the attraction of Slow Cities, however, resides in the fact that these pleasures are not presented as repackaged, 'heritage' experiences but that the experiences have a historical continuity. For example, a central pleasure of Slow Cities is the spatial experiences of the towns, whether a bustling market-place or a piazza. In many Città Slow towns, these spaces are commodified as they become attractions for tourists; the roving perusal of such spaces, with or without video camera in hand, is in some ways a historical extension of the spatial experiences of the *flâneur*, where the flux of urban existence was organized and attributed with meaning through the singular male gaze (Tester 1994). The meanings of such public spaces, however, are not limited to such 'observations': town squares and marketplaces are also important sites that facilitate community. These spaces work as civic spaces because their design 'collects' people – of diverse ages, genders and occupations – and, in turn, encourages social interaction and participation. As such, an important feature of these spaces is their *slowness*; market-places and town squares are nodal points in the flow of urban life, however bustling they may be. They act as destinations, unlike other social spaces such as a promenade or a shopping mall that are designed more to facilitate the flow of people.[12] It may be easy to appreciate the virtues and pleasures of such slow, civic spaces when one is sitting on the steps of the extraordinary Orvieto cathedral for several hours (ironically, 'slowed down' by a sprained ankle) but such virtues and pleasures can equally be found in more mundane circumstances, such as a weekly local growers' market.[13]

The towns of the Città Slow movement do, of course, easily provoke a cynical response for many; the figures of 'the city' and of 'utopia' have long been connected, with many utopian visions being based on the geographical scale of small-scale city life (Harvey 2000: 157). The Città Slow towns may embody the mythical ideal of community where there is a strong sense of place, where close and transparent personal relations give rise to real expressions of social unity and where traditional ways of living are maintained and consolidated through rituals and customs, the use of local resources, the deployment of particular skills, as well as the production and consumption of local produce. Such slow communities are defined through their opposition to the fast-paced, stress-producing communities in which most of us grimly battle on and seem to be a preservation and realization of the 'understandable dream' of community that has been destroyed by contemporary global culture (Young 1990: 300). Walking through the streets of Orvieto with mayor Cimicchi, we are certainly provided with a tangible sense of a 'slow' community, as the town's slower pace of life mingles with an animated civic culture, as we are introduced to shop owners and fellow councillors and observe quite heated discussion about local planning issues amid the weekly market stalls. And yet Slow Cities can also reflect the realities of much urban existence, as we discovered sitting in a park near the railway station at Bra which became the site of a common urban conflict: a territorial dispute between two groups of young men.

The very idea of a community is an easy target in many ways, given that it sits oddly in contemporary urban and global contexts. Young has argued that the normative ideal of community is a hindrance for transformative politics in contemporary mass urban societies. She instead argues for a model of 'the unoppressive city' that is defined through 'openness to unassimilated otherness' (1990: 319). The unoppressive city 'offers an understanding of social relations without domination in which persons live together in relations of mediation among strangers with whom they are not in community' (1990: 303). In this sense, Città Slow communities seem to embody the reactionary ideal of community criticized by Young. It is argued that this ideal of community posits social relations of transparency and thus denies difference between subjects and that it privileges face-to-face communication (seen as authentic) over mediated forms of communication (seen as inauthentic).

We argue, however, that Slow Cities cannot be so easily dismissed. While Città Slow communities do seek to protect a 'local identity', they are not insular entities closed off from outside influence and they should not be portrayed as a traditional form of community that rigorously pursues a unity based upon a violence of exclusion. Instead, we argue that slow communities are *themselves* the residues of exclusion from dominant expressions and structures of modern urban living. The human relations and social spaces that are promoted in Slow Cities are exactly those ways of life that are increasingly marginalized in modern urban contexts. The tremendous power of global culture to threaten cultural difference and standardize everyday practices gives rise to expressions of resistance in the form of entities such as slow communities. Città Slow, then, does not seek to promote 'static' cultures defined through their stubborn opposition to the 'monolithic fluidity' (if one can use such a phrase) of modern global culture but it is itself a 'fluid' organization, defining itself through its ongoing negotiation of emerging cultural change and traditional ways of living. A good example of such a negotiation is the adoption of new technologies, such as electric buses, in order to enhance public transport, reduce pollution and continue to improve the town's 'quality of life'. Città Slow represents not a refusal of contemporary global life but an active and critical interrogation of its values, practices, and ideologies and provides a site where agency can be exercised in the face of the 'inevitabilities' of global culture.

This discussion of Città Slow has foregrounded *Italian* places despite the recent growth of the movement outside its country of origin (see Chapter 2). Even within Italy, of course, there is no singular Italian sense of place, as the 'unity' of Italy is the sum of different local and regional realities (see Dickie 1996; Levy 1996; Capatti and Montanari 2003). While we are wary of national generalizations, it is not accidental that Slow Food and Città Slow arose in Italy, where slowness has been a more readily available cultural resource. In such a context, the clash between a culture of slowness and the increased frenetic pace of modern global life has been pronounced. Italy, however, arguably more so than other southern European nations, is also a nation constituted through radically different temporalities: both speed and slowness have been, and remain, intrinsic features of the culture since its rapid modernization in the post-war period. As a modern nation-state, Italy is also profoundly integrated into global capitalist networks, and, as such, Italian *national* structures and processes can be said to threaten slow living. Alternatively, the specific expressions of local and regional differences cumulatively do much to promote an 'Italian' cultural identity and way of life. This national identity, however loosely constructed through the collection of regional identities, can be mobilized by the nation-state in global competition with other nation-states, to further economic interests in sectors such as agriculture and tourism. Petrini's individual networking aside, it is not surprising that an organization such as Slow Food has attracted considerable governmental support from regional and national authorities who are recognizing the potential benefits that slow principles may offer their constituencies.

The towns of the Città Slow movement give expression to slow living in urban contexts but equally they derive much of their identity from linkages with surrounding countryside and from their manifestation of regional identities. Città Slow declare that they are committed to initiatives that encourage the protection of local products and the development of town markets to promote produce from the surrounding countryside. This represents much more than the simple enriching of the town's character with a rural aesthetic but rather it builds on a significant and distinctive Italian historical feature whereby the prevalence of urban centres throughout the land are important sites for the collection, representation and transmission of local and regional produce, cuisine and cultural identity. As Capatti and Montanari remind us in their discussion of Italian cuisine:

> In effect, the city constitutes a strategic setting for the creation and transmission of a culinary heritage that is at once local and national. ... The city ... represents the surrounding territory, and, in a more or less direct and often violent way, it appropriates the area's material resources and culture, including its culinary traditions, adopting them, exporting them, and perpetuating their use (2003: xv–xvi).

'The rural' remains an important space, not only for Città Slow, but also for the Slow Food movement, given its gastronomic basis together with its emphasis on the *terroir* of places. 'The rural' is, of course, often subject to romantic and nostalgic valorizations and this occurs around the world: in European countries such as France and Italy the countryside has particular cultural and aesthetic resonances while in Australia, the most urbanized country in the world, the rural has a mythic status and remains a privileged site in many downshifting experiences. Contemporary rural places are under considerable stress as agriculture becomes a declining force in national economies: in Italy, for example, the total number of farms fell 7.1 per cent between 1982 and 1991 (Capo 1995: 300). The rural, however, is also becoming a much more complex space, and its transformation through engagement with other places and global flows provides opportunities as well as threats:

> Concepts such as 'peri-urbanization, 'rurbanization', 'urban de-concentration' and 'urban exodus', clearly indicate that present-day rurality cannot be associated with the former 'peasant' society. The number of farmers has continued to shrink over the years while new categories of population have gradually appeared. ... The development of communications, along with significant improvements in productivity and production systems, have contributed greatly to opening up rural areas to the outside world. Rural populations have extended their networks, widening their social space and economic scope. (Bessière 1998: 22)

For Slow Food, the transformation of rural life in contemporary global contexts poses potentially disastrous consequences from standardized forms of mono-cropping by transnational agricultural conglomerates but the increasing openness of rural places, to more immediate urban contexts as well as global networks, also offers the means by which the distinctiveness of local cultural identity and local produce can be preserved and celebrated (see Chapter 6). Elena Saraceno (1994) argues that the rural/urban dichotomy is inadequate to account for the spatial logics of Italy and instead advocates a 'local economy approach' that considers a diversified countryside working in conjunction with urban centres of varying sizes within contexts of regionality. She demonstrates how it is increasingly untenable to simply collapse the spatial category of the rural with the economic category of agriculture and notes that over a twenty year period the percentage of the population in cities of populations over 100,000 actually decreased while the percentage of the population living in small and medium cities increased.[14] While Saraceno's analysis is nationally specific she also argues that such an understanding of spatial differentiation is not an 'Italian non-exportable extravagance' (1994: 455) but rather is more generally applicable to delineate diversified rural areas.

The fluidity of movement between Italian urban and rural places, this kind of *articulation* between the city and the country, points to an important factor in the establishment of the spatial contexts of slow living. Neither urban nor rural contexts are privileged here as the optimal sites for slow living but rather consideration of these spatial contexts lead us to an appreciation of the quality of everyday life that derives from a sense of *balance* where people have both a groundedness and a sense of belonging. Of course, both a connection with a specific territory and a sense of community are manifested in different forms in various kinds of places and are difficult to singularly evaluate, but they are features, nonetheless, that are absent from much of contemporary existence and they are invoked in the rebuilding and reconceptualizations of places. Many inner-city renewal projects, for example, attempt to reinvigorate local community life through the establishment of particular sites, such as city gardens. Our point here is that the mindful consciousness that we position as central to slow living generates an awareness of the specificity of place, and more particularly a material relationship to the land, as well as an attentiveness to those who coexist in the same territory and who collectively give their territory identity and value. This is not based upon a bourgeois, romantic valorization of either rural life or small, sophisticated towns in exotic locales, but is rather based upon a belief that in the contexts of our fast, deterritorialized, modern lives, we need to retain an ethical and political disposition that is grounded in an awareness of our fundamental relationships to the specificity of place, the land, its produce and each other.

–5–

Food and Pleasure

... inspiration is the best word we have for appetite, and ... appetite is the best thing we have going for us. ... It is appetite that makes things edible, just as it is imagination that makes lives liveable, once they are economically viable. And, as children take for granted, *lives are only liveable if they give pleasure*: that is, if we can renew our pleasures, remember their intensities.

Phillips (1998: 7, emphasis added)

As many others have noted in writing on the subject, food is never just about food. In this chapter, we do not want to rehash, so to speak, discussions of the multi-accentuality of food, important though they may be. Rather, we want to examine the significations, practices and contexts of food in relation to the discourse and practices of slow living, seeing food as a significant site for slow living, as what makes lives 'liveable', in Phillips's sense. While this chapter will draw on the literature on the sociology and anthropology of food, it will examine notions of pleasure through food from a cultural studies' perspective, influenced by Elspeth Probyn's work on food, culture and identities based on the concept of articulation (1998, 2000). Food's capacity to bring together, connect and emphasize disparate aspects of social experience and global politics makes it possible to think differently or beyond the current formations of family, economy or nation, to name a few (Probyn 1998: 171). Again, our central focus will be on Slow Food, as food and pleasure are the twin pillars on which all other aspects of the movement – including slowness – are built.

In this chapter, we will contend that the nexus of food and the body is central to the pleasures of slow living and its ethico-political agenda, and hence to the formation of slow subjects in the global everyday, but that these processes are complicated by assumptions about gender, family, class and nation. Through the stories and practices of food and eating derived from Slow Food we will interrogate how (and with what) the values of convivial and gastronomic pleasure are articulated and whether these articulations offer productive possibilities for slow subjects in the global everyday. The emphasis that emerges is what we will call 'situated pleasures', indebted to Donna Haraway's (1991) concept of 'situated knowledges'.

In relation to food and eating, situated pleasures are firstly grounded in the body – in the physicality and affectivity of the incorporation of food – and secondly based on an attentiveness to the *location* of the body, its association with other bodies in convivial settings, and an awareness of the nexus between the bodies that produce and consume food, in specific times and places. By using this notion of situated pleasures, we will be seeking to distinguish between traditional gastronomy, as an elite practice to cultivate taste based on an omniscient connoisseur's knowledge of world cuisines, and Slow Food's *eco*-gastronomy, based on an awareness of ethical connection with, and enjoyment of, the places and people who produce the cuisine.

Beginning with an exploration of the pleasures of food, then, this chapter will go on to examine the concept of authenticity which we argue is a core value in the role of food in slow living and in Slow Food in particular. We offer an account of authenticity as situated rather than essentialized, and as grounded in the historicity of sensory experience and material culture in everyday life (Seremetakis 1994). We are all repositories of past practices of food and eating (through, for instance, family, class, region and ethnicity) and yet also always connecting ourselves to practices and contexts in ways which are new to us and which may offer us the potential to reconsider our locatedness (Probyn 2000: 16). It is this dual perspective that food offers, its capacity to evoke the past and the new, the familiar and the other, which gives it the capacity to create new forms of knowledge, affectivity and connectedness (Labelle 2004: 86). Finally, this chapter will consider the more contentious aspects of food in slow living as notions of 'taste' and the 'shared table' invoke questions of class and gender. Eating is not only 'an act laden with affect' (Rozin 1999: 13) but, like all social practices, implicated with relations of power and distinction (Mintz 1996: 17–32). If slow living is to offer a form of dailiness that contests the paucity of pleasure in everyday life, its attention to food must be both reflexive and inclusive.

Pleasure

> It is axiomatic that in the late modern period Western individuals have come to expect to experience pleasure on a daily basis.
>
> Finkelstein (1999: 76)

On a nondescript street in an unfashionable part of Bologna is *La Scuola Vecchia* (literally 'the old school'), a Bologna institution, where the traditional pasta of the region (very rich egg pasta the colour of parchment) is made by hand, painstakingly rolled with long, thin rolling pins on large wooden blocks until the right texture and thickness is achieved, and hung to dry, or made into *tortellini* and its variations, which are a regional speciality. Classes are held daily and are open to food professionals or enthusiastic amateurs. The School also has a small dining room with one large table big enough to accommodate a group of a dozen or so people in homely surroundings, where dinners may be held or class members can taste their efforts. On a cold March evening we were to meet members of the Bologna Slow Food *condotta* who had arranged a dinner in our honour at *La Scuola Vecchia*, so that we could taste 'real' pasta, which they considered the cornerstone of traditional Bolognese cuisine. We were ushered into the premises where the proprietress waited to serve us a Bolognese feast of her day's handiwork: *tortellini in brodo* (small meat-filled parcels of pasta in a delicate broth), *tortelloni al pomodori* (larger versions in a rich tomato sauce), *tagliatelle al ragu* (which the English-speaking world knows as 'spaghetti Bolognese' but which bears no resemblance at all to the ribbons of delicate and yet robust egg pasta in a rich meat sauce), followed by a meat course, vegetables, dessert, coffee, all accompanied by wines from the Bologna hills, *piadine* (local flat breads) and plates of chunks of *Parmiggianno Reggiano* (one of which was consumed in its entirety by our two-year old son, to the delight of the locals and the horror of his parents). It is a cliché to refer to an 'unforgettable meal' but this evening is a sense-memory that will surely last, as every subsequent meal of pasta, since Bologna, has triggered unfavourable comparison with the memory of *La Scuola Vecchia*. Unlike the Proustian madeleine, which evoked a memory of connection with earlier times, the taste of pasta has become a disconnection, reminding us that some places and times are not repeatable. As remarkable as this pasta was, however, it was the evening of *ospitalità* which we recall most fondly. We had arrived in the city just a few weeks' earlier, having made email contact with the *fiducario* of the Bologna *condotta* before leaving Australia and hoping that we would be able to carry out some participant-observation at their events over the course of our stay. Instead, we found ourselves not only warmly welcomed, but the recipients of meals such as this, which our hosts organized for us around the region of Emilia-Romagna on a regular basis, allowing us to meet producers and experience food that as *stranieri* we would never have discovered by ourselves. Sitting around the dining table at *La Scuola Vecchia*, conversing in a mixture of English and Italian but connecting more effectively through the shared enjoyment of the food and wine, which seemed as much a heightened sensory experience for the locals as for us, it was easy to feel that food has a unique capacity to bring people together and that the pleasures of the shared table were a true gift.

It is hard not to idealize such a meal, as a glimpse of slow living that non-Italians all too often imagine is an everyday thing for Italians, given that Italy has been such a site of idyllic projections in literature and film (Parkins 2004a). For us, however, part of the pleasure of the evening was derived from the fact that it was a welcome respite from the stresses and frustrations of trying to settle (albeit temporarily) in a foreign culture, where time to work (and think) was a constant struggle without the usual temporal routines of work and family to anchor us and organize our day, and where the vagaries of Italian everyday life often made no sense to us. For our hosts, as well, it was something of an oasis from the busy professional lives of their working week (even though a culture of later dining hours and longer duration of meals meant that they may have had more such opportunities for 'slow time' even within the demands of contemporary Italian work culture).[1] One might assume, that is, that Slow Food members deliberately choose to organize their daily schedules so as to make slowness possible, especially in the area of food and eating. However, in the global everyday where speed and sociality – not to mention pleasure – are frequently pitted against each other, is this the case? Interviews with some Australian Slow Food convivium leaders found that while all espoused a passion for the philosophy of Slow Food and found it a source of meaning and value in their lives their everyday practices were not necessarily an exemplification of the slowness they desired (e.g. Bianchino 2004; Taylor 2004). This dilemma of how to achieve slowness on a mundane level has also often been aired in *Slow*, such as in an interview with Kerstin Müller, the then 38–year-old leader of the German Green Party and Slow Food member, who was asked how she finds the time to eat in her extremely hectic schedule. Müller replied: 'Usually food doesn't even cross my mind during the day. I don't eat breakfast and unless I have guests, I don't usually eat lunch either. Only when it gets to the evening do I find I'm getting really hungry' (Kriener 2002: 82). Met with some incredulity on the part of the interviewer, Müller concedes that she has a large fruit bowl in her office from which she may pick during the day. The interviewer persists:

> *Slow*: But eating something during the day would be a way of stopping for a moment. You could get off the treadmill and distance yourself from the rest of those fifteen hours that you spend working with your adrenaline at fever pitch. It could be a break that is as useful as it is enjoyable.
>
> Müller: It's just not possible. … there is simply no time to stop. So I prefer a good dinner in the evening with my husband or friends, when the day's work is over and I can eat in peace, and eat well. In the past few years, I've really learnt to appreciate the pleasures of a good meal and the sense of well-being it gives. (Kriener 2002: 82)

But does one meal a day eaten with others after a fifteen-hour work day bear any resemblance to the Slow Food philosophy of 'quiet material pleasure', which Müller supposedly supports? Although a member of Slow Food, Müller is in many ways a typical 'fast' global subject, for whom slow living is, apparently, a goal rather than a daily reality: she has no time to eat, does not even think about food, but worries about the effects of weight gain on her appearance (Kriener 2002: 82). In this instance, food, as represented by the good evening meal, is in fact the *only* signifier of slow living, the overdetermined image of its pleasures which, Müller says, can give a 'sense of well-being'.

Ironically for Slow Food, part of its appeal may in fact derive from the ways in which food can be seen as a 'shortcut' to a pleasure that is missing from many other aspects of daily life, as Müller's case makes clear. From the popularity of television celebrity chefs to the emergence of culinary tourism, the pleasures of food have a popular currency they may never have had before (Probyn 2000: 6). On a daily basis, media and visual culture link food and pleasure, if often in problematic ways for a range of variously situated consumers. The tedious monotony with which we are incited to indulge, succumb, be tempted or seduced by foods (which are almost always high in fat, sugar or both) not only attests to the impoverished imaginations of advertisers but a persistent cultural association between pleasure and guilt or sin. One does not have to be an unreconstructed Freudian to think that only a culture deeply ambivalent about pleasure could use the word 'wicked' so often to describe confectionery or dessert. For the ethical consumer as well as the fast-food junkie, moreover, food and eating can be associated with an absence of pleasure. As Probyn argues, the 'whiff of moralism' in much writing on food and globalization can result in the further relegation of pleasurable eating to a vice indulged by guilty privileged subjects (2000: 13). Attitudes towards the pleasures of food are also differentiated by gender and ethnicity. Cross-cultural research, for instance, has found that women worry more about food than men, while the French and Italians are more likely to associate food with pleasure than Americans (Rozin 1999: 19; Ochs, Pontecurvo and Fasulo. 1996).[2]

Pleasure, or at least preference, is, however, still central to food and eating in a very material sense. As Rozin argues,

> Almost all potential foods are either liked or disliked; we are rarely neutral. ... As a result, most people choose foods they like and hence eating is, for the most part, a pleasant, positive experience. Over and over again, although it is true that some foods are consumed primarily out of necessity or for instrumental reasons (gaining nutrition, losing weight, or being a member of the group), the principal basis for food choice is liking for the flavour. (1999: 15)

The centrality of pleasure to life in general is often something that adults 'forget', as Phillips reminds us, especially in a social context where bodily enjoyment is judged as inferior to the cultivated pleasures of taste and aesthetics (Bourdieu 2000: 22). Such a context has traditionally problematized the pleasures of food for the cultivated bourgeoisie, for whom gastronomy was a form of cultural capital and hence social distinction, and yet inevitably involved the 'taste of the tongue, the palate and the throat' which traditional aesthetics eschewed (Bourdieu 1984: 486, 490). This problem leaves traditional gastronomy with the absurd question of 'How to eat well without really taking nourishment?' (Revel 1992: 145), marking the extent to which the aestheticization of food, as distinct from a more embodied, affective experience, has been valued in the gastronomic domain.

With its originary narrative of an anti-McDonalds protest, Slow Food has been perceived by some as aligned with traditional gastronomy and hence with elitist tastes (e.g. Gaytán 2004; Laudan 2004). While the following section on 'authenticity' will return to this argument to elaborate on what specific foods and food sites are valued by Slow Food, here it is the assumptions about pleasure implicit in criticism of Slow Food's criteria of food values that warrant attention. Slow Food derides the evils of industrial agriculture that supplies and supports the fast-food industry, but its emphasis is often on the *consumption* rather than the production of fast food as a central issue (e.g. Petrini 2001: 26–33). The real problem with fast food, to paraphrase Daniel Harris on contemporary consumerism in general, is not that it is 'shamelessly carnal and sybaritic' but in fact it is not pleasurable enough (2000: xviii): whether through the hyperbole of advertising or the standardization of production which promises a 'perfect' product every time, the result is a kind of draining away of pleasure or at least reducing it to a one-note register. While Finkelstein has argued that eating at McDonald's offers social and semiotic pleasures rather than culinary ones (1999: 76), Slow Food's insistence on 'material pleasure' refuses such an 'either/or' approach to pleasure, emphasizing the range of pleasures associated with food, while enacting a critique of passive consumption by foregrounding attentive engagement and embodiment in eating practices.[3]

As discussed in Chapter 3, there is an explicit aesthetic in Slow Food discourse that serves, in part, to differentiate 'the good life' from (particular constructions of) the working life through denoting slowness as 'time to have a thought/experience whose productivity is subjective, connecting the sensorium to something that *feels* noninstrumental, absorbing, and self-affirming' (Berlant 2004: 449, original emphasis). Such a sensory aesthetic runs the risk of remaining in 'perfect consonance' with the privileges of contemporary social arrangements, even as it seeks to counterpose them (Berlant 2004: 449).[4] The question such an emphasis on sensory experience and pleasure in particular poses is the degree to which modern daily life makes pleasure – satisfaction, happiness – available to subjects who must 'earn' the free time necessary for aesthetic experience.[5] With the democratization of consumption, pleasure may no longer be the sole prerogative of the aristocracy (those historically with the time and resources to devote to its cultivation; Lefebvre 2000/1971: 80) but the palpable presence of negative emotions in contemporary 'affect worlds' (and their explicit mobilization for post-9/11 political agendas) makes issues of pleasure of new relevance (see Berlant 2004). This is the challenge Slow Food represents in the global everyday: by starting with the linkage of food and pleasure, an essential daily experience becomes the means for putting pleasure back into the quotidian, not as a bonus, nor a reward for hard work, nor a retreat, but as a central aspect of everyday life. Refusing to cede such pleasure to the domain of gastronomy, while distinguishing it from homogenized consumption, Slow Food prioritizes both aesthetic experience and corporeal enjoyment, thereby rejecting the traditional (Kantian) antithesis between the two.

One of the main ways that Slow Food tries to articulate food, pleasure and slow-ness in everyday life is through an attention to sensory experience. Take, for instance, the pleasure of biting into a peach – the instantaneous explosion of sweet flavour, dripping juice and soft flesh combined with the visual appeal of the orange-crimson hues across the dimpled curve and velvety fuzz of the fruit. At its heart, Slow Food is based on the notion that a sensory experience like eating a peach should be attended to. Not only would such attention expose the inferior quality of, say, the floury, tasteless, refrigerated peach from the supermarket and potentially instigate a desire for heirloom fruits or direct purchase from producers (leading to altered practices of consumption/production which other consumer or environmental groups also advocate). The 'peach experience' may also lead to a broader questioning of the place (or absence) of pleasure and beauty in our daily lives, and prompt a (re)new(ed) awareness of the senses, against the 'sensual logic of late capitalism', a context where hyper-consumption has 'privatized' and 'spe-cialized' sensory experience (Howes 2005: 293; Seremetakis 1994: 9–10). Coincidentally taking sensory memories of peaches in her Greek childhood as her starting point, Seremetakis has argued that the experience of objects laden with sense-memories 'interrupts' the flow of everyday life in non-synchronous ways because they seem to be 'out of the immediate continuum of socially constructed material presence and value' (1994: 12). The sensory experience of the bitten peach – or its memory – can be a moment of 'stillness', an alternative to dominant modes of experience, and offers us an encounter 'with cultural absence and *possi-bility*' (1994: 12, emphasis added). Seremetakis's evocative meditation on sense and material culture suggests, then, the practices of slow living can be understood as means of maximizing such moments of 'stillness' through experiencing 'inter-ruptive articles, spaces, acts and narratives' which are particularly associated with food (Seremetakis 1994: 12).

Such a sensory aesthetic differs from the tradition of aesthetics based on the 'senses of distance', instead favouring the senses of proximity (taste, touch, smell) (Bourdieu 2000: 22; Stewart 2005: 62). The difference between what could be called Slow Food's 'politics of the senses' (Seremetakis 1994: 13) and an 'aesthetic politics' may be illustrated by reference to an earlier Italian movement in which food and aesthetics were articulated. In 1932, Filippo Tommaso Marinetti's *La cucina futurista* (*The Futurist Cookbook*) insisted on the primacy of the aesthetic in the experience of food, to the almost total disregard of nutrition, in establishing a 'way of eating best suited to an ever more high speed, airborne life' (1989: 36). Futurists envisioned a utopian future in which Italians would derive nutrition from pills and supplements, and food would be valued solely for the aesthetic experi-ence it provided (Marinetti 1989: 38). Singled out for particular Futurist oppro-brium was the Italian penchant for pasta, an 'absurd Italian gastronomic religion', according to Marinetti (1989: 37). The Futurists called for the abolition of pasta on the grounds of its association with tradition and slowness (*'Pastascuitta* ... ties today's Italians with its tangled threads to Penelope's slow looms and to somnolent old sailing-ships in search of wind' 1989: 37), while also noting its supposedly detrimental effects on the virility and creativity of the body.[6] Marinetti's emphasis on shock value rather than corporeal enjoyment was a typical avant-gardist strategy to unsettle Italian traditions of convivial pleasure and to instead associate Italian culture – including food culture – with the symbols of modernity, such as the car, the aeroplane and the bomb featured in the names of recipes (for example 'Car Crash' was 'a hemisphere of pressed anchovies joined to a hemisphere of date purée, the whole wrapped up in a large, very thin slice of ham marinated in Marsala'; 1989: 119). Although Marinetti's attack was 'aimed at the entire panorama of indolent, provincial, self-satisfied gastronomy' (Capatti and Montanari 2003: 295), by its privileging of style, creativity and presentation, Futurist cuisine was in a sense the *reductio ad absurdum* of traditional gastronomy. Slow Food, then, inherits a tradition of culinary revolution (seen most clearly in its deployment of the manifesto form) but attempts to chart a different path in its goal to transform foodways by interweaving pleasure – aesthetic, sensual, convivial – with tradition and connectedness in a world of speed Marinetti could only have dreamt of.

Given the movement's emphases, it is not surprising that the Slow Food discourse of pleasure through food is a central theme in its quarterly journal *Slow*, and elaborated in books like Corby Kummer's *The Pleasures of Slow Food* (2002) in which lush photographs of food and countryside are juxtaposed with recipes and profiles of traditional cooks and food producers. It is easy to dismiss such texts as 'gastroporn' (Lawson 1999) – an unhealthy and elitist obsession with food, its preparation and consumption – and the linkage of food and sex seems to be one of the few ways our culture can conceptualize pleasure.[7] Indeed, in researching this book it has been surprising to find how *little* literature exists in cultural studies and everyday life on pleasure per se, not sexual pleasure or what might be called the pleasure of resistance but ordinary, everyday, garden-variety pleasure. Even Luce Giard's account of the pleasures of the table is articulated with and through an extended metaphor about food and sex, noting that 'the table and the bed often seem to serve a common purpose' (1998: 196). The pleasures of food are of course a highly sensory and sensual experience and Giard is right to stress the 'intimate proximities', both corporeally and emotionally, bound up with our food experiences from earliest childhood (1998: 195). It nevertheless strikes us that the thinking and doing of pleasure in everyday life remains a relatively unexplored area of analysis, to which the expanding literature of Slow Food adds a welcome dimension.

In this literature, *Slow* occupies a central place and exemplifies Slow Food's philosophy in its layout, imagery and production values as much as its content. *Slow* describes esoteric food and wine practices around the world, nostalgic memories of past meals, and culinary landscapes but it has also devoted issues to themes such as inebriation, butchering, garbage and leftovers. In *Slow*, the pleasures of food are not only diverse but can be messy, unsettling or even dangerous. The issue on inebriation (1996), for instance (complete with cover image of the Queen sipping champagne), begins with the 'pleasures' of drunkenness before dissecting and exploring the topic in sixteen articles by food writers, poets, scientists and anthropologists, while the issue on butchering (2002) contains many graphic images from abattoirs around the world which confront the reader with the realities of meat consumption one might associate with an animal liberation campaign. As Capatti puts it in the editorial to this issue: 'Dedicating an issue of *Slow* to blood, the art of cutting meat and the fingers of butchers, carvers and carnivores is tantamount to breaking a taboo. In these years of anguish over farming methods and their consequences for the consumer, it means taking a good look at the way we organize pleasure and disguise death' (2002a: 4). Pleasure in *Slow* is not only polysemous but a means of beginning an interrogation of contemporary food practices which for Slow Food leads inevitably to broader questions of the ethics of everyday life in a global context. In a recent issue, Petrini argued that Slow Food is seeking to redefine gastronomy by 'deem[ing] pleasure a subject worthy of study' (2004b: 6): 'In the light of the new definition of gastronomy we are trying to build, consumption demands reason if it is to be sustainable for the land and avoid contributing to social injustice. But it must also be pleasurable' (Petrini 2004b: 8).

The most elaborated and explicit account of the centrality of pleasure in the movement is in fact by Petrini in his book *Slow Food: The Case for Taste* (2001), which warrants a lengthy quotation:

> pleasure was, and is, a thorny subject: moralistic people feel itchy at the sound of the word; if you are involved in any sort of social cause or movement, your fellows will rebuke you for mentioning it; others will cite health concerns; and almost anyone will regard an interest in pleasure as a sign of superficiality. They all make the mistake of considering pleasure as synonomous with 'excess'. ... Above all, dedication to pleasure is theoretically impossible, for excess is simply incompatible with a steady routine. This is true in biology (our senses, for example, can become so accustomed to smells pleasant or unpleasant that we no longer perceive them) and in psychology too, for there is no form of pleasure that the passage of time will not make us take for granted or even dislike, no matter how lovely it may be at first. If habit blunts pleasure, then obviously we can't organize our lives around it. What is the consequence? *Simply that in order to live pleasurably, we need to broaden the range of things that give us pleasure, and that means learning to choose differently, even to live differently.* From there to gastronomy is an obvious step: alimentary monoculture ... blanks out the pleasures of the palate, because, no matter how much we like them, it makes them

habitual. So embracing variety and difference really means performing an impossible trick every day – that of making an ephemeral and voluptuous pleasure last. (2001: 20–1, emphasis added)

Petrini's emphasis here on a variety in diet that is distinct both from excess and unthinking habit is a clear articulation of the link between Slow Food's philosophy and the Epicurean life of *ataraxy* (contentment and tranquillity) based on 'the prudent pursuit of pleasant experiences' (Bennett 2001: 87). As Foucault has explicated at length in *The Use of Pleasure*, for Greeks in the classical period it was the avoidance of excesses associated with the body – whether an excess of food, wine or sex – that diet or regimen as a 'whole art of living' (1985: 101) was intended to balance. Hence moderation was valued as 'an art, a practice of pleasures that was capable of self-limitation through the "use" of those pleasures that were based on need' (1985: 57). Just as Petrini emphasizes embracing variety and difference, so too did ancient regimens guard against a uniform approach to diet: 'A regimen was not good if it only permitted one to live in one place, with one type of food, and if it did not allow one to be open to any change,' Foucault argues, 'The usefulness of a regimen lay precisely in the possibility it gave individuals to face different situations' (1985: 105).

Slow Food's 'pleasure principle' of food (Capatti 2002c: 5) has, then, deep historical roots in classical approaches to diet based on the 'use of pleasure' but is also imbricated in both Christian and post-Kantian attitudes to pleasure and the body. As Parasecoli notes, until at least the end of the 1960s, 'Among the Italian Left a "cathocommunist" attitude prevailed, which united Catholic morality with Communist ideology' (2003: 29) and this ascetic-conservative orientation of the Left was an initial motivation for Slow Food's founders to articulate an oppositional, celebratory approach to pleasure, food and community. More generally, the discipline of extreme abstinence from food has been a recurring one throughout the history and various traditions of Christianity indicating 'a profound ambivalence about food and flesh' (Griffith 2001: 36). While the food refusal of the 'desert fathers' and medieval saints has been well documented (see, for example, Walker Bynum 1987), more contemporary examples of an intersection between, say, American Protestantism and modern dieting are also now receiving attention (see Griffith 2001 and 2004; Murray Berzok 2002; Nemeroff and Graham 2002). More generally, as Montanari points out (while stressing that the Christian tradition is 'not univocal') there has been a persistent recommendation 'not to look for pleasure in food [and] not to pay too much attention to it' (1996b: 58).

Outside of religious traditions, the suspicion towards pleasure which Petrini noted has also had a long history on the thoroughly secular Left and is particularly associated with the work of the Frankfurt School, such as Horkheimer and Adorno's *Dialectic of Enlightenment* where they argue that pleasure is antithetical to critical thinking. Pleasure, Horkheimer and Adorno state, 'always means not to think about anything, to forget suffering even where it is shown. Basically it is helplessness. It is flight; not ... flight from a wretched reality, but from the last remaining thought of resistance' (1982 1944: 144). As we argued in Chapter 2, however, Slow Food sought a different articulation of pleasure and politics, gastronomy and social change, from its origins in the Italian Left.[8] As Petrini wrote in *Gambero Rosso* in 1987:

> Many would like to teach communists the right way to act. According to these 'masters of life', a good communist should mortify himself in clothing, in enjoyment, and above all in frequenting good restaurants. ... Well, I have the impression that these people will always confuse Communism with Franciscanism. Such confusion, after all, favours those who believe that the precious elements of Italian gastronomy should always be a privilege for the usual few. (quoted in Parasecoli 2003: 35)

Parasecoli has considered the question of how the appreciation of food and wine came to be articulated within a broad Leftist perspective as an oppositional discourse in the 1980s in Italy, despite the earlier pejorative approach to pleasure and culture. Tracing back to the influence in Italy – as elsewhere – of the counter-cultural movements which emerged in the 1960s and 1970s in which values such as pleasure and creativity were seen as the key to social transformation, Parasecoli argues that from the 1980s on, food became a way of 'absorb[ing] and neutraliz[ing] the disruptive forces unleashed by the new attention to pleasure' (2003: 34). Such a shift was consonant with the rise of a 'reflexive' middle class in the 1980s in Italy, with a growing awareness of the interrelations between consumption, everyday life and global risks (Ginsborg 2001: 43).[9] For many intellectuals, formerly part of what Parasecoli calls the 'pleasure-allergic Left' (2003: 33), food could now be considered not simply in terms of exploitation or inequitable distribution but within a different conceptual framework in which pleasure and community were (re)valued:

> The new emphasis on food as a social and cultural practice constituted an effective antidote to the damage suffered by traditional political identities or, even more importantly, to the painful disclosure of a fundamental lack of identity, a lack that had been concealed in the past by hegemonic practices and a political project that collapsed along with the Berlin Wall. Food became a focal point, condensing a symbolic network that connects various heterogeneous elements. ... (Parasecoli 2003: 35)

Today, in Slow Food's emphasis on pleasure, traces of the 1960s' conception of pleasure as disruptive and liberating coexist with an insistence on the *right* to pleasure, as a means of challenging the industrialization of food, the global agglomeration of agriculture, and the privilege of 'the usual few' (Parasecoli 2003:

35). For Slow Food, taste has revolutionary potential precisely because of its capacity to command our attention to the experience of the body and its affects in the present moment, to mobilize a 'politics of the senses' through 'stillness'.[10] In this way, it differs from the 'hyperaestheticization of everyday products' of late 'capitalist sensualism' in which marketers and designers seek to engage as many senses as possible, thus overwhelming consumers with sensory stimulation in order to facilitate indiscriminate consumption (Howes 2005: 296). Attention to sensory experience is not a dry aestheticism for a cultured elite but an attempt to restore agency to subjects inundated by the sensory profusion of late capitalism in which pleasure may be all too fleeting. The malleable and nuanced significations of pleasure in Slow Food discourse, then, attempt to make everyday life a site of potential plenitude, consonant with Bennett's sense of 'enchanted materialism', in which a cultivation of openness to the sensory and material opportunities made available by the world becomes an 'ethical task to en-joy life with discipline, ... and to add, by one's actions, to its stock of joy' (2001: 88).

Authenticity and Taste

By celebrating the immense capacity for pleasure food affords as a means of restoring enjoyment to everyday life, Slow Food associates food with three of the four realms of gratification attributed to food consumption: the sensual, the social and the contemplative (Warde and Martens 2000: 183).[11] The only type of gratification which Slow Food derides in relation to food is the 'instrumental', a type of enjoyment derived from a food experience that involves putting that experience to some use for gain, other than the pleasure of flavour or company (such as material advancement or a successful performance of class; Warde and Martens 2000). Slow Food attempts to define itself *against* the instrumental realm of gratification (which would include food snobbery) as an 'inauthentic', relation to food. As the denigration of instrumental gratification suggests, however, there is a binary of authentic/inauthentic, which Slow Food uses to promote its philosophy of eco-gastronomy, that clearly privileges some foods and foodways over others and links the pleasure associated with Slow Food to values such as knowledgeability and attentiveness (see Chapters 2 and 6 for further discussion of eco-gastronomy). This is a position that is also expressed by conservative American writer, Wendell Berry, who argues that a greater pleasure can be derived from informed eating than what he calls 'industrial eating' (1992: 375).[12] 'The pleasure of eating,' Berry argues,

> should be an extensive pleasure, not that of the mere gourmet. People who know the garden in which their vegetables have grown and know that the garden is healthy will remember the beauty of the growing plants, perhaps in the dewy first light of morning when gardens are at their best. Such a memory involves itself with the food and is one

of the pleasures of eating. ... A significant part of the pleasure of eating is in one's accurate consciousness of the lives and the world from which food comes. (1992: 378)

Berry's description of dewy gardens places strong value on the immediacy and proximity of the earth as the guarantee of authenticity in food and food practices. So how closely does Berry's notion of authenticity match that of Slow Food? While Berry's work explicitly celebrates traditional American values in advocating simplicity and a return to the land (see Shi 1985), Slow Food's notion of authenticity is more consciously articulated in the detraditionalized contexts of the global everyday.[13] If much of the contemporary interest in food 'combines a yearning for authenticity with a recognition of its impossibility' (Probyn 2000: 3), we will argue in this section that Slow Food adopts a reflexive and nuanced conception of authenticity grounded in the material culture and history of everyday life. We will then consider how notions of taste are figured as ways of acknowledging the place of food and suggest that such an approach to taste and authenticity offer productive possibilities for privileging and sustaining networks of social relations in which slow living may be practised.

On a warm spring morning, we were escorted to a small farm outside Reggio Emilia in time for the morning cheese-making, to watch rounds of *Parmigiano Reggiano* formed by hand with traditional cheesecloths by the couple who had been making cheese that way on that farm for nearly forty years. We and our local hosts watched intently, transfixed by the skill and yet the simplicity of cheese-making in this way, with milk produced by a breed of cattle unique to the area (the *Vacche Rosse* – 'red cows' – of the Reggio breed), housed in the adjoining barns and fields. Like the cultures at work in the cheese, here was a tradition that was alive, thriving and sustainable. The farm shop did steady business throughout the morning and yet production was limited by the milk produced each day (which varied according to season; only two rounds of cheese were made and added to the vast cheese room on the day we observed them). When we tasted the matured cheese – the piquant richness, with the added surprise of the occasional crunch of crystals that denotes a traditional *Parmigiano* – it was as if we had never really tasted *Parmigiano* before but only insipid, overly salty or smelly imitations. In a detraditionalized global everyday of food scares, the 'routinization of the exotic' (Warde 1997: 61) and 'gastro-anomy' (Fischler 1980: 948), this story may seem like a nostalgic evocation of the value of tradition, or what Rachel Laudan calls 'Culinary Luddism' based on 'turn[ing] back the clock' (2001: 36, 43 and 2004).[14] In order to develop our conception of Slow Food's deployment of authenticity as situated but not nostalgic or essentialized, it is necessary to critically engage further with Laudan's argument.

Against the nostalgic reaction that is 'Culinary Luddism', Laudan posits its opposite, 'Culinary Modernism'. Leaving aside for the moment the asymmetry in a binary between Luddism (as a political protest movement) and Modernism (as a heterogeneous, aesthetic-cultural movement) to describe different approaches to food production, here is how Laudan delineates Culinary Modernism:

> Culinary Modernism reshaped the world. Settlers appropriated the temperate grass-lands of North America, Argentina, Australia and New Zealand to raise wheat and cattle for distant urban centres. Migrants moved from country to town and from Europe to the overseas colonies. The acreage under the plough shot up. Merchants opened up new commercial channels and institutions to bring wheat and beef to market. Inventors and industrialists found new ways to process them. People's lives changed in England and the United States as they began to take for granted the white bread and roast beef their great grandparents only have dreamed of. .... (2004: 135)

In apparently summarizing the development of industrialized agriculture and food production, Laudan effectively erases imperialism and capitalism as benign land 'appropriation' and 'opening up' of markets that only changed people's lives for the better (all the white bread you dreamed of!). The absence of differential power relations between settlers and indigenes, margins and centre, industrialists and 'people', renders this a very partial historical account. A far more accurate denom-ination for such processes would in fact be 'Culinary Global-Capitalism', were a single descriptor for such a complex set of global socio-economic processes not overly simplistic. 'Culinary Modernism', moreover, becomes an agent of history, if not effectively anthropomorphized in phrases such as: 'Culinary Modernism's attempt to provide white bread and beef for all' (2004: 136). Accusing Slow Food of a 'romanticized version of history', then, Laudan's repudiation of Slow Food stands or falls on her account of Culinary Modernism as the progressive, demo-cratic form of food production and thus its differentiation from Culinary Luddism as the uncritical celebration of 'the sunny rural days of yore' (2001: 36) and the equivalent of 'breeding fine horses, or patronizing chamber orchestras' (2004: 134). Laudan's account of Slow Food creates the impression that it has never spread beyond Piedmont and has no cognisance of, or response to make to, glob-alization (2004: 139–42).

By refusing to consider the complexities and potentials of Slow Food's still-developing engagement with globalization, industrial agriculture and threats to biodiversity, Laudan's caricature of the movement, and her consequent indictment of it, rests, then, on what she assumes to be the contradictory deployment of the concept of authenticity by Slow Food. On the one hand, Laudan sees Petrini's fas-cination with the French notion of *terroir* purely as a cynical marketing strategy (2004: 136–9); on the other, she regards the movement and its adherents as naive and ignorant of history for opposing 'Culinary Modernism'. On both charges, Laudan fails to consider the complex notions of place and the local which are implicated in Slow Food's valuation of the authentic and artisanal in food and foodways. New food projects and the networks they foster not only create a new awareness of place and locality (through linking production and consumption) but in the process also complicate notions of place and connectedness as people become more aware of the diversity which exists within 'the local' (Labelle 2004: 86–7). Whether through farmers' markets exposing diverse ethnic traditions of foodways in the same geographical area, or through Slow Food *convivia* meeting with different producers of the same regional product, designations of typicality or *terroir* are not understood as simplistic guarantees of a pre-given 'authenticity'. As Chapter 4 argued, moreover, the notion of *terroir* as it was understood by Slow Food from the outset meant that it did not denote an inherent meaning in certain foods or practices but was a matter of stressing the *connectedness* of food to specific contexts. Such connectedness – of place, people, history, culture – constitutes a dynamic set of social relations that is under threat by the changes represented by globalization and its capacity to erase cultural specificities. It is hence the dominant 'logic of industrialization' underlying the global food and agriculture system that Slow Food rejects (Hendrickson and Heffernan 2002: 362), rather than an ignorance of the historical realities that have ensured that dominance. As Hendrickson and Heffernan (2002) have argued, alternative approaches to food are not motivated by a naive belief that global agriculture can be remade through practices organized around concepts of the local and the authentic described here. Rather, such alternatives, which seek to reembed food production within a community,

> can position [themselves] in the spaces where the global [food] system is vulnerable by eschewing the attributes that make the global system strong (mass production, access to capital and a profit-oriented long-range vision). By doing so, alternative groups can potentially strengthen, create and maintain spaces of action that will potentially become more important in an increasingly unstable dominant food system. (Hendrickson and Heffernan 2002: 365)

Laudan's final charge against Slow Food – that it has not cured world hunger (2004: 141) – thus profoundly misunderstands the kinds of responses that alternative food projects can make and are making to food practices in the global everyday. In Slow Food, food and foodways are not preserved as 'cult objects' (Petrini 2001: 59), nor as theme-park attractions divorced from historical realities. Rather, they are recognized for their *historicity*, as a testament to their viability, and their *locality*, as embedded in specific networks and relationships. For Slow Food, an 'authentic' food is one produced in a specific space and time, a specific material culture, known to the consumer and producer and linking both in a social as well as economic exchange based on trust and mutual knowledge (see Labelle 2004: 85; Heldke 2003: 202). Petrini's mobilization of a French notion of *terroir* in his own region of Italy represented, then, a particular articulation of authenticity and food, an articulation through which a critique of the homogenization of tastes and the erasure of place through global agribusiness could be forcefully declaimed: 'Local cultures are the answer to the drive to standardize inherent in the fast-food model; their variety and diversity are the key by which our members all over the world acknowledge and understand each other' (Petrini 2001: 38). In this formulation – one which also underpins Slow Food objectives such as the Ark of Taste and Presidium projects – authenticity is *not* a defensive means of retreat from a world which threatens to contaminate the purity of local culinary traditions, nor simply a marketing and tourism strategy, but refers to the ways in which food is embedded in social, economic and ecological relationships between actors in specific food systems and communities (Hendrickson and Heffernan 2002: 361). Mobilizing such a conception of authenticity, then, becomes a means of connecting local cultures, producers and consumers in a form of cosmopolitan exchange distinct from global capital (Hendrickson and Heffernan 2002).[15]

A desire for authenticity in the global everyday is, however, also often linked with the rural and the traditional and this linkage both informs the context in which Slow Food is developing its profile and plays on the connotations of Italian culture and heritage. The recent popularity, for instance, of a popular genre of travel writing, charting life in a Tuscan villa, is a good example of the ongoing resonance of these connotations. The best known example is Frances Mayes's *Under the Tuscan Sun* (1996; also a 2003 feature film) in which Tuscany is reconfirmed as a utopian space of rural simplicity and convivial pleasures in the Anglo imaginary and the discovery of cultural authenticity is inextricably linked with food. The appeal of such narratives of acquired heritage and belonging is that they are able to reflect a desire for slow living outside the reader's experience of everyday life by tapping into a post-Romantic tradition of rural, peasant life as the source of authenticity. In Mayes's account the accretions of cultural authenticity pass metonymically from the landscape and architecture to the expatriate narrator through her adoption of local practices and objects, often centred on food, in what Appadurai has called the subtle transference of *patina* – as a signifier of high cultural value and historical continuity – from objects to owners (1993: 22). The temporal and spatial authenticity seemingly guaranteed by this transference is, in fact, based on an 'imagined nostalgia' – 'nostalgia without lived experience or collective historical memory' (Appadurai 1993: 25) – which relies on a temporality of lost or distant times and leads to a heightened sensory experience of the present for Mayes's narrator.

Such a desire for authenticity and its location in rustic Italian life is not, however, confined to the Anglo imagination but also demonstrated in the recent revival of folk festivals and traditions in Italy itself, suggesting that 'peasant Italy has finally achieved the same status within the urban post-modern Italian imaginary which it has long enjoyed abroad' (Bennetts 2003: 5). Stephen Bennetts reads such revivalism as attempts to negotiate a position of cultural autonomy within modernity through participating in practices derived from Southern Italian peasant tradition (from Calabria, Southern Puglia and Campania) which are seen as more 'authentic' than those within modern Italian society (2003: 2). Emerging from the mid-1990s, the revivalist milieu in Italy comprises urban hippies, left-wing students and *portatori della tradizione* ('bearers of the tradition', elderly local people from peasant backgrounds), as well as including participants from a range of social and political groups, such as supporters of Slow Food and Città Slow (Bennetts 2003: 3, 8). Folk revivalism is also situated in a context of reemergent Italian regional identity, marked, for instance, by the influence of the Northern League on contemporary moves towards devolution and by the Bassolini administration's programme of urban renewal in Naples. Given the multiple interests with a stake in current revivalism and the increasing support revivalist projects are now attracting at local and regional levels, the success of revivalism could itself become a symptom of the globalization of culture it opposes because it is premised on a notion of authenticity that can only be defined and guaranteed by a lack of contamination from the outside world (Bennetts 2003: 9–10).

Such evidence of a desire for a (lost) authenticity that is believed to be embodied in Italian rurality and peasant cultures intersects with Slow Food in a common concern with the preservation of tradition and a critique of the standardizing impact of globalization. There is also, however, a sharp divergence in the two impulses towards authenticity. In Italian revivalism, there is an explicit privileging of folk culture and the virtues of 'the people' in a conscious attempt to preserve a pre-industrial *il mondo popolare*. In narratives like *Under the Tuscan Sun* there is a similar tendency to essentialize and ossify a traditional culture. For Slow Food, by contrast, while the rhetoric of the imminent loss of valued practices and products is frequently invoked (and the metaphor of the Ark is the best example of this), there is also an insistence on an active and dynamic engagement with the global everyday, rather than a retreat from it. In the discourse and philosophy of Slow Food, authenticity is not a pristine or timeless state but a quality derived from *terroir*, understood as a distinct cultural and historical identity in which 'the resources of the past are activated to build the future' (Bessière 1998: 31). Rather than an aura that can be simply lost, or rediscovered by true believers, authenticity is a vital connection between a specific place, history and people which can be embodied in an object but does not timelessly inhere in it. It is, above all, a social process whose history, meaning and practice may always be contested by those who claim it (Terrio 2000: 17; see also Heldke 2003).

While a notion of locality and artisanal production is closely related to Slow Food's conception of authenticity it does not constitute a 'return to the land' movement. One of the challenges of any form of slow living is the possibility of implementation in the urban/suburban realms which for so many people is where the global everyday occurs. An increasing attention to the plight of small producers and traditional farmers around the world has been evident in Slow Food over the past few years (as the *Terra Madre* meeting of food communities in 2004 and its continuation attests), suggesting that a more complex response to the ethical responsibilities of consumers and producers in global economies and contexts is developing. A good example of this reflexive approach to authenticity is a project undertaken by Gary Nabhan (a speaker at the Naples Congress of Slow Food in 2003 and contributor to *Slow*) who embarked on a year-long undertaking to eat only locally-sourced foods, charted in his book *Coming Home to Eat: The Pleasures and Politics of Local Foods*. Nabhan was first prompted to begin this project after an experience of cognitive dissonance while eating in an international restaurant in Beirut. Contemporary food practices for many in the affluent West, he speculated, reflected 'a desire for a life unsoiled by local, regional, cultural, or even nationalistic constraints, where one could pick and choose from the planetary supermarket without any contact with local fishermen or farmers, let alone any responsibility to them' (2002: 22–3). Returning to the United States, Nabhan boycotted the supermarket, emptied his larder and undertook a subsistence life of growing, foraging, bartering, cooking and preserving based on sourcing foods only within a limited radius from his home in Arizona, encompassing desert and mountain landscapes and extending south to the Gulf of California. In the course of this obsessive (and somewhat idiosyncratic) narrative, however, Nabhan's food isolationism gives way to a more nuanced and reflexive approach to both the local and the authentic:

> My earlier, naïve hope had been to form a food economy isolated from all others, a bubble in space and time, nested within the canyon. Yet many current forces and historic events would not allow us to achieve a sense of complete isolation... I conceded that I did not even wish to be part of any economy that excluded urban areas, immigrants, or other traditions: I simply wanted all of us to have some wedding with the land. (2002: 205)

Nabhan's reflexive localism is still premised on the significance of territory, as a means of rejecting a rootlessness that he associates with contemporary subjects and sees exemplified in their consumption habits. But his notion of territory expands from simply the landscape and its indigenous inhabitants to include the diversity of the history and culture it contains, which he wants foodways to reflect. This notion of territory corresponds closely to the idea of the 'foodshed' as a metaphor to describe the area generating our food supply, denoting its (social, economic, ethical and physical) embeddedness both in a particular place and a 'moral economy' (Kloppenburg, Hendrickson and Stevenson 1996: 118, 114–15). It is within such reflexive localism that the notion of the authentic is employed, and this leads to an important distinction in Nabhan's narrative between the local/authentic and the 'organic' food item. That the authentic can never be a 'bubble in space and time' is matched by an awareness that neither is organic produce necessarily an embodiment of a desired authenticity through food. Organic food, Nabhan argues, is not necessarily more 'ethical' than its mass-produced equivalent, if it has travelled thousands of miles before you purchase it (2002: 47). For Nabhan, the value of authenticity can never be an iron-clad 'guarantee of freshness or quality', but is realized in the spatial and temporal relations attached to it, linking producers and consumers in a shared and mutually dependent network of times and places.[16]

By such an emphasis on the 'relationship of food with territory' (Gho 2002: 32), Slow Food's construction of authenticity not only seeks to distinguish the movement's sense of culinary pleasures from fast food and industrial agriculture but also from the elite section of the food industry. The celebration of local *osterie*, an important priority for Slow Food since its inception, is concerned with protecting the moderate price and scale of these eateries with a cross-class clientele, as well as the local food cultures they represented. The *osterie* were thus positioned positively against the gastronomic values of a *nouvelle-cuisine* style of cooking (Miele and Murdoch 2002: 317). Nouvelle cuisine may now itself have become passé, but the more recent culinary fad of so-called 'fusion food' has frequently been discussed in the journal *Slow* as a kind of test-case for Slow Food's philosophy to resist globalization by promoting authenticity, with debate hinging on a question raised by Barbara Santich: 'Does one individual have the right to borrow and transform recipes and practices that might be considered the "birthright" of others?' (2002: 88). One issue of *Slow* which focused on fusion cuisine featured a cover image by French sculptor Alex Angi, who uses only plastic garbage (heated and moulded). The amalgam of different brightly coloured plastic strips resembled different forms of pasta fused together in one shiny but unappetizing ball. The message that fusion food was plastic (and hence contemporary and inauthentic) could not have been clearer and was followed by Capatti's editorial, which described fusion food as a 'Babel of cooking styles and flavours' (2002b: 4), an oft-repeated metaphor.[17] Fusion cuisine was not, however, unthinkingly dismissed by contributors. Philip Sinsheimer's article, more guardedly titled 'It depends what you mean', cautioned against the dangers of any notion of cultural purity, making the obvious point that all culinary heritages have borrowed from, or fused with, others over history (2002: 24–31). Even an article that recounted horrible experiences of expensive fusion cooking (illustrated with further images of Angi's food-like plastic sculptures) concluded with Luca Vercelloni's 'golden rules' for food and dining, the last one being: 'There is no such thing as copyright in the kitchen. A good recipe belongs to everyone' (Vercelloni 2002: 15).

Slow Food's reflexive understanding of place, food and tradition is perhaps best illustrated by the article by Paola Gho, editor of *Osterie d'Italia* (Slow Food's best-selling guide to the *osterie* of Italy). Defining fusion cuisine as aiming 'to define a global gastronomic code through the theory and practice of an uninhibited intermingling of traditions, ingredients, techniques and flavours' (2002: 32), Gho supports instead a slow approach which 'focuses on protecting local gastronomic practices', while 'shy[ing] away from nostalgia and fundamentalism' (2002: 32). Even as she pits the celebrity chefs and food fashions of fusion cuisine against 'honest artisans, the descendants of popular cultural tradition' (2002: 32) in Slow Food *osterie*, Gho does not position these local food cultures as frozen in time with pristine traditions but rather as evolving and reinterpreting traditional knowledges and practices. Moreover, Gho argues that it was not so much a case of Slow Food preserving *osterie* but rather mobilizing a particular construction of such eateries as the best site in which local food cultures could flourish, by fostering networks of connections between consumers, restaurateurs and local produce. The publication of *Osterie d'Italia* was not a historic register but a means of making public, and therefore asserting the cultural value, of such food practices: 'If today we can assert without fear of contradiction that such a thing as an Italian *osteria* actually exists ... it is also true that we have witnessed these eateries evolve, albeit in the brief time span of little more than a decade' (Gho 2002: 34).[18]

If this conception of Slow Food against which fusion food is contrasted is a far cry from a view of authenticity as timeless tradition untouched by modernity it nevertheless relies on a contrast between speed and slowness to stress the differences between the two styles of food. In Slow Food discourse, the problem with fusion food is not simply its decontextualization of culinary traditions, but that it is symptomatic of 'fast life' and the relentless need for novelty and innovation in fashion cycles which, paradoxically, erase differences (Gho 2002: 32, Sinsheimer 2002: 30). While in gastronomic terms, 'fast life' dates at least from the time of Brillat-Savarin, who favoured innovation as a sign of true gastronomy (claiming the invention of a new recipe was as important as the discovery of a new planet; Vercelloni 2002: 14), the appeal of the new is a continuing response to modernity, which coexists with the contradictory appeal of the familiar or the traditional (Warde 1997: 64). The existence of such contrasting responses provides global subjects with a range of resources from which to fashion a lifestyle in which novelty and tradition are mutually imbricated. As Warde argues, 'the appreciation of novelty requires one to postulate the existence of a traditional past imagined to exhibit permanency, even though no such fixed past may ever have existed. Conversely, people perceive perpetual flux while living and consuming in a profoundly routine manner' (1997: 71). By positioning fusion food on the side of speed, innovation and extravagance, Slow Food aligns it with those aspects of contemporary life it considers 'inauthentic' – disconnected from relations with place, people and territory – which can only be enhanced and made meaningful by slowness (awareness, attention, engagement). In this construction, sites like the *osteria* are symbols for the kind of sociality Slow Food encourages, as distinct from the fleeting or instrumental forms of social contact it associates with fast-food or *haute-cuisine* restaurants. There is also, however, a recognition by Slow Food of what it calls 'slow fusion' (Ruffa 2002: 115; Santich 2002: 89) to describe the complex formations of culinary heritage in nations characterized by migration from various cultures (such as the USA, Canada, South Africa, Australia) which rejects any sense of rigidly quarantining culinary heritage in its deployment of authenticity.

Slow Food's linkage of authenticity with time and space means that its hierarchy of food values does not simply result in the valuing of organic or biodynamic produce per se, but requires a consumer with a knowledge of *terroir* and the global networks of food. In what sense, then, is this knowledgeable consumer different from the traditional connoisseur? Is the knowledge of the Slow Food member just another form of cultural capital? There is no doubt that part of the appeal of Slow Food to non-Italians lies in the persistent association of Italy as a place of fine food and wine – indices of high cultural value – despite the movement's founders being motivated by what they saw as the increasing *precarité* of their food culture. Is Slow Food's notion of authenticity, then, anything more than a branding exercise and an attempt, as Laudan charges, to impose 'elite culinary preferences on the rest of the population' (2001: 42)? The importance of a sense of place to Slow Food's notion of authenticity is both emphasized and complicated by the increasing reflexivity of the movement in response to its spread to new national and cultural contexts. Ideas of culinary heritage, for instance, cannot be isolated as a univocal value for all Slow Food members when such heritages may vary from hundreds of years to less than a century but must be reinterpreted and applied in varying contexts. The increasing emphasis in Slow Food events on bringing together producers and consumers from disparate parts of the world – most notably, the *Terra Madre* World Meeting of Food Communities in 2004 – is one response to the need to develop a more nuanced understanding of *terroir* and its networks of connection in a framework of eco-gastronomy (see Chapter 6).

The problem lies, however, in the way that a product from a particular *terroir* is transplanted by/for a cosmopolitan subject, and in the process becomes a sign of cultural capital for that subject (see Donati 2004; Leitch 2003). Is the stylization of food – the use, that is, 'of styled items to express, in a predominantly aesthetic manner, group membership' (Warde 1997: 184) – always unethical? Is there an ethical way in which a cosmopolitan subject can support culinary tradition and authenticity? That consumption practices can construct an identity based on an ethical or political commitment is accepted when it comes to practices like consumer boycotts or veganism but the purchase and consumption of, say, artisanal olive oil is usually only interpreted as the sign of a bourgeois 'commitment to stylization' (Bourdieu 1984). While others have noted the importance of relations of trust and knowledge in fostering alternative food practices (Hendrickson and Heffernan 2002; Labelle 2004), disentangling food knowledge from distinction, or culinary authenticity from the 'gentrification of taste' (Terrio 2000: 56) is not an easy matter. It seems to us, however, that there is more than a trace of Bourdieu's class-ification of meals in some of the wariness expressed concerning Slow Food. Gaytán's observation, for instance, that the first Slow Food *convivium* meeting she attended was 'Needless to say, … not what I expected' because of the presence of cocktails and 'people with PhDs' (2004: 99) explicitly expresses an unease with the middle-class conviviality of the event which implies that the event should either have been less festive (like a business meeting) or less bourgeois. In *Distinction*, Bourdieu pitted the honest hospitality and enjoyment of the working-class meal against the bourgeois equivalent (1984: 195–9), arguing that there was no neutral viewpoint in these 'two antagonistic approaches to the treatment of food and the act of eating'; that food is either 'claimed as a material reality, a nourishing substance which sustains the body and gives strength' in an environment of 'trusting openness', or that style is elevated over substance in an exercise of social distinction (1984: 196, 198–9). Simply, working-class earthiness good, bourgeois stylization bad. While Gaytán's event was clearly a celebration of food rather than the cold social ceremony of the bourgeoisie Bourdieu described, her social dis-comfort is presented as evidence of the bourgeois limitations of the movement, and perpetuates a binary between conviviality and (alternative forms of) politics which Slow Food seeks to counterpose.

Slow Food cannot, however, be simply aligned with one or the other of these classed positions on the happy eater. The pleasures, plenty and bodily freedoms of appetite and expression that Bourdieu attributes to the working-class table are celebrated in Slow Food's exhortation to spend more time at the table. The bour-geois emphasis, however, on the aestheticization and tempo of a more structured meal time, in which each dish is served with due care and ceremony, is also advo-cated in Slow Food's insistence on attention in the preparation and consumption of food. But whereas Bourdieu saw in the bourgeois practices a censorship of the pleasure of eating, Slow Food urges an attentiveness in food practices in order to accentuate and increase the pleasures of the table, in all their complexities of flavour, sequence and aesthetic appeal within a context of mutual enjoyment. While, as discussed in Chapter 2, like other forms of 'life politics' Slow Food is primarily middle class in its membership, it is important to distinguish between membership and the class implications of the approach to food taken by the movement. Slow Food's eschewal of the kind of sharp class differentiation Bourdieu makes may be a pragmatic attempt to broaden its appeal by celebrating differently classed approaches to food and eating, or a reflection of the differ-ences between Italian and French culinary culture, or it may be – as we believe – a more ambitious attempt to marry what are often antagonistic attitudes to food, eating and pleasure in what might be called a 'practical aesthetic' (Miele and Murdoch 2002: 313).[19]

There is no denying, however, that such situated pleasures and the stylization of food can be associated with economic privilege (although they do not necessarily have to be). The question may then be: how is the privileged subject to eat ethically? Unless we adopt the position that only asceticism in food consumption is ethically sustainable, then we would have to conclude that if a consumer has the luxury of being able to pay more for her food it is not automatically ethically suspect to do so. It may in fact be an ethical imperative for the economically privileged to do just that if by such economic support traditional food communities can be maintained (although this is by no means to argue that this is the *only* ethical response required).[20] In exploring such issues in an ethics of eating Nabhan asks: 'What if each of us, day by day, fully fathomed where our food comes from, historically, ecologically, geographically, genetically? What would it be like if each of us recognized all the other lives connected to our own through the simple act of eating?' (2002: 163). In a sense, these are the questions which Slow Food poses and the diversification and proliferations of its projects reflects varying attempts to answer such questions. Having marked the movement's shift to what it has called eco-gastronomy, Petrini has repeatedly stressed that it has not abandoned 'the principle that makes Slow Food unique: the defence of the right to pleasure, claiming it everywhere in the world for everyone' (Bogliotti 2002: 117). Is this insistence political naivety? Or mere bourgeois stylization? Or is it an insistence that defies easy categorization, itself troubling such distinctions between politics and pleasure, aesthetics and carnality?

The valorization of slowness by Slow Food combines an insistence on the simple pleasures of good food and commensality with an awareness of the enormity of our ethical and political investments in food (Probyn 2000: 4–5). Take the instance of 'food miles', an important concept in ethical eating in the global everyday where produce may travel thousands of miles before reaching its intended consumers. A commitment to reduce food miles can be a way of prioritizing local production over global marketing, as well as signalling a commitment to reduced consumption of fossil fuels (Purdue et al. 1997: 652; on this point, see also Chapter 6). Does a reduction in food miles mean, however, the only ethical diet is one limited to one's immediate vicinity, as in Nabhan's original experiment? This dilemma – 'is it better for people to travel or products to be shipped?' (Petrini 2001: 58) – brings us back to the question of the privileged consumer who has the means to travel to eat the produce *in situ* as well as to purchase it at higher cost as an import in their own neighbourhood. Petrini answers as follows:

> it is better for people to travel, as long as they move attentively, choosing their route with intelligence and seeking to acquire as much cultural stimulus as possible from the land in which they find themselves. That resources are limited, and that we have to pay a fair price to enjoy them, is something we just have to accept if it means that those willing to devote themselves to the work of producing basic foodstuffs can make a

living without succumbing to the industrial ethos. And doing without may sometimes be an act of respect. (2001: 58)

In other words, prudent pleasure is again the underlying value expressed by Petrini as the slow philosophy that does not advocate a provincial attitude but at the same time recognizes the ethical limits of cosmopolitanism.[21] To the charge of elitism associated with global travel, it again needs to be reiterated that the articulation of travel and privilege – meaning, a privileged experience divorced from local realities – is not a necessary or inevitable one and ignores the paradigm-shifting capacity that travel may offer the mobile subject. Alice Waters, for instance, Vice-President of Slow Food and the force behind the Edible Schoolyard, has told of how a trip to France in the 1960s not only inspired her passion for food – best represented by her restaurant *Chez Panisse* – but first alerted her to the ethical importance of the local in food production and consumption (Harris 2003: 53). Such a paradigm-shifting travel experience exemplifies that form of ethical cosmopolitanism which responds to the cultural specificities and social inequities of global culture by making links between local and global contexts. Waters' travel, like Nabhan's experiment, is an action undertaken by privileged, affluent Western subjects, but the ethical dimension of such practices can be multiply determined.

Pleasure and authenticity – both mobilized by an awareness of the interconnectedness of food, territory, culture and people in the act of eating – are core values not only in Slow Food philosophy but in its pedagogy: enhancing pleasure and recognizing authenticity must be learned or at least cultivated and developed. In this sense, Slow Food comes closest to the 'reflective eating' of traditional gastronomy (Santich 1996: 180). But the 'reflective eating' encouraged by Slow Food is not the same as the connoisseur's appreciation taught by traditional gastronomy nor the meditative practice urged by writers on the ethics of eating.[22] While Slow Food encourages attention, thoughtfulness and appreciation it has attempted to develop a somewhat different approach to taste education, defining taste as 'pleasure that evolves into knowledge and knowledge that turns into pleasure' (Petrini 2001: 77). Such a strategy is fraught with the risk of being confused with food snobbery and class distinction. If, as Bourdieu argued, the embodiment of taste helps to shape the classed body (1984: 199), then the very concept of 'taste education' and discussions of 'quality' may be irredeemable for some, as signalling the imposition of certain class values disguised as ethical eating. But what does Slow Food mean by 'quality'?

Slow Food will teach you how to distinguish between one kind of quality and another. There is the kind we may call 'hard,' because of its huge environmental and energy costs. Quality of that kind could never be produced in adequate amounts, at least not the way it is presently conceived of and consumed. ... And then there is the kind of quality that Slow Food wants to promote, a 'soft,' renewable kind that improves quality of life for the largest possible number of people. (Petrini 2001: 25–6)

Within the discourse of eco-gastronomy, then, 'quality' can never be an inherent property of an object from which it derives an absolute value, to be considered in isolation from the social and environmental contexts in which it is produced. 'Soft quality' is a value linked to both sustainability and access: how can the best possible food be available to the greatest number of people? One of the ways that Slow Food seeks to achieve this is through connecting education with pleasure by insisting that the pleasure of eating involves the politics, aesthetics and ethics of food; 'The education of taste is the Slow way to resist McDonaldization,' as Petrini puts it (2001: 69).

While, as discussed in Chapter 2, Slow Food has adopted a multi-pronged approach to what it calls 'taste education' – from school gardens and tasting programmes to *convivium* workshops and the University of Gastronomic Sciences – the focus on taste education has often been articulated with widespread concerns about children, obesity and nutrition in developed countries (and has become a particular focus of attention in Slow Food USA). It is because pleasure is at the 'foundation of [Slow Food's] project to transform society' (Capatti 2000c: 4) that children need to be given the opportunities to develop what Slow Food calls 'sensory literacy' within a context in which they also become aware of the global consequences of their food choices and preferences. As one writer in *Slow* puts it, 'How can you like something you don't know anything about?' (Methfessel 2002: 16). Children, of course, do like things without knowing anything about them, or at least what adults consider 'knowing'. (Ask a child why she likes something and chances are she will reply, 'Because I do'.) To paraphrase Freud (1999/1905), the customary task of adults is more often to teach a child that it is unacceptable to like something that she enjoys. Encouraging children to develop a taste for foods, moreover, is not the invention of Slow Food but has long been a principle of 'progressive' theories of education which, for instance, encouraged children to 'experience' their food (involving touching and handling the food to learn its different textures and viscosities) and, like such theories, is based on a common assumption that childhood experience shapes subsequent pleasures. Bourdieu argued that tastes in food are probably

the strongest and most indelible mark of infant learning, the lessons which longest withstand the distancing or collapse of the native world and most durably maintain nostalgia for it. The native world is, above all, the maternal world, the world of primordial tastes and basic foods, ... in which pleasure-giving is an integral part of pleasure and of the selective disposition towards pleasure which is acquired through pleasure. (1984: 79)

While other research has disputed this assumption of the centrality of the mother to later (food) pleasures (e.g. Rozin 1999: 15), it is widely held that the socialization of children through food can have a significant impact not only on adult eating patterns but the broader processes of subject-formation. Taste education, then, may offer the possibility to foreground and renegotiate the whole issue of pleasure in eating. Slow Food USA, for instance, has attempted to critique the dichotomy which tends to position food as *either* 'good for you' *or* 'good to eat' but never both in the American imaginary (Chrzan 2002: 26), where dessert is often constructed as a 'conditional pleasure' (or reward, when one has done one's 'duty' by eating the main course, especially vegetables; Ochs et al. 1996: 23).[23]

In a sense, then, Slow Food's taste education project is – paradoxically – to teach children a more child-like approach to food, in the sense of foregrounding the sensual experiences of eating and the social pleasures of doing it with others (Venturi 2002). Italian taste education projects, for instance, have included intensive programmes of teacher-training in courses of 'sensory literacy' and are based on a commitment to 'help young people to relate to food on the basis of pleasure, conviviality and the awareness of cultural values connected to food and diet' (Venturi 2002: 59).[24] This is one domain, however, in which cultural differences within Slow Food constituencies may be apparent, with different social contexts of family structures and food practices inflecting taste education differently. In the literature associated with taste education, particularly deriving from the school gardens' projects in the USA, pleasure is not foregrounded to the same degree as nourishment, responsibility and intellectual development. For instance, the mission statement of the Edible Schoolyard, the model for subsequent school gardens in the USA initiated by Alice Waters, is to

> create and sustain a vibrant organic garden and landscape that is wholly integrated into the school academic curriculum and lunch program. In the garden, students are involved in all aspects of planting and cultivation; and in the kitchen-classroom they prepare, serve, and eat food they have grown themselves. These activities are woven into the daily lesson in almost every subject and are part of the normal school day. (Edible Schoolyard 2004)

The foregrounding of the pedagogic over the pleasurable may well reflect an understandable concern to justify the educational benefits of such an innovative programme to school authorities and parents alike, but the danger is that school garden projects could become entirely co-opted to prevailing attitudes to food and eating which positions 'good eating' with nutritional science and health campaigns (as in, 'eat your broccoli, it's good for you and you grew it in the school garden!'). By potentially overemphasizing the intellectual and the educational aspects, the Slow Food USA ethos of taste education could be seen as consonant with broader cultural imperatives in which the governance and surveillance of children by adults is a valued civic duty (Spigel 1998: 114).[25] In somewhat of a contrast to the American model, which begins with the garden, Barbara Methfessel's approach to children's taste education, as outlined in *Slow*, begins with the body, with fostering children's awareness of their own bodies, their likes and dislikes, and linking food and eating with care for the body's well-being and pleasure. Employing methods such as children keeping food diaries or writing biographies, Methfessel argues that it is important to give attention to foods children hate as well as food preferences in order to foster a reflexive attitude to food, pleasure and the body (2002: 21). If taste education is to be more than just another part of the 'civilizing process', in which children learn to eat like adults, it will need to support and encourage the childish demand for more pleasure by showing children how an expanded repertoire of tastes and sensations gives them more pleasures to choose from, as well as expanding their practical and intellectual pleasures through increasing their skills and knowledges of the garden, kitchen and table.

In this context, the adoption of taste education programmes in schools will need to be monitored closely, to ensure it does not become just a variant on the 'health and nutrition' classes that proponents of taste education are at pains to distinguish it from. There are currently signs that taste education is well on the way to becoming a more widely accepted part of both school curricula and catering. As noted in Chapter 2, a Slow Food USA initiative passed at the Slow Food International Congress in Naples, 2003, urged all *convivia* worldwide to become involved in school garden projects. In Germany, after a meeting between Petrini and Renate Künast, German Minister for Agriculture and Consumer Protection, in 2003, a government programme for Taste Education in schools has been implemented, with the support of Slow Food Germany. Currently, a pilot programme is underway in 10,000 schools across Germany in which students are offered 'a healthy diet based on organic or locally grown products', as well as a related campaign which emphasizes the pleasures and sociality of eating (Künast 2004: 78).

In conjunction with other Slow Food campaigns like the Presidia projects, taste education forms a context in which taste, pleasure, authenticity and the ethics of 'soft quality' may be explored (Perullo 2003). The valuing of authenticity and sensory awareness, then, are not simply markers of distinction for elite tastes but are mobilized by Slow Food to foster a greater awareness of the relations and networks between land and table, producer and consumer. By situating pleasure in this way, some of the ethical implications of slow living may be foregrounded. Within a framework of ethical cosmopolitanism, the need for interrogating the micro-political practices of everyday life remains a task for slow subjects, mindful of the privilege attached to the capacity for choice on a daily basis. Attending reflexively to the implications of those choices will include mundane meals as well as heightened sensory experiences and it is this aspect of slow living which the following section addresses.

The Shared Table

Women, who everywhere else, make up society's charm, find themselves out of place at a dinner of gourmets, where the attention, far from wanting to be shared, is based entirely on what garnishes the table and not on what surrounds it.

Grimod de La Reynière (quoted in Giard 1998: 218)

If there is a single image which – apart from the snail – encapsulates Slow Food it would be the shared table. The Slow Food approach to food and pleasure celebrates two distinct but interrelated pleasures: the pleasures of food itself (such as taste, smell, texture and presentation) and the social pleasures associated with it (such as conviviality, exchange of knowledge and shared preparation). Slowing down for convivial pleasure is an appealing image to those overwhelmed by the 'time bind' of 'fast life': the concept of the shared table seems to crystallize a contemporary desire for time to connect with others. But does the shared table, like charity, begin at home? To what extent, that is, is the Slow Food ideal of conviviality based on a familial model or a gastronomic model, both with their attendant assumptions about gendered participation as the epigraph from Reynière makes clear? We will consider here this central concept of the shared table as an overdetermined metaphor for hospitality and conviviality in the movement and its broader implications for slow living. Beginning with a consideration of the value placed on the 'family meal', we will critically examine how the values of slowness can be negotiated around the cultural specificities of family, gender and sociality in which Slow Food is situated and in which it seeks to intervene.

Over the past few years, there has been a considerable expansion of the market for quick-serve meals, such as the 'six-minute pot roast', whose signification differs markedly from that of fast food (Day 2003). While this is a growing section of the food business, with sales totalling $150 million in the USA in 2002, quick-serve meals may not yet be a threat to fast-food corporations but they similarly offer a solution to 'fast life' while insisting on the value of tradition in the form of the 'home-cooked' meal. Tyson's, the American company currently dominating the quick-serve meal trend, has identified its target market as what it calls 'frenzied families', traditional nuclear families of at least four people in which no one has the time or energy to cook a 'family meal' (Day 2003: 1). Reflecting this research, the company ran a television advertisement in which a mother and father watch as their daughter boards the school-bus while the voice over says: 'We know how time flies. That's why Tyson's has introduced ready-to-eat beef and pork roasts' (Day 2003: 1). The nostalgic connotations of such meals evokes a time when families ate together and offer the possibility for time-poor families to slow down to eat, even if not to prepare the meal. The widespread perception that the 'family meal' is in decline (despite the fact that there does not seem to be any large-scale and reliable longitudinal research to support this view), forms the background against which the shared table idyll is often situated (Murcott 1997: 35–6; Crang 2001: 191; as opposed to Falk 1994: 29–30). What existing research *does* seem to support, however, is the persistence of 'the idea of the family meal as an aspiration', a symbol of family unity in a fragmented, fast and hostile world (Murcott 1997: 41, 32). Added to this is the common conflation of the family meal with the 'proper meal' as home-made, requiring time and effort to prepare and involving 'good food' (Keane and Willetts 1995: 17). Together, the 'proper meal'/'family meal' conjunction derives from a certain construction of the family and become mutually constituting: a 'real family' is one who eats a 'proper meal' together as a regular practice (Charles and Kerr 1988: 17, DeVault 1991: 79).

As the advertising campaign for Tyson's quick-serve meals showed, the commodification of the 'family meal' positions the 'family as the privileged site of consumption' (Probyn 1998: 167) even as it erases (or conceals) the gendered labour that produces it. In the words of a Tyson's executive: 'The family dinner wasn't all about mom standing in the kitchen cooking all day and then cleaning up the dishes for several hours. ... The family dinner was about sitting down and eating a good meal together' (Day 2003: 1). This statement conveniently renders the woman's labour invisible, 'backstage' to the main event, in order to emphasize the desired outcome – the family meal as idyll – which, it is suggested, is still possible to achieve without changing the schedules or time allocations of today's family members. As Bender and Poggi remind us, however,

> it behoves one not to criticize the impersonal consumption of food at a McDonald's purely as an aspect of a colonized life-world without reflecting on the contrasting model, implicit in this critique, of a wife and mother who in the past willingly and lovingly cared for the material well-being of her dear associates. Sure, she may have done so; but did she have any choice? (1999: 26)

The binary of fast food/slow food, that is, which underpins the ideal of the shared table, needs interrogation in order to consider whether this ideal is dependent on a traditional demarcation of domestic labour, in which the woman/mother is the cook rather than a full participant in slow conviviality. As discussed in Chapter 3, the contemporary desire for more meaningful time, which we see as linked to slow living, is often differentially available along gender lines. In a comparative study of food writing in British women's magazines in 1968 and 1992, Warde was unable to conclude if food preparation times had decreased from the 1960s to the 1990s because, unlike today, in 1968 'cooking times were generally not recorded' (1997: 151). It could be taken for granted that someone had the time necessary for the daily activity of meal preparation, in contrast to today when food writing, whether from nutritionists or celebrity chefs, often assumes that we all want 'fast, fresh recipes for busy people', in the words of Australian food writer

Donna Hay who offers solutions to 'the daily dilemma of what to have for dinner – and quick!' (Hay 1999: n.p.). As both these instances of an overdetermined evening meal remind us, the imbrication of food and sociality is always linked to assumptions about family and gender identities. To emphasize the pleasures of the shared table, therefore, is also inevitably to problematize them, as who will sit at the table – and for how long – requires 'food-work' ('planning, choosing, buying, cooking and cleaning-up'; Crouch and O'Neill 2000: 186).

As many television advertisements for fast food or reheat meals demonstrate, the smiling woman/mother who serves/prepares the meal is clearly responsible both for the family's eating and togetherness. In an influential study, Marjorie DeVault has argued that food-work in the home, almost always carried out by women, involves 'the skill that produces group life' (1991: 130). Feeding a family, DeVault maintains, 'involves not just the physical care and maintenance of house- hold members but also the day-to-day production of connection and sociability' (1991: 230). As the image of the smiling woman at the shared family meal implies, women's status in relation to food-work is overdetermined. Her smile attests to her own pleasure but also reassures the viewer that the family is being cared for. Even though her labour may be minimal (putting fried chicken and chips on a plate), the woman's emotional and domestic labour is both elided and required in such repre- sentations to construct the notion of family through the family meal. Despite recent resignifications of feminine domesticity, which attempt to accommodate care for the self alongside caring for others (Hollows 2003), women are still often depicted as having the capacity and the responsibility to transform their families' habits and lifestyle, serving both to reemphasize the primacy of the private sphere and women's 'natural' place within it (Sandilands 1999: xii).[26] One question which needs consideration, however, is to what extent the Italian origins of Slow Food influence its idealization of the shared table, in practice and representation, and its implications for slow living more generally?

Within the 'spatial and emotional proximity' of Italian families the shared table has been a valued site of family life (Ginsborg 2001: 74). As one of the intervie- wees in Carole Counihan's study of Florentine families put it, '*Mangiare insieme è la base della famiglia*', 'Eating together is the foundation of the family' (2004: 116). In the decades since Italy's rapid modernization, Italian family life has itself changed significantly, due to a range of factors such as legislative changes con- cerning equal rights and family law, and changes in education and labour partici- pation (Passerini 1996: 144–9; Ginsborg 2001: 71). One of the most obvious signs of change has been the decline in fertility rates to the lowest in the world (from an average number of children per woman of 2.42 in 1970 to 1.21 by 1993; Ginsborg 2001: 69; see also Saraceno 1991: 509). The sociocultural impact of these changes has often been discussed in the Italian context through the concept of *la doppia presenza*, 'dual presence', to describe the way that women inhabit 'two worlds:

that of the family and that of work', while men's family responsibilities remained largely unchanged (Saraceno 1991: 513, 515–16). Like elsewhere, the role of the father in contemporary Italian society is currently under some negotiation, but mothers remain 'at the centre of Italian families, the providers of a constant flow of totalizing care, directed primarily towards their child or children, but also towards their husband, their parents and often their husband's parents as well' (Ginsborg 2001: 77). The centrality of the mother in the Italian family is notably marked by the 'oral dependency' which ties the family together around the mother's food-work, a dependency which may continue, especially for sons, throughout adult life (Ginsborg 2001: 77–9).[27] So while the shared table figures importantly in constructing an image of family cohesion through the pleasures it offers, in the Italian context in particular it may entrench dependencies that could compromise the possibilities for slow conviviality for all participants, especially the mother as the primary food provider.[28]

Outside the family home, however, there is also a somewhat different sense of the demarcation between public and private dining in the Italian context than in Anglo-American culture, which perhaps derives in part from a different understanding of restaurants, particularly *osterie*, as occupying a distinctive and important place in community and family life. As described earlier, an *osteria*, a relatively modest restaurant, is without parallel in Anglo-American culture as an important site of everyday life in both rural and urban contexts (the closest equivalent in British culture may well be the pub but without the same degree of family-friendliness *osterie* imply). To give one small example of cultural contrast, while Sunday lunch has been an important site for the performance of family in many Western cultures (in Anglo-Australian culture, for instance, 'lunch at mum's', typically involved roast meat as the centrepiece of the meal), in Italy it may be shared in an *osteria*-type restaurant, its 'family' status seen as undiminished by the commercial setting in which the family gathers. As Helstosky has described in her history of food in modern Italy, a culture of collective eating developed in distinctive ways in twentieth-century Italy and since the rapid modernization in the 1960s, Italians have eaten outside the home more frequently and in ever increasing numbers (2004: 132, 148). For younger Italians, in particular, eating outside the home is now common, as it is with young adults and students in many other national contexts where, especially in urban areas, the large number of small, inexpensive eateries effectively creates a highly-visible and sociable food community (Counihan 2004: 126, 184). The notion of the 'shared table', then, includes a potentially wider range of sites and participants than just the domestic family meal, which may offer differing opportunities for convivial participation.

Similarly, in the literature of Slow Food the shared table is not confined to the home, but is discussed as a general principle or site of sociality which, it is implied, could be located in a range of settings. A good example of this is the Slow

Food manifesto on hospitality, written by Capatti, which begins from the premise of the *impossibility* of hospitality in the global everyday and considers how Slow Food could reinvigorate it. As with the manifesto on rest discussed in Chapter 3, 'In Praise of Hospitality' does not conform to the generic conventions of the manifesto so clearly displayed in Slow Food's founding manifesto, but was originally an editorial in *Slow* and is now featured on the Slow Food website alongside some of the more recent manifestos (e.g. the Ark manifesto or the manifesto on biotechnologies). Does a *convivium* event, Capatti asks, constitute an act of hospitality? 'Not in a traditional sense,' he concludes, as members pay for their share of the meal and the *convivium* leader does not fulfil the role of host, since her/his 'gift of time and effort is implicit, invisible.' Rather than encouraging members to return to the domestic practice of hospitality, however, 'In Praise of Hospitality' urges greater dialogue between restaurants and their consumers. Locating hospitality in the public rather than the private sphere, then, seems to be the preferred site of the shared table.

Such apparent acceptance of the commercialization of hospitality seems at odds with the concept of slow living as we have described it, and as Slow Food has itself sketched out as a preferred way of life. Like quick-serve meal advertisements, which seek simultaneously to value family conviviality and commodify it, Capatti seems to be resigned to the commodification of the shared table as the only way it can be maintained in the overcrowded schedules of global subjects. How, then, can Capatti's sentiments – and their apparent endorsement by Slow Food signalled by the manifesto's presence on the website – be explained? As noted earlier, the spaces of conviviality in Italian culture are not always as sharply gridded across a public/private binary as in Anglo cultures and this may in part account for such a conception of the shared table. Locating conviviality in the public domain also circumvents the gendered inequities of the familial shared table and its (unpaid) food-work in the domestic space, which mainly falls to the woman/mother. Capatti's conclusions may be ultimately due, however, to the fact that Slow Food has to date, and by its own admission (R. Sardo 2003; Barbero 2003), not paid sufficient attention to the private spaces of everyday life in relation to its philosophy of slowness. While a broader understanding and implementation of slowness was advocated in the early years of the international movement – as the discussion of the meanings of slowness in Chapter 3 examined – and remains a theme in more recent writings and interviews with Petrini (e.g. Petrini 2001; 'Interview' 2004), the proliferation and diversification of Slow Food's aims over the last four or five years especially has seen a significant shift of emphasis to the larger international projects, such as those generated through the Presidia.

At the level of local *convivia* and the everyday lives of individual members, however, the shared table remains a central principle, signifying a commitment to taking time to prepare and eat food with others. In our interviews with Australian *convivium* leaders, all strongly expressed such values (e.g. Bianchino 2004; Hale 2004; Meyer 2004; Taylor 2004). Interestingly, all were women, whose passion for good food, cooking, conviviality and family were central to their identification with Slow Food and their hopes for the future success of the movement.[29] While these women's commitment to Slow Food could be due to their own relation to food-work (both domestic and commercial), motherhood and community, it would be true to say that the broader implications of slow living for family and gender have yet to be fleshed out by Slow Food. In this regard, the school garden projects may emerge as a particularly important site from which to consider the implementation of slowness in everyday life. By largely leaving the issues of slowness in the private sphere unexplored, Slow Food avoids the danger of making 'the social' coterminous with 'the familial' in contemporary public discourse (Riley 2002: 1) but it also leaves the valuing of conviviality and 'quiet material pleasure' open to charges of elitism and exclusivity if the issue of who is facilitating and participating in these pleasures is not more fully considered. The large-scale events staged by Slow Food, most notably the biennial *Salone del Gusto* in Turin, thus become the showpieces of conviviality, exemplifying the pleasures of food and sociality on a grand scale (see Chapter 6). The notion of place and the importance of local networks in Slow Food discourse, however, suggests that there would be fruitful opportunities in paying more attention to home environments as sites of cooking, gardening and conviviality and that such opportunities to promote connectedness, relations of trust and the 'place' of food could be lost by concentrating so much on larger-scale conviviality.

The discourse of material pleasure through food is a connecting thread running through the sweep of Slow Food projects and campaigns, from taste education to *convivium* events, and remains a potent strategy for a broad critique of the practices and structures of everyday life, as well as a significant form of appeal to time-poor subjects. Such an emphasis on everyday pleasures is an important component of any formulation of slow living. For this reason, we believe that the Slow Food emphasis on pleasure, while central to its philosophy, remains underdeveloped both in its public discourse and the private practices of its membership and employees. In order for Slow Food to more effectively mobilize the concept and practice of slow living it needs not only to address more explicitly the everyday practices of its adherents but also to develop a more nuanced consideration of the gender, familial and cultural assumptions which underpin its commitment to conviviality and to pay more attention to the place of the home – however it is configured – in (re)valuing the local. As Probyn states, 'food reminds us of others' (2000: 12) and hence food and foodways provide a unique opportunity to articulate the possibilities for slow living – both ethical and political – in the global everyday. These possibilities form the subject of the concluding chapter.

–6–

The Politics of Slow Living

In this final chapter, we turn to an explicit discussion of the politics of slow living. As we have noted in regard to the themes of other chapters, we are very conscious that focusing on the politics of slow living may create a false impression that it is a domain that can be studied in isolation from other aspects but we hope our discussion here brings to the foreground and develops the ethico-political implications of slow living in the global everyday. This chapter, then, allows us to turn a more focused attention to political practices and possibilities which we consider both at the level of the global politics of food in relation to Slow Food, and in the related everyday life practices of slow subjects.

To do so, we begin with a discussion of what *kind* of politics are possible for global social movements and stress the centrality of strategies of publicness and visibility for promoting the philosophy and agenda of Slow Food. We will then analyse Slow Food's deployment of the notion of eco-gastronomy. Implicit in eco-gastronomy, we will argue, is the imbrication of global and local, collective and individual, and we will evaluate how successfully Slow Food has used this concept to reframe and intervene in global issues (such as sustainability of environments, communities, and cultures) at both the macro- and micro-political levels. We argue that movements like Slow Food generate a public debate about matters of personal practice, public values and social organization, 'contesting the norms by which we live our lives', with the potential to reinvigorate everyday life (Crossley 2003: 295–6). Unlike the order of discussion in previous chapters, that is, here we begin with an analysis of the politics of Slow Food before we return to a consideration of the everyday politics of slow living. Revisiting the idea of life politics, in which the practices of everyday life are reflexively interrogated in order to 'remoralize and repoliticize politics' (Crossley 2003: 295), we will consider the possibilities of slow living as an achievable, and desirable, option in the global everyday.

Visualizing Global Social Movements

As a movement, Slow Food embraces a plurality of responses to globalization and global political issues which may be construed as anti-corporate (e.g. the original McDonalds protest) as well as more traditionally political (e.g. partnership with the Brazilian socialist government in its 'Zero Hunger' programme) or cultural (e.g. food events and festivals). While it has not generated the kind of 'shock' publicity that some other anti-globalization, anti-corporate movements have (the smashing of McDonalds on the evening news, for example), Slow Food relies on a complex range of strategies to represent its values to a media-saturated world. Amory Starr (2000) has identified two broad formations in anti-corporate movements, contrasting the 'AgriCulture' formation, which focuses on traditional forms of food production and cultures in a critique of global corporate power, with 'PopCulture', comprising more of an emphasis on cultural politics and media imagery. Starr's binary of more and less legitimate forms of anti-corporate movements, however, fails to engage adequately with how 'the public sphere has been reshaped through the globalizing, mediated forms of communication that constitute the representational infrastructure for today's public spaces' (McLaughlin 2004: 157).[1] In such a context, Slow Food's philosophy of eco-gastronomy – intimately connected with a range of global political issues such as sustainable agriculture (Pretty 1998, 2002), genetic engineering (Lappe and Bailey 1999; Purdue 2000), biodiversity (Shiva 1997) and fair trade (Ranald 2000) – has been an important means of *visualizing* its concerns as well as arguing its philosophy. While the next section offers a more detailed analysis of the concept of eco-gastronomy, here we briefly address the role of events in the politics of Slow Food, where events are understood as significant moments of cultural formation and innovation which may constitute new interventions in culture or politics (Terrio 2000: 8).

Modern public life is a mediated phenomenon: the media are the sites where the meanings and values of politics and public life are generated and evaluated, and it follows that we cannot oppose an 'authentic' unmediated public life with an 'inauthentic' public life that is constituted through the mass media, whatever its shortcomings (Craig 2004). The politics of a global social movement such as Slow Food, therefore, relies on the organization of media events and the implementation of strategies of promotion and visibility. It is easily overlooked that, from its beginnings as Arcigola, Slow Food was a movement that embraced a range of promotional strategies and used mass media to advance its causes. The Arcigola movement was distinguished from traditional gastronomic clubs by its left-wing political origins and its lack of insularity, fuelled by a desire to initiate widespread changes in food cultures and intervene in public, political debates. Arcigola also differed from more traditional leftist strategies, not only through its embrace of food and pleasure, but also by enthusiastic use of mass media. Aided by Petrini's early interests in radio and theatre (Kummer 2002: 18), Arcigola (gaining its name partly from the innovative *La Gola* magazine) grew rapidly due to this awareness of the centrality of publicity for any such organization, an awareness most clearly manifested in its publications, such as the *Gambero Rosso* wine guide. The success of Slow Food, then, has been always partly derived from its canny publicity skills (Kummer 2002: 23). Now, the organization excels not only at large-scale food events but also at other forms of communication, such as the movement's comprehensive and ever-expanding web site.[2]

Slow Food's mobilization of a range of contemporary media forms, imagery and events is a good example of a movement attempting to intervene in a global civil society and to use that intervention to foreground the plight of traditional food producers around the globe, as well as establishing networks of exchange and solidarity between them, to encourage a form of 'globalization from below' (McLaughlin 2004: 169; Falk 1993). When 140,000 people visited Slow Food's biennial *Salone del Gusto* (Hall of Taste) in Turin in October 2004, they were attending much more than a conventional food and wine fair. The event, claimed to be the world's largest of its kind and with over 2,000 accredited journalists, is not only Slow Food's premiere function but also its most important promotional vehicle, representing an agglomeration of the promotional, political, economic, and educational strategies of the movement.[3] The 2002 *Salone* featured 500 exhibiting producers from over thirty countries, including many Presidia products, plus an *Enoteca* with 2,500 wines available for tasting, and over 300 Taste Workshops (*Salone* Official Program 2002: 9). By connecting artisanal producers with consumers, the *Salone* is able to embody the relations of knowledge and networks of trust that Slow Food, like other alternative food projects, seen as crucial to remaking food culture and production. In addition, the *Salone* also enables producers to meet *each other* and share information and experiences. As Anya Fernald from the Presidia/Ark office told us:

> In the international projects the most amazing thing for me is that the producers get to feel that they are part of a community. It's an emotional thing – they come to an event and they meet forty people like them from around the world and they're people who don't get to travel. It's a really mind opening experience for them. (2003)

The *Salone del Gusto* is also the site where strategies and initiatives are made public. Every major new initiative has been announced or launched at a *Salone* event: the Ark was announced in 1996, the Presidia introduced in 2000, the Foundation for Biodiversity inaugurated in 2002, and the first *Terra Madre* gathering was held in 2004. Through this combination of the visual display of producers and the associated discussion of Slow Food philosophy and praxis, then, the *Salone del Gusto* marks an *intervention* in the food politics and agricultural economy of Italy and beyond. The size and scope of *Salone* – as a kind of culinary-agricultural public sphere – is an important means of demonstrating that Slow Food does not merely represent a niche market for elite consumers but is an aspect of a kind of transnational civil society distinct from the transnationality of global corporations.

Events like this represent Slow Food's attempt to marry 'event' pleasures with the 'traditional' pleasures of food (Warde and Martens 2000: 217–18), in order to offer participants an enhanced sensory and affective experience, as well as promoting the movement to a wider audience. Slow Fish in Genoa in 2004, for instance, was not only a festival of seafood but a platform to draw attention to the imperilled status of much of the world's fish stocks and to debate the vexed issue of fish farming as a solution or a contribution to the depletion of biodiversity in the ocean. Such food events, however, occur in a context described as the 'experience economy' which increasingly seeks to attract consumers by presenting them with experiences that engage, entertain, educate or absorb, with the aim of creating memorable personal experiences based on heightened sensations and active participation (Pine and Gilmore 1999). Similarly, Florida has identified a trend among affluent Western subjects for a lifestyle based on a 'passionate quest for experience' (2003: 166), where what is most sought after is not the kind of 'pre-packaged experiences of the sort Disney provides' but 'more active, authentic and participatory experiences' (2003: 167). Sampling the smorgasbord of exotic tastes and festival atmosphere at *Salone* or picking fruit in a heritage orchard at Barossa Slow in South Australia could be seen as forms of this 'quest for experience'. In an experience economy where the aim of business is increasingly to create a total experience for customers, Slow Food events, while aiming to present a unique opportunity to engage with local and traditional food cultures, could be caught up in this commodification of 'authentic' experience currently manifested in everything from wilderness vacations to themed restaurants (see also Heldke 2003).

It is difficult to provide any singular conclusion about the meanings and effects of the promotion that occurs through Slow Food events. On the one hand, given the mediated basis of contemporary global culture, Slow Food must adopt a public orientation and implement strategies of visualization, and festival-style events effectively foreground the importance of pleasure and conviviality the movement seeks to return to food. On the other, in making the *Salone*-style events the centrepiece of Slow Food's profile there is a risk that Slow Food could become just another food event provider, offering leisure activities to privileged subjects seeking a new experience devoid of ethico-political implications. Moreover, the deleterious effects of sudden, substantial media coverage on sustainable gastronomy projects in remote areas also poses dangers, leading to suggestions that 'alternative forms of public recognition' should be developed (Scarpato 2002: 147; Leitch 2003). As we noted in Chapter 4, however, the spatial contexts of slow living involve the combination of a valuation of geographical specificity with a global consciousness and this extends to the public life of Slow Food where there is a valuation *both* of more immediate social relations *and* the construction of a 'publicness' that occurs through media discourse and representation. While the resources of its media liaison office and Slow Food Editore have been effective in connecting events to campaigns and initiatives beyond the festive, Slow Food cannot avoid differing interpretations of its events being made by observers. Nonetheless, we believe that a strengthening of Slow Food networks at the local level of *convivia*, where a more sustained attention to practising slowness at the micropolitical level of food production and consumption is possible, supported by a clearer articulation of such initiatives in the public discourse of Slow Food International, would allow the larger, more spectacular events to continue to provide an important resource for the movement without occluding other emphases.

The media and promotional strategies of Slow Food highlight some of the ways in which the idea of slow living arises from a necessary engagement with contemporary global culture and an engagement with public life. The success of Slow Food owes much to its representations and portrayals in contrast to dominant lifestyle patterns and values and such representations should be considered as part of the political project of Slow Food, as they embody and visualize 'slowness' to a wide audience. The growing prominence of organizations such as Slow Food and Città Slow, reflected in considerable media coverage, as well as the appearance of popular books such as Carl Honoré's *In Praise of Slow* (2004), are evidence that a space is being carved out in public discourse to question the assumptions of everyday life and to explore alternatives to a multitasking, conspicuous consumption version of daily existence. If such prominence is not to result in a simple renegotiation of the 'quality of life' for privileged subjects, however, such questioning needs to be located in the *global* everyday. How the politics of food, in particular, is used to explore these kinds of political implications is the subject of the following section, which examines Slow Food's concept of eco-gastronomy in this context.

The Politics of Eco-gastronomy

Today, the politics of the Slow Food movement derive specifically from its self-proclaimed status as an 'eco-gastronomic' movement and therefore we need to explore in more detail the concept of eco-gastronomy as it is mobilized in the politics of food.[4] As we stated in Chapter 2, Slow Food has always promoted the connections between the pleasures of the table and the production of food but in recent years it has focused more on the politics of the environment by working, for example, to preserve biodiversity and promote sustainable systems of agriculture. As Petrini has noted:

> we quickly realized that the flavours we wanted to save were closely connected to the work of people – of farmers, who with their ancient knowledge are the true custodians of biodiversity and the land. We had this fundamental realization of the connection between sustainable agriculture and gastronomic culture. Anyone who thinks of themselves as a food lover but does not have any environmental awareness is naïve. Whereas an ecologist who does not enjoy the pleasures of culture certainly has a sadder life. ('Interview' 2004: 51)

Even though it is axiomatic that the consumption of food is a fundamental human act that is always implicated in social relations and an orientation to the physical environment, the distinctive political identity of Slow Food stems from this 'unusual' articulation of 'gastronomy' and 'ecology'. While traditional gastronomy advocated a thoughtful approach to food, eco-gastronomy goes beyond an attentiveness to the plate to locate food in a global context of risk and its networks of relations – to cultures, places and ecosystems – which require an ethical response (Donati 2004: 28).

For all its environmental awareness, however, Slow Food's valorization of the pleasures of food consumption sets it at odds with the general asceticism of the environmental movement (Maniates 2002b).[5] While the unusual conjunction of pleasure and ethics in Slow Food has already been discussed, here we want to foreground how this kind of conjunction involves a profound problematization of political categories and existing political value-systems. The slow and mindful orientation to life of Slow Food shares much with movements such as Voluntary Simplicity but it remains clearly differentiated through the latter's privileging of 'frugality' (Maniates 2002b: 199). As we have previously noted, Slow Food's promotion of pleasure is not a promotion of luxury or excess but rather a celebration of the corporeality and conviviality that is associated with food consumption. Some are keen to dismiss Slow Food as an elitist organization because of its gastronomic basis and its preoccupation with notions of food quality and taste (Gaytán 2004), and the movement is itself aware of the perils of perceptions of elitism (Sonnenfeld 2001: xiv), but there is an ethical edge to its assertion of the democratic right to pleasure and taste for all ('Interview' 2004: 52). Slow Food's anti-globalization stance, moreover, is another significant distinction from the Voluntary Simplicity movement which has been characterized as overly focused on private consumption practices and resistant to 'seizing on the more broadly political character of simplicity' (Maniates 2002b: 228). By connecting resistance to the frenetic pace of life that exists in much global culture – and which simplifiers also oppose (Maniates 2002b) – with campaigns for cultural and biological diversity in opposition to transnational agricultural corporations, for instance, Slow Food is attempting to articulate more coherently 'the micropolitics of everyday life with the macropolitics of global economic and political processes' (Mohanty 2002: 509).

It is apparent from such an overview that Slow Food can be many things for many people and that such a multifaceted organization can be analysed from a variety of theoretical perspectives. Our purpose here in an analysis of the politics of Slow Food is to show that any account of the movement that does not encompass its diversity fails to adequately grasp its articulated political character. For all its plurality, however, Slow Food is informed by a coherent political philosophy: the movement's broad range of concerns represents a holistic response to many of the political and social exigencies of contemporary life, not just a crowd-pleasing 'something for everyone' approach. Fundamentally, Slow Food seeks to reembed economic forces in their social contexts and emphasize networks between, and linkages across, socio-political terrains and categories in order to promote local economies and cultures. Slow Food is only 'anti-business' and 'anti-globalization' when the primacy of market forces threaten to destroy the fabric of local communities, environments, and food cultures.

In this way, Slow Food, like other anti-corporate movements opposed to the unbridled growth of global corporate capitalism, values a 'substantivist' (Emmison 1983) position on the economy where economic forces are not 'abstracted' from the social activity from which they derive. As Karl Poyanyi has noted, this wider understanding of the economy derives from our dependence upon nature and other human beings for our survival and the satisfaction of our wants (quoted in Emmison 1983: 141). Such an argument taps into calls for new understandings of the 'economic' (Thrift and Olds 1996) that ground economic analysis in the specifics of social activity, as well as emphasizing the heterogeneous range of networks, practices and values that constitute that activity. This new approach would mean finding ways 'to write social practices (like trust, reciprocity and knowledge) into the economic; to show markets as complex operations with moralities and histories from a myriad of overlapping time frames; to describe performative agents in relational terms; [and] to watch the moments and motions of consumption and production relations merge' (O'Neill and Whatmore 2000: 124). We see something of this imbrication of the social and economic in Mara Miele and Jonathan Murdoch's case study of the Slow Food affiliated *Ristorante Bagnoli* on the southwest coast of Tuscany in which the restaurant is the focal point of a series of networks involving ecosystems, political authorities and economic institutions at the local level (2002: 322). Such a successful eco-gastronomic venture depends on a diverse but interconnected network of aesthetics, ethics, labour and economics. The restaurant promotes the local economy through bringing together rural producers with urban actors and authorities; advocates the ethical value of only using produce from the surrounding countryside; highlights the pleasures of the taste and quality of the food; and demonstrates a 'practical aesthetic [that] animates the labour process in ways that work with, rather than against, tradition and typicality' (Miele and Murdoch 2002: 323).

Beginning from such an understanding of the complex imbrication of the economic in the increasingly global production and distribution of food, Slow Food – like other agricultural activists (Hines, Lucas and Shiva 2002) – is primarily concerned with installing what might be termed 'relocalization' as a means of overcoming the inequities and deficiencies resulting from global agriculture.[6] As the term suggests, '*re*localization' foregrounds the idea that much agriculture has been '*de*localized' as production is geared towards export rather than local needs, exacerbating a situation where the resources of the developing world service the consumption needs of the developed world and the profits of large corporations. In the words of Vandana Shiva: 'Relocalization implies, very simply, that what can be grown and produced locally should be used locally, so that resources and liveli-hoods can be protected' (2000: 37). The idea of relocalization incorporates many of Slow Food's key projects, including the promotion of sustainable agriculture, the preservation of biodiversity, and the battle against genetically modified food. Relocalization is an explicit counter-proposal to the dominant agricultural system that operates in much of the developed world and is promoted through institutions such as the World Trade Organization (WTO). If agriculture is increasingly 'framed as a masculinist (and white) moral project of "feeding the world" – a moral project that is ideologically in the service of international trade' (McMahon 2002: 205), relocalization, by contrast, emphasizes 'feeding your communities', through the empowerment of local communities rather than global corporations.[7] Relocalization does not, however, seek to insulate local communities from the rest of the world; its philosophy is very much informed by a global consciousness as it seeks to rework the structures of global agriculture. Slow Food may not advocate the direct-action approach of some anti-globalization protests but, like much of the anti-globalization movement, it promotes an understanding of food that involves 're-embedding people in time and place by linking them to particular farmers whom they know, and through them to specific pieces of land, the ecology of place and the seasons. It is a form of resistance to the commodification of life and farming under capitalism' (McMahon 2002: 203–4).

Such processes of reembedding involve the establishment and strengthening of networks and linkages between participants. This can occur at the local level, as we have just seen with the example of the *Ristorante Bagnoli* and its explicit iden-tification with Slow Food, but it also extends to a more global orientation. Sarah Whatmore and Lorraine Thorne (1997) argue that 'alternative geographies of food' are cast as more plausible if we adopt a 'network' rather than a 'systems' per-spective on globalization. Totalizing representations of transnational corporations and their supporting regulatory institutions implicitly render alternative ideas about global agriculture as weak and ineffectual against the might of global capital (Whatmore and Thorne 1997: 302; see also Hendrickson and Heffernan 2002; Barndt 2002). Such representations in fact misunderstand the non-deterministic, partial and necessarily situated nature of globalization:

> there is nothing 'global' about such corporations and bureaucracies *in themselves*, either in terms of their being disembedded from particular contexts and places or of their being in some sense comprehensive in scale and scope. Rather, their reach depends upon intricate interweavings of *situated* people, artefacts, codes, and liv-ing things and the maintenance of particular tapestries of connection across the world. Such processes and patterns of connection are not reducible to a single logic or

determinant interest lying somewhere *outside* or *above* the social fray. (Whatmore and Thorne 1997: 288, original emphasis)

Accordingly, alternative agricultural models need to attend to a range of social practices, skills and knowledges that animate different points in networks, and reemphasize the importance of human actors and relations of trust in such networks (Whatmore and Thorne 1997; Hendrickson and Heffernan 2002).

Like other alternative food projects, then, Slow Food seeks to encourage networks of social relations and market forces not only in specific, local contexts but by linking local projects into global networks of production and consumption, in an attempt to link an 'ethics of taste' to an 'ethic of production' (Donati 2004: 42). The Slow Food Awards, for instance, recognize those people who have played an important role in the preservation of biodiversity while the Presidia, the primary concern of the Slow Food Foundation for Biodiversity, supports projects to assist artisan producers (for example through providing infrastructure, equipment or training). There is frequent exchange between the Slow Food Awards and the Presidia: often an Award nominee who fails to receive an Award would be considered for a Presidia project (Scaffidi 2003a). In accord with the idea of social and economic networking mentioned above, the Presidia not only support producers and their traditions but also assist local economies and communities. Supporting specific Presidia projects, moreover, may also involve lobbying at governmental agency level, for instance, lobbying the EU to acknowledge traditional production methods and gain exemptions from hygiene regulations for artisanal producers (such as producers of raw-milk cheeses).

Of course, Slow Food's involvement with marginalized farmers and their communities raises many difficult issues of North–South power relations for the movement. This is particularly the case as the number of Presidia projects increase, extending from a concentration on European projects to a more global orientation, focusing on countries in the developing world. Slow Food's Piero Sardo has described the challenge in this way:

> we know what we are talking about, and the areas we are dealing with, when it comes to wild smoked salmon, raw milk Cheddar cheese or French potatoes. This issue is very different when we shift to second and third world countries. In these situations, we are not dealing so much with saving marginal specialities as with ensuring the survival of agricultural techniques, fighting desertification, getting reasonable prices for productions that are snapped up cheaply by large international buyers, and so on. (2003: 141)

Any scrutiny of NGOs working in the developing world raises ethical and epistemological difficulties associated with 'that stubborn "Doing Good?" question', as Donna Murdock has put it (2003). In seeking to resolve such difficulties, it is important to 'focus on the lived experience of NGOs, with particular attention to social actors' ongoing negotiations of meaning and practice' rather than moral or political absolutes (Murdock 2003: 508). Presidia projects, in the process of attempting to 'do good', do initiate relations of dependency, at least in the short term, and a politics of 'othering' is always perpetuated, to some extent, in encounters where Slow Food is an agent that bestows assistance and valorizes Presidia and Slow Food Award winners as 'needy' or 'deserving' recipients. The process of protecting global cultural diversity through ethical consumption could also potentially become another (post-colonial) form of fetishizing diversity. Contemporary global capitalism bears more than a trace of the logic of a European imperial past, continuing to 'appropriate the local for the global' and to commodify cultural diversity for its exotic value (Dirlik 1996: 32; see also hooks 1992). The question has therefore been raised whether Slow Food is complicit in such processes, rendering the post-colonial Other as an object of desire and source of pleasure in order to overcome the North's cultural *anhedonia* (the loss of the capacity for pleasure or happiness)? (Donati 2004: 60). The goal of such projects, however, is to have them as 'producer-run organizations' linked with and sustained by those who are 'integrated into the local community' (Fernald 2003) and Slow Food has explicitly acknowledged a need to maintain a vigilant awareness of postcolonial contexts and implications in its projects (Scaffidi 2003b).

The Slow Food Awards and the Presidia projects, then, share many of the political and ethical dilemmas that aid organizations and NGOs face in relation to North–South encounters, but there are still important differences that derive from the eco-gastronomy principles of Slow Food and the movement's promotional skills. As Fernald puts it, '[Producers also] want to know how to ... sell their product; they don't know how to say that their product tastes better, how to market it' (2003). Of course, such producers cannot compete with global agribusiness conglomerates, nor do they necessarily wish to, but they can generate strategies to ensure their own survival. Exposure to an audience on a global scale through the Awards, *Salone del Gusto* or coverage in *Slow*, may result in the ventures of small or marginalized producers gaining considerable success. While the aim of Presidia projects is to facilitate the economic independence and viability of the producer – so, as Fernald says, ' they're not dependent upon aid and they're able to sustain their lifestyle, what we call their slow lifestyle' (2003) – it remains an open question whether producers will choose to continue with their 'slow lifestyle' once they assume greater autonomy. Slow Food acknowledges that its intervention in Presidia projects, particularly through the marketing of products, can change the lives of producers, and that it is a 'tough balance' (Fernald 2003) between ensuring the ongoing viability of producers and their products while maintaining the integrity of their identity and ways of life. Ironically, such survival may depend on linking producers into global networks in a form of 'virtuous globalization' (Fernald 2003; also 'Interview' 2004: 52) but as Slow Food international office executive director Renato Sardo insists: 'We are not defensive: we are about globalization with people keeping their identity' (2003).

An example of a Slow Food Award winner illustrates well some of the complexities between tradition and development, North and South, in establishing new agricultural projects. In 2002, Raúl Hernández Garciadiego was an Award recipient for his work in the Tehuacán valley, Mexico. In this impoverished agricultural area, Hernández Garciadiego identified amaranth, a crop forbidden by the Spanish conquistadores for its links to indigenous religious practices, as an ideal crop to revive: it requires minimal water; is rich in nutrients; and assures higher earnings for farmers as the grain fetches a good price and has value-adding potential (Bogliotti 2003). Hernández Garciadiego then established the Quali project to set up cooperatives for sowing, harvesting, processing and marketing amaranth, as well as educating farmers and locals on the cultivation and cooking of the product, given its long disuse in the area. Now, over a 1000 farmers in the Tehuacán valley produce amaranth, with over 100 more currently employed in marketing and associated tasks, including a factory which produces amaranth-based cakes sold in cooperative shops (Bogliotti 2003). The multiple benefits from such a project, which is able to combine improved living standards for the local community with the revival of an endangered historical variety and protection of scarce water resources, aptly represents the networks and linkages Slow Food seeks to foster in response to global, industrial agriculture.

Such a slow politics of production does not seek to isolate and segregate marginalized farmers and communities but to help them combat the global forces that threaten their annihilation. Slow Food encourages those 'who are working … *against* the economic logic of modern life but *in* this "modern" world' (Petrini 2001: 109, original emphasis). Ultimately these projects are about interventions in global systems of agriculture and trade in order to protect, and demonstrate the viability of, the 'slow lifestyle' that encompasses traditional and sustainable forms of farming, the preservation of quality produce and food cultures, and the immediate contexts of local economies and communities. They do not seek to 'preserve' traditional practices as a living museum but to maintain the diversities and specificities of food cultures in sustainable and enriching ways. The preservation of traditional farming methods is approached in a pragmatic way, combining tradition with modern techniques and knowledges where necessary in a form of 'technology-blending', where there is a 'mixture of labour-saving and labour-intensive technologies' that are environmentally sustainable and in harmony with the community's values (Biel 2000: 308). Other Award recipients have exemplified this combination of old and new technologies, showing that Slow Food is not a simplistic 'back to the land' movement that idealizes peasant cultures. For example, Regassa Feyissa of Addis Ababa, Ethiopia, won an Award for Biodiversity in 2003 for his development of a germoplasm bank to recover lost crop varieties and establish agricultural systems and germoplasm that are compatible with arid conditions. Feyissa's Ethio-Organic Seed Action (EOSA) now involves a cooperative of 4,500 farmers who sell their crops directly, resulting in more consistent profits. Feyissa's EOSA means that farmers no longer have to rely on imported agricultural practices that involve costly fertilizers and other chemicals and, importantly for Slow Food, the EOSA technology remains locally controlled (Scaffidi 2003c; see also Donati 2004: 74–6). Such a politics of slowness is, then, 'grounded' in *terroir* – in a fundamental connection to the land, an understanding and valuing of the uniqueness of place, together with its ensuing cultural diversity – but it is also situated within global modernity.

The politics of eco-gastronomy projects, then, involves negotiating how to support local agricultural practices and food cultures while also using global market forces and consumption to enhance the project's viability. As Petrini notes, this is a large and difficult quest, 'bringing together ancient and marginal professions and a new class of consumers disposed to pay a fair price in exchange for quality and outstanding flavour, and sensitive to the need to protect the environment and the food supply' (Petrini 2001: 97). The nurturing of the local producers often means an active intervention in their farming practices, production methods or distribution and marketing. One example of such intervention is the case of *Ventricina del Vastese*, a traditional cured pork meat from the Abruzzi region of Italy, which is produced on a small scale and consumed directly by the producers or by knowledgeable outsiders for astronomical prices. Petrini argues the product could be an important economic resource for the area and that the Presidium has to 'convince the producers to raise more pigs organically and sell more Ventricine into the market, at a more affordable price' (Petrini 2001: 94).

Such a 'bringing together', as Petrini puts it, of traditional producers with newly aware consumers can, however, engender problems for producers and their communities, as well as triggering difficult issues regarding global trade and consumption. The promotion of the gastronomic delights of a particular food product, for instance, can elevate it into something of a status symbol: quality can subsequently sometimes suffer because increased demand and higher prices may result in importation to supplement locally sourced product, a proliferation of producers, or large-scale commodification of the product. Alison Leitch (2003) has studied the case of *lardo di Colonnata*, a type of cured pork fat from Carrara in central Italy, threatened by EU hygiene regulations due to its traditional preparation in marble troughs unique to the area. The designation of the *lardo* by Slow Food as an Ark product (and hence unique and endangered) elevated its popularity, triggering a proliferation of imitations by big butcheries throughout Italy. The local *lardo* producers sought unsuccessfully to protect the name through a collective trademark but a group has now acquired legal copyright to the name *lardo di Colonnata* (Leitch 2003: 445–8).

In addition, an associated problem is that the enhancement of unique, quality produce and the promotion of the territory from which it emanates sometimes results in an influx of tourists wishing to consume the produce and have direct experience of the traditional lifestyle and the pleasures of the region's *terroir*. While this connection between food and territory is successfully deployed in wine tourism, for instance, it can have deleterious effects on a community. In an attempt to address the problems associated with increased tourism, Slow Food has advocated 'gastronomic tourism' that provides people with pleasures, experiences and knowledges in accord with the mindful and environmentally aware ethic of slow living: 'the kind of tourism that Slow Food promotes with its guides, its tasting tours, its gastronomic strolls is meant to be aware and well-informed about the places visited: respectful, slow, reflective, and as distant as possible from the culture of "use and discard"' (Petrini 2001: 57).[8] From the point of view of the local communities, one way to prevent the deleterious effects of tourism is to limit growth and be conscious of the need to strike a balance between development and the traditional, environmental and social identity of the community. In the Italian context, for instance, where agriculture has been transformed over the last twenty years into either 'agribusiness or agritourism' (Helstosky 2004: 161), the fostering of eco-gastronomic tourism may in fact offer greater opportunities for farmers and farming communities to maintain their livelihood and autonomy in sustainable ways.

While Slow Food may cautiously advocate the positive experiences of eco-gastronomic tourism, contemporary consumption is also informed by the transportation of produce and goods over considerable distances, and many marginalized producers have been assisted by the global marketing of their produce and access to markets beyond their local province, while also benefiting from the reduced impact of the tourist 'footprint' on their local environment. This, in turn, raises another difficult dilemma for the movement: the environmental, political and quality problems associated with the increased levels of transportation of food around the planet, commonly known as 'food miles' (see Chapter 5). The dramatic energy and pollution costs associated with the shipping of produce around the world have been well documented: the distance food is transported by road has increased over fifty per cent in the last twenty years (McMahon 2002: 205). Global food conglomerates also use their economies of scale in transportation at the expense of local, small-scale farmers and food producers (Schlosser 2001). The purchase and consumption of organic produce, moreover, favoured by some consumers for environmental or health reasons, is no solution to the 'food miles' issue: 'one shopping basket of organic products could have travelled 241,000 kilometres and released as much carbon dioxide into the atmosphere as an average four-bedroom house does through cooking meals over eight months' (Hines, Lucas and Shiva 2002: 38; see also Guthman 2003). In addition, while some types of food can be transported around the world without excessive diminution of quality due to the speed of transportation and refrigeration technologies, in some cases quality is sacrificed, as in the example of the live transportation of animals where the stress and cruelty of shipping adversely affects the quality of the meat. Advocates of an alternative global agricultural system acknowledge that the issue of food transportation and food miles cannot be overcome completely. With products that are generally not grown in the North, such as coffee, tea and bananas, it has been argued that the principle of 'fair trade miles' be followed; 'this would combine the requirements of Fair Trade with "food miles", with a guaranteed quantity of goods to be purchased by each buying country within a guaranteed range of prices' (Hines, Lucas and Shiva 2002: 40).

Slow Food also argues that the global distribution of food involves a standardization of consumption, destroying the spatial and temporal orientations of local food cultures and seasonality. While, as the seventeenth-century Bolognese chef Bartolomeo Stefani noted, it has always been possible to obtain food out of season given a 'full purse' and 'fast horses', modern forms of transportation have made such consumption commonplace (Montanari 1996a: 70). As we argued in Chapter 5, the valuing of local, seasonal produce as 'authentic' is ultimately informed not by notions of 'organic' status, or even by the 'quality' of the food, but by the way it realizes particular local spatial and temporal relations which in turn are tied to ethico-social relations (Nabhan 2002). In this sense, for Slow Food members, the politics of 'food miles' and the alternative privileging of 'seasonality' stems from a philosophical and ethical framework where a mindful and attentive orientation is given to one's local and everyday contexts. The consumption practices of Slow Food members needs to be situated, then, in an understanding of consumption as having the potential to initiate political and economic change. As Daniel Miller has argued, we need to disengage consumption from the 'myths' that often circulate it, in order to posit its transformative potential for politics and everyday life (1995: 18). Instead, we should think of consumption as 'a use of goods and services in which the object or activity becomes simultaneously a practice in the world and a form in which we construct our understandings of ourselves in the world' (Miller 1995: 30). Consumption is not, of course, the only means of identity construction, and sometimes consumption shapes our self-understandings through our deliberate distancing from, as well as participating in, commodity cultures (Humphery 1998: 12). People operate in complex ways in consumer culture, that is, 'while attempting also to keep separate other aspects of their lives and to retain an *imagined outside*' where they might register anger or resentment at the imperatives of the market, for instance (Humphery 1998: 12, original emphasis). Thinking of consumption as a 'practice in the world', then, assumes an agency for the consumer – to pay more for an artisanal product, or to boycott GM-foods, for instance – which facilitates a different form of consumption through which a sense of global embeddedness and obligation may be expressed, as well as having a positive impact on food production networks.[9]

Through its eco-gastronomy projects Slow Food has certainly 'succeeded in creating the cultural space for the performance of a new kind of consumer politics' (Leitch 2003: 456) but ultimately the significance of the politics of Slow Food resides in its insistence on bridging the gap between production and consumption. Slow Food shares many characteristics with other consumer movements, most notably those informed by an environmental politics where there is a desire to overcome the alienated nature of contemporary Western consumption, instil an ethic of individual responsibility, and bring about subsequent change in processes of production. In addition, however, Slow Food celebrates consumption as a site of pleasure. Such a valorization of pleasure sets Slow Food apart from other social movements and consumer groups who, informed by an ascetic consciousness, identify the *pleasure* of consumption in some ways with the *problem* of consumption. The pleasure of consumption in Slow Food is a multifaceted phenomenon, incorporating the aesthetic and sensory pleasures of taste together with the pleasures of knowledge that trace consumption back through to the contexts of production and its human agents. By contrast, the simplifiers – adherents of Voluntary Simplicity (Maniates 2002b) – ultimately dissociate consumption from production, seeing consumption in isolation as a *means* to bring about the political changes associated with a change in production. Slow Food, alternatively, offers a more integrated understanding of consumption and production in the global everyday, mixing pleasure, taste, conviviality, ecology, agriculture, *terroir* and community in the politics of eco-gastronomy.

Life Politics

Such an articulation of food in the global everyday is consonant with the micropolitics of slow living. This is a politics that foregrounds the importance of the individual subject and the contexts of their everyday life, including their interaction with the processes and networks of global culture. This politics, we argue, is a form of 'life politics', as delineated by Giddens (1991), that recognizes, and attempts to capture, the processes of self-formation in a world characterized by the declining significance of traditional structures and value-frameworks, and increasing degrees of social indeterminacy. In this section, we explore further the 'life politics' of slow living, arguing for the possibilities of political transformation in everyday life.

As we noted in Chapter 1, the respective works of Giddens, Connolly (1999) and Bennett (2001) throw light in different ways on the possibility of what we have termed the 'slow arts of the self', where processes of self-formation arise from the implementation of values (such as care and attention) and the cultivation of everyday pleasures. This process of self-formation is, in turn, the basis from which the possibility for broader cultural and political transformations arises. We argue that the politics of slow living are a response to the accelerated pace of modern existence and its accompanying features of stress, over-scheduling and distraction. Much has been made by some theorists of the formation of an efficient, flexible and mobile neo-liberal subject in response to the increased tempo of contemporary life and a global culture of risk that is characterized by greater individual autonomy and reflexivity (e.g. Beck, Giddens and Lash 1994). We argue, however, that a context of speed and global risk also highlights natural, human and social limits, prompting fundamental reassessments of the allocation of time and attention with regard to individual lifestyles and social relations. In a range of current debates in both popular media and academia – about the intensification of a work culture, the importance of parents reading to children in the development of infant literacy, or the merits of fast-food restaurants – there is evidence of a politics of 'time' emerging across a diverse and proliferating range of social life (see e.g. Hochschild 1997: 245–52; Tanner 2003) and which is clearly articulated in the politics of slow living.

The idea of slow living foregrounds the very concept of 'life' – the meanings and values of contemporary existence, the spaces and temporal rhythms of everyday life, and the organization of lifestyles – and in this sense is one manifestation of a problematization of 'life' in contemporary culture.[10] This problematization of life has often occurred through processes of commodification, relating for instance to care of the self and body regimes, but it is also a more generalized phenomenon. In post-traditional societies characterized by greater degrees of reflexivity, 'lifestyles' have taken on a growing importance. While the concept of 'lifestyle' is often associated with popular media, consumerism and particular class habitus, such emphasis overlooks lifestyle as a generalized feature of modernity, as 'patterns of action that differentiate people' (Chaney 1996: 4). The legitimacy crises of traditional institutions and values, the greater segmentation and mobility between the locales of social life, and the centrality of mediated experience are all factors that contribute to the increasing indeterminacy of modern life and, in turn, impose the necessity of making choices in the organization of individual lives. Lifestyles, then, are structuring devices in identity formation, they are 'existential projects ... [with] normative and political as well as aesthetic implications' (Chaney 1996: 86; see also Chaney 2002).

To advocate a position that gives the individual subject, and matters of lifestyle and consumption, a significance in the politics of globalization is counter to many analyses of the way we live now. Michael Maniates, for example, bemoans what he terms the '*individualization of responsibility*' (2002a: 45, original emphasis) in the politics of environmentalism, where the privileging of a neo-liberal account of the individual precludes structural analysis and change: 'when responsibility for environmental problems is individualized, there is little room to ponder institutions, the nature and exercise of political power, or ways of collectively changing the distribution of power and influence in society' (Maniates 2002a: 45).[11] The slogan 'think global, act local', Maniates argues, too often involves 'feeling bad and guilty about far-off and mega-environmental destruction', and naively buying a 'green' product that 'will somehow empower somebody, somewhere, to do good' (Maniates 2002a: 58). Such a caricature of ethical globality, however, effectively perpetuates the very neo-liberal conceptualization of the subject that Maniates set out to critique. By setting the subject positions of 'consumer' and 'citizen' as mutually exclusive, and blaming the predominance of individual consumption solutions to environmental problems for contributing to the dessication of the concept of citizenship, the transformations to subjectivity in second modernity which have been called 'individualization' are overlooked.[12] Individualization not only impacts on the lives of subjects themselves but has significant implications for the social bonds and networks that are also constructed through 'a paradoxical collectivity of reciprocal individualization' in a culture of risk and indeterminacy (Beck and Beck-Gernsheim 2002: xxi). Without such an understanding of the individual subject's complex positioning in contemporary culture, the imbrication of the 'global' and the 'local' cannot be adequately acknowledged and hence the politics of everyday life is reduced to isolated and ineffectual acts of consumption, denying any political efficacy to the everyday.

The processes of individualization in fact generate a raft of ethical and political issues that are negotiated in different ways by subjects. The idea of slow living privileges the attentiveness of/to everyday life regarding those decisions about how time is used, how personal relationships are developed and sustained, how food is produced, prepared and consumed. Slow living acknowledges, that is, the politics inscribed in such decisions and actions. Such attentiveness, we would argue, not only makes possible a 'repoliticization' of everyday life but demands a consciousness of the global contexts in which such decisions and actions are made. This is a form of 'cosmopolitanization' where individual moral life-worlds are fundamentally informed by a global consciousness (Beck 2002). Of course, one can argue that there remains a substantial gap between individual *consciousness* of the political ramifications of individual acts and actual *forms* of political and social change, and we acknowledge that the establishment of connections and networks between micro- and macro-political levels remains a pressing problem and a requirement for any kind of progressive politics. A functionalist understanding of the individual, however, also works against the establishment of such connections and, as we have tried to demonstrate throughout this chapter, inadequately represents the changing political and social dynamics of contemporary life in the contexts of global culture.[13]

In such contexts, the politics that derives from particular relationships between individual beliefs and actions and their expression in informal, yet collective forms take on a new significance. Social movements, while a significant feature of late modernity, do not fully encompass the expression of social protest, which may take the forms of an extraordinary range of informal networks in everyday life that contribute to processes of individual identity formation, the establishment of new social milieux, and new collective identities (Purdue et al. 1997: 647). Such 'networks of renewal' are attempts to negotiate the challenges of everyday life that have arisen in response to the emergence of the features of second modernity, namely globalization, individualization, underemployment and ecological crisis (Purdue et al. 1997: 646; Beck, Bonss and Lau 2003). Examples of such networks would include organic food box schemes, local exchange trading systems (LETS) and festivals, through which milieux are formed where individuals are loosely bound together in ways which facilitates the enactment of political agency (Purdue et al. 1997). As Purdue et al. argue with regard to box schemes: 'What unites members ... is not necessarily direct contact with each other within the network, rather it is a milieu they share, where their social competence is expressed in taking responsibility for their own life politics' (Purdue et al. 1997: 653). The flexible affiliations of such networks of renewal can be manifested, of course, in a variety of ways. To be a member of a Slow Food *convivium*, for example, is to be part of a broader social movement and the purpose of the group (as the name suggests) is partly to experience conviviality but it also often assumes the form of a milieu that facilitates in more informal ways the individual life politics of members. Here, then, is an attempt to chart the subtle and complex expressions of a form of political activity that is not captured in conventional party political affiliation or protest action. It is a more individualized expression of political value that is nonetheless not disconnected from social contexts; it is a form of life politics, a series of lifestyle choices, that are informed by a state of glocalization where individuals attempt to negotiate, in ethical and politically conscious ways, the intersections between a grounded, specific locality and global forces.

The politics of slow living, then, cannot easily be demarcated between spheres of life politics and more conventional political struggles, nor can it be cast as a politics that occurs outside of global capitalism. As a form of life politics, slow living represents choices that are made in contexts beyond the dictates of tradition, relatively independent from basic material needs, and to some degree beyond the urgency of emancipatory issues. It is also a politics of lifestyle that assumes prominence in people's daily lives once the costs of global capitalism – whether a decline in food quality or an increase in work stress – impinges on their social contexts and everyday routines. Slow living is one answer to existential dilemmas in the global everyday where self-actualization and matters of authenticity are posited not as a luxury of an elite but the necessary work of all in the processes of identity formation. The politics of slow living, however, cannot be fully contained by the concept of life politics because it is also concerned with the politics of development and represents a response to the social and economic injustices that result from contemporary global capitalism. As embodied by Slow Food for instance, the politics of slow living also concerns a commitment to marginalized producers and communities who encounter the market forces of global capitalism and who are threatened with extinction or dislocation. Struggling farmers in both the North and South may choose traditional production processes, not only because of their desire to ensure cultural continuity, but also because there is a rediscovery and recognition of the values of such production processes. Such farmers cannot be dismissed as subjects who have had slowness imposed on them or who have no choice other than to assume newer, faster ways. Instead, they too are understood as subjects who have decided to choose slowness because of their recognition of its strategic value in niche global markets. To live slowly in this sense is to protest against the homogenization of global capitalism as it destroys biodiversity and the specificities of local cultures and ways of life.

As we have stressed throughout this book, then, slow living is a relational concept, given meaning through its contrast with the exigencies of 'fast life'; it does not represent a retreat from the world but rather involves an active engagement with the contexts of contemporary existence. For us, the politics of slow living are practised across a broad spectrum, involving matters such as the growing influence of new social movements, the relationship between food consumption and production processes, as well as myriad choices about the allocation of time and attention in everyday life. The politics of slow living are not containable in a singular 'position', nor are they restricted to a particular sphere of society or type of social activity, but they represent an oppositional discourse in as much as they attribute value to a 'quality of life' – manifested in ideas of pleasure, mindfulness and ethical relations with others and the earth – counter to the structures and demands of much modern existence. As such, slow living may not single-handedly overturn the structures and rhythms of contemporary life; rather, it may open to question the organization and values of everyday lives in the more indeterminate contexts of second modernity (Beck et al. 2003).

Conclusion: Rage Against the (Bread) Machine?

I think we need to find ways of not being so impressed by wealth and success. Until we find persuasive accounts of this, everybody is going to feel they must organize their lives around these things, whether enviously, or self-righteously, or taking a moral high ground, or getting wholeheartedly rich and successful. Money and success, stories from which none of us can exempt ourselves, are soporifics, and exhilarations and opportunities. They are narcotics. *We need alternative stories about what makes a life good.* Not stories which say it is better to be poor or better to fail. But stories which get us out of this whole language.

Phillips (2000: 195, emphasis added)

Slow living, and its manifestation in the Slow Food movement, is one such attempt to offer an alternative story about what makes a life good. It is a story of the quotidian location of the good life, of the pleasures of present-ness in the global everyday. As Honoré noted in his recent popular book on the slow movement, the biggest appeal slow living has going for it is its emphasis on pleasure (2004: 278–9). Its insistence that fast life is not only bad for the planet or our health but robs us of the time and energy to live with attention and enjoyment, wonder and generosity, urges us to interrogate the consequences of the pace of our lives. If we rage against the bread machine, it is not because it makes bread too quickly, but because it makes bread *badly* – it not only deprives us of the taste and texture of hand-kneaded bread but the tactile pleasures of kneading the dough and an awareness of time passing as it rises. In its place, it gives us beeping and flashing lights, extra washing-up and bland bread, which goes stale in twenty-four hours. We are not, however, calling for an outbreak of machine-breaking, still less of driving women back to the kitchen for hours of bread-making every day. What we need is to break the equation of bread machines (or the latest technological toy) with the good life. Making space for slowness (Eriksen 2001) does not mean abolishing speed, or even demonizing it, but allowing the possibility for other temporalities and making space for different ways of operating in the global everyday.

We have insisted throughout on the importance and centrality of everyday life as a site of 'ethical en-joyment' (Bennett 2001), a place to recultivate wonder and generosity, through practices of slowness. Recently, everyday life has taken on a renewed prominence in cultural studies more generally, as evidenced by the recent special issue of the journal *Cultural Studies* devoted to the topic (18 (2/3) 2004). In that issue, Highmore considered the ambiguous possibilities for daily, domestic activities to provide value and meaning in modern life. 'Can domestic routines become precious moments snatched from more thoroughly exhaustive work practices,' he asked, 'or do their rhythms constantly signal their lack of value? And how, supposing we wanted to, would we call attention to such "non-events", without betraying them, without disloyalty to the particularity of their experience, without simply turning them into "events"?' (2004: 207). Highmore's questions indicate that a reinvestigation (and reinvigoration) of the concept of everyday life does not simply endorse an 'aestheticization of everyday life' in which the goal is to 'efface the boundary between art and everyday life' (Featherstone 1992: 268). In stressing the value of attention in everyday life, neither are we offering only an aesthetics of existence, as so much of our dailiness includes routine which aestheticization excludes and excoriates. Slow living needs to attend to the humdrum as well as the evanescent if it is to find opportunities for both pleasure and ethical engagement. In such negotiation of routine, slow living – like cooking in Highmore's example – is characterized by 'multiple calls on the attention ... suggest[ing] that the inattention that we might associate with routine is better described as a peculiar layering of attention' (Highmore 2004: 318).

In a global everyday characterized by violence, displacement and deprivation for so many, the ethical possibilities of daily attention may seem unsustainable. Part of a 'living politics of social life,' however, as Highmore reminds us, may start by '"doing justice" to the complex bodily, social and temporal experience of the routine care of others' (2004: 319, 320). It is the sphere of everyday life which can provide the social relations and practices out of which collective forms of political opposition may arise (Burkitt 2004: 224: Melucci 1996b). In his influential book, *The Playing Self* (1996b), Melucci contended that it was no longer possible to imagine forms of collective opposition to existing power relations which 'did not involve individual experience':

> Being strictly related to individual experience in everyday life, these forms of collective action are apparently very weak and certainly they do not seem to much affect the structure of society and its political decision-making. But their apparent weakness is in fact the most appropriate way to oppose a power that has become molecular and penetrates individual lives. (1996b: 153–4)

The limits of capitalist consumption may be particularly exposed by the practices of so-called 'alternative lifestyles', such as slow living, from which can emerge new social movements, or more loosely formed milieux, with a focus on a politics of time and space (Burkitt 2004: 224–6). From challenging work culture to reclaiming public space for leisure or community, the aim is to refuse 'attempts to constantly rationalize the time and space of work and life' (Burkitt 2004: 226; see also Melucci 1996b: 144; Hochschild 1997: 245–52).

We have resisted delineating a set of practices that would constitute or define slow living, even as we have used a number of examples throughout (cooking, knitting, walking, gardening, cycling, reading, meditating – although, with the possible exception of meditation, all of these activities can also be done *quickly!*). Rather than defining slow living by its practices, then, we have proposed that slow living is a way of cultivating an ethical approach to the everyday. Thought of in this way, slow living becomes as much an attitude or disposition as an action, one that combines wonder and generosity. 'Fast life' so often precludes time for wonder or generosity – the kind of time, that is, that allows us to invest time in ourselves and others as a recognition of our worth and in response to our environment. Such time makes more possible a rediscovery of the enchanted materiality of the world around us and our connections with it.

Our chief example of the possibilities of slow living here has been the Slow Food movement because of the ways it addresses and connects the 'global' and the 'everyday'. As we have shown, Slow Food has successfully promoted an articulation of everyday pleasures with global responsibilities. As a global social movement, Slow Food responds to the risks and opportunities of second modernity – characterized by detraditionalization and individualization, as well as globalization – at both the macro- and micro-political levels. Alongside the processes of reflexive modernization, however – in which, even in 'our most intimate everyday experiences, ... what we once took to be given appears now as the arena for our conscious intervention' (Melucci 1996b: 86) – we need to remember the limits imposed by the 'finite capacities of the body' (Highmore 2004: 323). In a climate of 'instantaneous time', 'frenzied families' and 'time-poor subjects' where the fragility of bodies and social relations may be all too apparent, the conscious cultivation of slowness may be a salutary reminder of how our rhythms and routines have the potential to either challenge or perpetuate the disaffection of everyday life. Above all, ethical relationships *take time* (Ahmed 2002: 559; Bauman 2001: 71–2).

As we have observed at several points, however, the realm of the everyday still presents a challenge to the Slow Food movement to consider more fully the implications of both slowness and eco-gastronomy at the level of the personal, the domestic, the familial, the social.[14] In its attention to the threats posed to communities, territories and the environment by global agribusiness, for instance, Slow Food is exemplary in its negotiation of 'big-picture' issues, given its limited resources. The micro-politics of slow living, by contrast, remains an everyday dilemma, by which we mean not that meaningful action is impossible but that we need to find ways to manage our dilemmas, rather than waiting for a complete resolution of them (Melucci 1996b: 154). As Melucci puts it,

> we cannot choose between nature and technology, we can only manage different blends of technological intervention and respect for nature. There is no possibility of escaping the necessary link between these two poles. In the same way, we cannot choose between globalization and particularism. The respect for differences and the necessity of reaching a global integration of the world system and making it work cannot be separated. We can only manage different political solutions to cope with these dilemmas. In our lives and in our politics courage and hope will be our companions. (1996b: 154)

Slow living, then, is about keeping open the everyday possibilities for plurality and pleasure, change and justice, through ordinary ways which may also have extraordinary consequences.

Appendix

Official Manifesto for the International Movement for the Defense of and the Right to Pleasure (9 November 1989)

Our century, which began and has developed under the insignia of industrial civilization, first invented the machine and then took it as its life model.

We are enslaved by speed and have all succumbed to the same insidious virus: *Fast Life*, which disrupts our habits, pervades the privacy of our homes and forces us to eat *Fast Foods*.

To be worthy of the name, Homo Sapiens should rid himself of speed before it reduces him to a species in danger of extinction.

A firm defense of quiet material pleasure is the only way to oppose the universal folly of *Fast Life*.

May suitable doses of guaranteed sensual pleasure and slow, long-lasting enjoyment preserve us from the contagion of the multitude who mistake frenzy for efficiency.

Our defense should begin at the table with *Slow Food*. Let us rediscover the flavours and savours of regional cooking and banish the degrading effects of *Fast Food*.

In the name of productivity, *Fast Life* has changed our way of being and threatens our environment and our landscapes. So *Slow Food* is now the only truly progressive answer.

That is what real culture is about: developing taste rather than demeaning it. And what better way to set about this than an international exchange of experiences, knowledge, projects?

Slow Food guarantees a better future.

Slow Food is an idea that needs plenty of qualified supporters who can help turn this (slow) motion into an international movement, with the little snail as its symbol.

Notes

Preface and Acknowledgements

1. The recent listing of Carlo Petrini, head of Slow Food, as one of the twenty nine contemporary 'heroes' by *Time* is one indication of the media attention Slow Food is currently receiving (Ducasse 2004).

Chapter 1 Slow Living in the Global Everyday

1. In the discourse of Voluntary Simplicity, both consumer culture and its antithesis are often framed as conflicts over what truly constitutes American culture. As an example of the American-ness of this discourse, which may have become more prominent in a post-9/11 context, the title change of Jerome M. Segal's influential book on the subject is revealing. First published in 1999, Segal's book *Graceful Simplicity* had the subtitle *Toward a Philosophy and Politics of Simple Living* but in the 2003 revised edition the subtitle had changed to *Toward a Philosophy and Politics of the Alternative American Dream*. Voluntary Simplicity also, however, puts an emphasis on global social justice and equity – as reflected in the movement's most widely known slogan 'Live Simply That Others May Simply Live' (http://www. simpleliving.org) – making its location in American culture and politics difficult to define as simply conservative. For an overview of the movement, see the following websites: 'The Simplicity Resource Guide' http://www.gallagherpress.com/pierce/lbp.htm; www.simpleliving.org; http://www.seedsofsimplicity.org. See also Maniates (2002b) and Etzioni (1998).
2. Our delineation of attention and its ethical dimension in slow living owes a debt to the emphasis on an ethics of attention to the other (and the world) in the work of Simone Weil (1951) and Emmanuel Levinas (1998). For recent engagement with Weil and Levinas, which considers some of the implications of their work for contemporary ethics (and politics), see, respectively, Hermsen (1999) and Bell (2001).
3. Barthes specifies as 'idle' practices painting and knitting, the latter which he describes as 'the perfect example of a manual activity that is minimal, gratuitous, without finality, but that still represents a beautiful and successful idleness' (1985: 341). On knitting as a slow practice, see Parkins (2004b).

4. The study of everyday life has a long history in sociology as well as cultural studies (see Gardiner 2000: 2, Felski 1999–2000: 15). For the best overview of this rich field, see Highmore (2002). The most obvious problematic element of this tradition of everyday life is its treatment of gender, as Felski (1999–2000) and Langbauer (1992) have charted. To take one example, Lefebvre's oft-quoted statement that 'Everyday life weighs heaviest on women' (2000/1971: 73) can be seen to exclude women from the transformative potential everyday life can offer (Langbauer 1992: 51).

5. Other recent theorists of the everyday have similarly emphasized the non-containable dimension of everyday life, what Michel Maffesoli calls its 'plurality of rationalities and sensations' (1989: 6). David Chaney refers to this 'messy particularity' as the 'irrationality' or 'creativity' of everyday life, which is incompatible with the 'drive to order and control, the rationalism, of dominant public discourse' (2002: 37, 50): 'Everyday life is a creative project because although it has the predictability of mundane expectations, it is simultaneously being worked at both in the doing and in retrospective reconsideration' (2002: 52).

6. This is not to conflate the personal and the everyday. While there is significant overlap here, not everything personal is everyday (e.g. giving birth, terminal illness) and the everyday is also defined by practices which take place outside the personal domain (e.g. the world of work or community involvement).

7. It may be worth reiterating here that Beck and Beck-Gernsheim also stress the differences between their concept of individualization and the neo-liberal individual in the 'free market'. Their understanding of individualization refers to a 'sense of *institutionalized individualism*' where 'human mutuality and community rest no longer on solidly established traditions, but, rather, on a paradoxical collectivity of reciprocal individualization' (Beck and Beck-Gernsheim 2002: xxi, original emphasis).

8. We do not want to rehash debates over definitions and distinctions between modernity, postmodernity, second modernity or late modernity. While there is a place for such differentiation, we have generally in this book used the terms second modernity or late modernity. In this, we follow the lead of Melucci who, emphasizing the provisionality of such terms and warning against the comfort of fixed definitions, sees the proliferation of terms as social theory's attempt to capture the complexities of contemporary society and, 'somewhat provocatively' uses various terms to describe present society interchangeably in his own work (1996a: 485–6).

9. Such an understanding of the mutual imbrication of the global and the local in Beck and Tomlinson is also, therefore, to be distinguished from the cosmopolitan subject described by Ulf Hannerz as a person who, for all their cultural competence and their 'openness toward divergent cultural experiences', always 'knows where the exit is' (1990: 239–40).

10. See Hoggett's (2001) critique of Giddens's structuration theory and Craib's critique of an assumed unitary self in Giddens' account (Craib 1992: 171–7).

11. See also Fisher 1998; Curtis 1999; Dumm 1999.

Chapter 2 Slow Food

1. The name 'Arcigola' has a rather complex origin. 'Arci-' comes from the acronym ARCI, which stands for the Recreative Association of Italian Communists, the social-cultural wing of the Communist Party. 'Gola' is an Italian word meaning both 'throat' and 'appetite for, enjoyment of food' (and often inaccurately translated as 'gluttony' with the pejorative connotation of a sinful desire for excessive food consumption not present in Italian; see Counihan 1999: 180). *La Gola* (1982–89) was also the name of an interdisciplinary journal of food and wine run by an editorial cooperative including Petrini (see Petrini 2001: 6–7; and also Leitch 2003: 448–9).

2. It would be more accurate to term the protest groups that have arisen in recent years, for all their diversity and myriad differences, an 'anti-global capitalism' movement (see Craig 2002) or 'anti-corporate movements' (Crossley 2003).

3. Deborah Barndt calls 'the other globalization' a 'mobilization of civil society across borders and around common visions of social justice and environmental sustainability' (2002: 57). Another term to describe positive globality, which would also reflect some of Slow Food's concerns, would be 'globalization from below' which 'consists of an array of transnational social forces animated by environmental concerns, human rights, hostility to patriarchy, and a vision of community based on the unity of diverse cultures seeking an end to poverty, oppression, humiliation, and collective violence' (Falk 1993: 39).

4. In both Australia and the UK, for instance, press coverage of *Salone del Gusto* featured details of local producers who had travelled to Turin to exhibit, thus raising their profile and offering the endorsement of an international food fair which could have positive effects on their economic sustainability (see e.g. Ripe 2001).

5. The study of fifty-four Italian Presidia (roughly half of the projects undertaken in Italy) was undertaken in 2002 by the Bocconi University of Economics and Business in Milan.

6. There are probably a number of reasons for this, the first being the expense of the courses, which depend on sponsorship from producers to provide the tasting products, and secondly the capacity to organize within Italy where Slow Food has a more integrated relationship with producers due to the strength and size of the movement within regions.

7. The full name of the movement is Città Slow: International network of cities where living is easy.

8. In his popular book, *In Praise of Slow* (2004), Carl Honoré conflates the various organizations and social-cultural phenomena he describes as a 'slow movement'. While such a denomination is an effective shorthand way of sketching a series of complex cultural responses to the acceleration of everyday life, we differ from Honoré in distinguishing between broader social trends and a more coherent movement like Slow Food.

9. The extensive literature on social movements in recent years has developed an expanded taxonomy to describe the multiple and diverse forms of social-political organizations that have emerged since the latter half of the twentieth century, distinguishing, for instance, between social movements, new social movements, social movement organizations, global social movements and anti-corporate movements.

For simplicity's sake, we will refer to Slow Food as a social movement. While theorists like McCarthy and Zald (1977) distinguish between social movements and 'social movement organizations' we do not find this a useful distinction in the case of Slow Food primarily because McCarthy and Zeld's delineation is dependent on an overly vague and minimal definition of social movement (as 'a set of opinions and beliefs in a population which represents preferences for changing some elements of the social structure...' 1977: 1217), which almost then requires a corollary term in order to capture the coherent aspirations and organized activities of social movements.

10. As Mohanty reminds us, however, and Crossley omits from his pertinent critique of the ethnocentricity of analyses of new social movements, such analyses are often gender blind as well, despite the fact that, as Mohanty says, it is girls and women around the world, especially in the Third World/South, that not only 'bear the brunt of globalization' but also responses to it, such as the anti-corporate consumer movements, the small farmer movements against agribusiness and the anti-sweatshop movements (Mohanty 2002: 514, 529).

11. We follow Mohanty (2002) here, who uses Dirlik's (1997) formulation of North–South 'to distinguish between affluent, privileged nations and communities and economically and politically marginalized nations and communities. ... as a metaphorical rather than geographical distinction' (Mohanty 2002: 505).

12. Edwards in particular argues against Habermas's view of the distinctiveness of new social movements: 'while system-lifeworld conflicts may spark public-sphere generating social movements, these movements do not have to be distinct from capital-labour struggles. In denoting the tensions between state, economy and everyday life in the process of capitalist modernization, system-lifeworld conflicts fail to mark a shift from capital-labour conflicts; on the contrary, they encompass them' (2004: 114). Acknowledging this critique, we will still use the term 'new social movement' in the context of this discussion to reflect the emphasis on culture, identity and everyday life associated with them.

13. See, for example, the positive coverage in *The Ecologist* in launching an ongoing relationship between the magazine and Slow Food in the April 2004 issue.

Chapter 3 Time and Speed

1. In the nineteenth century, for example, both W. R. Greg and John Ruskin associated a diminished quality of life with the culture of speed associated with the railway. Greg castigated the dominance of 'SPEED' and the 'hurrying pace' associated with catching trains (1877: 263, 267) while Ruskin made the following famous assessment of rail travel:

The whole system of railroad travelling is addressed to people who, being in a hurry, are therefore, for the time being, miserable. No one would travel in that manner who could help it – who had the time to go leisurely over hills and between hedges instead of through tunnels and between banks... The railroad is in all its relations a matter of earnest business, to be got through as soon as possible. It transmutes a man from a traveller into a living parcel. (quoted in Schivelbusch 1986: 121)

Ruskin's comparison of the alienated, instrumentalist rail passenger with the carriage traveller who has a keener aesthetic sense and the time to travel slowly was also in the tradition of the Romantics' valorization of walking (see Jarvis 1997).

2. 'Pace of life' has been defined as 'relative rapidity or density of experiences, meanings, perceptions and activities' (Werner, Altman and Oxley 1985: 14).

3. The importance of speed in the areas of visual culture and military operations should also be noted but is beyond the scope of the current discussion. On these, see Bartram (2004) and Virilio (1986a).

4. This concept is not dissimilar to Virilio's notion of the emergence of a 'one time system' (1991).

5. As in the case of the railways when the 'discovery' of new pathologies or disorders expressed corporeally the perceived impact of technological changes ('railway shock'), so too with the bicycle: 'bicycle face' was identified in 1896 as a condition that could be incurred by moving against the wind at high speeds (quoted in Kern 1983: 111). In an interesting inversion/perversion of this modern association of speed and the bicycle, the first issue of *Slow* included an article on the virtues of slowness, 'The Art of Coming Last', as exemplified by the *Giro d'Italia* (Tour of Italy) in the post-war 1940s, in which the cyclist who came last and was awarded the black sweater became the most celebrated of the race, earning only slightly less than the winner (and much more than the other place-getters). Dario Ceccarelli argues that the popular support for the rider in the black sweater (most famously, Luigi Malabrocca) symbolized a sympathetic identification with his struggle, corresponding to the hardships of life for many in post-war Italy (1996: 42–5).

6. An example of such a repudiation in contemporary culture would be the cultural type/phenomenon of 'slackers' who reject the dominant model of work and subjectivity in contemporary everyday life. Richard Linklater, director of the 1991 movie *Slackers*, described slacker culture as in part 'a desire … to question the grinding down effect society has on its inhabitants, to formulate your own code of decency and *spending time*' (quoted in Wilson 1999: 21, emphasis added). For a useful discussion of this phenomenon and its complex relation to contemporary work culture and capitalism, see Heiman (2001).

7. As Cannon concluded, it may be argued that young people have a different sense of temporality, without the sense of a long-term future that their parents/grandparents may have had, inhabiting 'real time' in which life is envisaged as a series of 24–hour periods in which to eat, sleep, work and play (quoted in Urry 2000: 128). The links between this view of temporality and the appeal of the 'non-stop' city, in which each 24 hour period offers a multiplicity of potential activities or (pre)occupations may not then be coincidental.

8. Specifying an 'ethics of time' here is not intended to foreclose the political but rather, indebted to Levinas, to emphasize the ethical as a response to the other. The ethical relies on maintaining the alterity of the other while, as Derrida (1999) points out, political formulations must necessarily generalize to some degree (see Levinas 1986, Levinas 1998, and also Bell 2001 and Raffoul 1998 for very useful discussions of these distinctions).

9. On the modernization and Taylorization of housewifery and domestic management in the twentieth century, see Schneider (1997) on the German context; Ross (1995)

on the French; Arvidsson (2000) on the Italian; and Graham (1999) on the American.

10. For a related argument concerning the cycle of acquisition and consumption of goods in contemporary society, see Schor's (1998) account of 'competitive consumption'.

11. Michel de Certeau has also considered time wasting as a practice of everyday life, seeing it as a tactic which, unlike a strategy, has no explicit goal or aim (Certeau 1984: xx). While the deployment of slowness may be viewed as unproductive 'delay' from the point of view of a 'fast' subject, it cannot be described as 'tactical' in Certeau's sense because it is based on a conscious aim of constructing the good life.

12. Other examples of the 'Italian farmhouse' narratives would include Matè (1998), Hawes (2001), Dusi (2001), Parker (2001) and Gervais (2000). The forerunner of such Italian narratives is clearly Peter Mayle's *A Year in Provence* (1987) (see James 1996).

13. Mayes, for instance, makes much of a Renaissance paradox, 'Festina Tarde', which translates as 'Make haste, slowly', to illustrate a notion of balance she sees as fundamental to Tuscan culture (1996: 93).

14. For Levinas, "It is alterity, ... not shared attributes, that is the key to social life" (1989: 55).

15. Our conception of generosity here is indebted to La Caze's interpretation of Cartesian generosity (2002).

16. Critiques of communitarianism (e.g. Young 1990) have long noted the serious political problems that arise when an ideal of community results in the imposition of specific community values on others. Like the myth of the transparent democracy of the Athenian agora, such an apparent univocity conceals and refuses the expression and inclusion of difference. Hence Bell's delineation of Levinas's 'ethics of non-(in)difference' (2001).

17. For this society, speed is associated with deleterious practices in agriculture and medicine, a decline in democracy and the standard of public debate, and increased 'tensions and antagonisms' at work. Even daylight saving is criticized for disrupting the more 'natural' time rhythms of farmers and children. It remains an open question as to whether such a society represents a reactionary desire for the 'good old days' or a gentle form of urban guerrilla tactics.

18. For example, Leavis and Thompson write: 'The great agent of change, and, from our point of view, destruction, has of course been the machine – applied power. The machine has brought us many advantages, but it has destroyed the old ways of life, the old forms, and by reason of the continual rapid change it involves, prevented the growth of new' (1942/1932: 3).

19. Originally an editorial by Petrini which appeared in the first issue of *Slow* (1996: 7–8), 'In Praise of Slowness' now appears in the manifesto section of the Slow Food website, signalling its status as a proclamation of core Slow Food values.

20. This is why we disagree with Chrzan's contention that Slow Food members and writers use the word 'slow' indiscriminately, with 'mantra-like rhythmic repetition' (2004: 121). The interrogation of 'slowness' has been a feature of Slow Food discourse from the beginning and allows for productive exploration of the term's polysemy.

21. This may also be a case of Slow Food inheriting a different tradition of the imbrica-

tion of aesthetics and politics in everyday life. See Bolt Rasmussen on the Italian movement of the 1970s, *Autonomia Creativa*, which distinguished itself both from traditional left politics and the Situationists in favouring a 'playful attitude to life and society' and urging the 'freedom to choose one's lifestyle and recreational activities' (2002: 351).

22. One solution to the diverse temporalities in the global everyday, however, has been the establishment of 'time offices' in some municipalities in Germany and Italy in the 1990s. These time offices attempt to coordinate the temporalities of a municipality, such as opening hours of schools, libraries, public offices and shops, with public transport schedules and working hours. Their aim is to respond to time needs and the lost communal rhythms of citizens, to synchronize daily life and hence increase the perceived quality of city life (Reisch 2001: 375). Such practices are also featured in some Slow Cities. On the diverse temporalities of cities, see also Crang's (2001) discussion of the rhythms of collective life (deriving from Lefebvre 2004).

Chapter 4 Space and Place

1. In Australia, over 20 per cent of people work unpaid overtime and 60 per cent spend time working in the evenings or on the weekends (Tanner 2003: 51–2). In America, one study noted that for workers with children twelve years and younger only 4 per cent of male workers and 13 per cent of females worked less than forty hours a week (Hochschild 2003). Hochschild found in her study of an American corporation with 26,000 employees that the average working week was between forty-five and fifty-five hours and managers and factory workers often worked up to sixty hours per week (Hochschild 2003: 200–1). See also Schor (1991).

2. Perhaps part of the initial problem is, as Aronowitz and Cutler note, that it simply 'strikes us an unimaginable that we could have policy ideas centered on providing human happiness' (1998: 68).

3. See also Craig (2003) for a discussion of the workplace of the international financial news, technology and data corporation, Bloomberg.

4. Studies of transnationalism stress, however, that processes of deterritorialization also occur within more limited relations across specific individual nation-states (Kearney 1995; Jackson, Crang and Dwyer 2004) and that transnational processes are both *'anchored in* and transcend one or more nation-states' (Kearney 1995: 548, emphasis added).

5. Deterritorialization in fact cannot be disengaged from processes of reterritorialization. Inda and Rosaldo capture this in their neologism of 'de/territorialization' (2002: 12). They argue that 'the root of the word always to some extent undoes the action of the prefix, such that while the "de" may pull culture apart from place, the "territorialisation" is always there to pull it back in one way or another' (2002: 12).

6. One attempt to create contemporary slow spaces is the 'New Urbanism' movement that 'evokes the streetcar suburbs of the early twentieth century' (Honoré 2004: 110–18) in the United States. See Knox (2005), however, on the problems of creating a kind of 'slow' community in such enclaves.

7. Indeed Massey, drawing on Chantal Mouffe's understanding of the articulated basis

of individual subjectivity, argues that 'if places are conceptualized in this way and also take account of the construction of the subjects within them, which help in turn to produce the place, then the identity of a place is a double articulation' (Massey 1994a: 118).

8. Tomasik gives an overview of the complex etymology of the term *terroir*. Originally 'denoting land or an expanse of land' from the 'popular-Latin *territorium*' it began to be associated with 'agricultural land' at the end of the thirteenth century and in the sixteenth and seventeenth centuries 'was being applied to the positive and negative qualities of people associated with a particular provincial region'. Now, however, 'English has no satisfactory equivalent for *terroir* and so must fall back on more general terms such as "soil" or "land" with, at times, references to something rural' (Tomasik 2001: 523). O'Neill and Whatmore describe how the term *'cuisine de terroir'*

> challenges the notion that food preparation is a service which is increasingly able to be reproduced from place to place according to venue and demand. Instead, it sees food preparation and consumption as grounded in the landscape – soil, climate, growers and suppliers that have been historically assembled and nurtured into a complementary and evolutionary network keenly tuned to local growing conditions, markets and each other's needs. (2000: 133)

9. Here we must respond to Rachel Laudan's (2004) attack on the mobilization of the 'The French Terroir Strategy' by Petrini and Slow Food. Laudan asserts that 'The French Terroir Strategy' was a fictional device used in order to 'prop up the French wine industry' and to 'encourage culinary tourism' between the 1860s and 1930s although she provides no source material to support this view (2004: 138). Laudan also argues that the validity of the *terroir* of a place is undermined because it is exploited for 'marketing' purposes. As we have stated, the meanings of places always involve representation, and while we must guard against inaccurate or misleading representations, we would reject the belief that experiences and events are less 'authentic' because they are 'mediated' (Craig 2004).

10. Upon gaining membership of Città Slow, the mayor of Ludlow in England declared that the local leisure centre should offer local food products rather than 'endless fizzy drinks, ice creams and factory-made chips' (Kidd 2004: 5).

11. The revivals of industrial cities such as Glasgow, Dublin and Manchester not only involve the physical reclamation of factory spaces and docklands but the creation of a particular 'spirit of enterprise' which revolves around attracting specific kinds of industries and promoting a certain cultural and civic identity (Rose 2000).

12. For an overview of the 'urban public realm', see Montgomery's (1997: n.p.) discussion of Gehl, who argues that 'good public spaces are characterized by the presence of people staying or lingering when they have no pressing concern (or "necessary activity") to keep them there.'

13. The rapidly growing popularity of such markets, in both city and country locations, occurs in no small way because they offer a space for community formation. The increasing popularity of growers' markets is also not limited to Italy but is occurring in many other countries such as Britain, Australia and the United States. In the

United States, the number of farmers' markets grew 79 per cent from 1994 to 2002 and there are currently 3,100 markets operating across the nation. In Britain, the city of Bath held the only farmers' market in 1998 but six years later there were around 380 (Paul 2003).

14. Between 1971 and 1991 the percentage of the Italian population living in towns of 10,000 to 50,000 increased from 27.6 to 31.0 per cent. In towns of 50,000 to 100,000 the percentage of the population grew from 8.1 to 10.1. Alternatively, the percentage of the population in cities between 100,000 and 500,000 fell from 13.7 to 12.3 per cent in the corresponding period and in cities of over 500,000 the percentages fell from 15.5 to 13.2 (Saraceno 1994: 458).

Chapter 5 Food and Pleasure

1. Our companions that evening, all members of the Bologna *condotta*, were almost all of the professional middle class, apart from one restaurateur.

2. Research on women's relation to food has consistently found a discomfort with the pleasures associated with food, figuring eating as a battleground or a site of temptation (e.g. Murray Berzok 2002: 22, 28). In a survey of eating patterns among American college students, Rozin et al. found that 'over 10% of women claim[ed] that they would be embarrassed to buy a chocolate bar in the store, and about 30% [said] they would be willing to opt for a nutrient pill, safe, nutritionally complete, and cheap, as a substitute for eating' (quoted in Rozin 1999: 18). Ventura's research on the eating habits and practices of Italian women made similar findings on women's unease with the pleasures of food. Food avoidance and the classification of foods as dangerous or forbidden seemed to cross social levels and commonly manifested itself as an avoidance of pasta, with its connotations of pleasure, comfort, tradition and – most worryingly – fat (Ventura 2002: 32–3).

3. We do not mean to imply, of course, that Slow Food is alone in its opposition to fast food. In mobilizing culinary and political protests against fast food in Italy, Slow Food has both fostered and tapped into a wider cultural opposition to fast food and its values. In Italy as elsewhere McDonalds has been a site of protest by a range of causes and organizations in recent years, such as farmers protesting EU and Italian agricultural policies and environmentalists opposed to genetically modified foods. In addition, in 2003 McDonalds sued Edoardo Raspelli, food critic for *La Stampa*, who criticized the quality and nutrition of the chain's food in a newspaper interview (Helstosky 2004: 160, 215, n.13).

4. Through, for instance, maintaining existing class distinctions associated with privileging certain tastes and the practices that maintain them; or through valuing 'slow time' as free time without challenging the hegemony of work time that necessarily precedes other forms of time ('slow time' as reward).

5. See Lefebvre's analysis of leisure in *The Critique of Everyday Life*: 'So we work to earn our leisure, and leisure only has one meaning: to get away from work. A vicious circle' (1991/1958: 40).

6. Not coincidentally, Marinetti's condemnation of pasta also corresponded with the Fascist government's push for increased rice production and consumption: 'And

remember too,' Marinetti wrote, 'that the abolition of pasta will free Italy from expensive foreign grain and promote the Italian rice industry' (1989 1932: 37). An extensive programme of 'rice propaganda' was initiated under Mussolini, including the introduction of a 'National Day for Rice Propaganda' in 1928 (Helstosky 2004: 79).

7. It should be noted, however, that Lawson is not critiquing the supposedly excessive pleasure in food connoted by the term 'gastroporn'. As she puts it, 'it makes perfect sense that in our puritanical age the last allowable excess should be gastroporn' (1999: 154). In both her writings and television programmes on food, Lawson is a notable exception in articulating the multiple and diverse pleasures of food in different contexts, and in placing women at the centre of culinary *pleasures*, not just culinary preparation (see Hollows 2003).

8. There is perhaps also another historical echo detectable in Slow Food's insistence on the right to pleasure. As Simonetta Falasca-Zamponi has argued, Mussolini's Fascism explicitly rejected happiness as a legitimate goal of politics or social transformation. 'Fascism denies the materialistic conception of "happiness" as possible,' Mussolini wrote, 'it denies, that is, the equation wellbeing = happiness which would turn men into animals who only think about one thing: to be fed and fattened, reduced, that is, to vegetative life purely and simply' (quoted in Falasca-Zamponi 2002: 157). Such a philosophy dovetailed with Fascist austerity programmes and other means of food control associated with the policy of autarky in the 1930s (Helstosky 2004: 4). A focus on material pleasure and food, therefore, implicitly locates Slow Food outside and opposed to the anti-materialism of Fascism in the Italian political imaginary.

9. Ginsborg describes the emergence of two distinct middle-class 'voices' in Italy in the 1980s. One 'heavily concentrated among entrepreneurs and shopkeepers, was localistic, consumerist, strongly oriented both to self-interest and an overriding work ethic' – 'Thatcherist without Mrs Thatcher' (2001: 66). The other 'reflexive' element of the middle class (prevalent among those in education, social services, and fringes of the professions and salariat) adopted a perspective of global environmental concerns and the negative consequences of consumerism (2001: 66). On the development of conspicuous consumption in the 1980s and its ramifications for Italian politics, see also Helstosky (2004: 156–7).

10. On the 'presentness' of pleasure through food, see also Albert O. Hirschman who argues: 'Food has a special ability to provide pleasure that is based on the body's recurring physiological need for the energy it supplies. Foodstuffs disappear precisely in the process of conveying their energy to the body, and *their disappearance is essential to the pleasure felt in the act of consumption*' (1982: 29, emphasis added). Hirschman is best known for his work on consumer dissatisfaction and his 'exit-voice-loyalty' thesis (put simply, when dissatisfied with a purchase, consumers will either take their business elsewhere, express dissent in a variety of ways or suffer in silence), which may also account for some of the appeal of Slow Food. Although we dispute the classification of Slow Food as a 'consumer movement' (Leitch 2003 and Chrzan 2004), Hirschman's account of how the 'exit-voice' responses may go together, reinforcing each other and creating a significant linking between private consumption and public action (1982: 65), is one explanation for how the kind of cultural politics Slow Food practises is instigated. Originating in disappointment

with the inferior quality of homogenized, industrialized food and an incitement of others to similarly demand high-quality, sustainably produced food, Slow Food has been able to mobilize such responses in an effectively positive form, without being branded simply as a protest movement.

11. To summarize Warde and Martens's taxonomy of gratification: the sensual realm includes bodily pleasures; the instrumental involves achievement, material advancement or successful presentations of self; the contemplative includes a range of experiences, from dreaming and fantasy to aesthetic appreciation and religious ecstasy; and the social is comprised of pleasures associated with participation, mutuality and companionship (Warde and Martens 2000: 186–7). While in one sense Warde and Martens's taxonomy could be seen as an overly complex way of arriving at the unsurprising conclusion that people enjoy some things more than others, it does remind us of the complexities of pleasures associated with commensality, highlighting how a polysemous notion of pleasure enhances the philosophy and appeal of Slow Food. In particular, Warde and Martens's contention that degrees of gratification may correspond to whether the experience is a routinized or reflexive one corresponds with Slow Food's insistence on attentive engagement with food practices.

12. Berry defines the 'industrial eater' as 'one who does not know that eating is an agricultural act, who no longer knows or imagines the connections between eating and the land, and who is therefore necessarily passive and uncritical' (1992: 375). A 'responsible eater,' by contrast is one who learns the origins of food, best farming practices and life histories of the food species we eat (1992: 377).

13. Despite the fact that Berry has recently been a contributor to *Slow* (2004: 98–9) we would contend that his writings suggest significant differences with some aspects of Slow Food philosophy due to their explicit location within what Berry describes as specifically American, Christian values (e.g. Berry 2002).

14. In arguing that Slow Food is a form of 'Culinary Luddism' which is based on a misunderstanding of history, Laudan herself perpetuates the myth that nineteenth-century Luddism was simply a futile and simplistic campaign to 'turn back the clock'. On the complexities of Luddite protests against the industrialization of artisanal skills, see the classic account by E. P. Thompson (1968: 600–5). For a similar charge from an unexpected quarter – given his endorsement of 'slow life' – see Agger (2004), who sees a 'premodern pastoralism' in Petrini's position. As we argue here, however, we understand Slow Food's discourse of food as situated within a reflexive engagement with modernity, as precisely an attempt to 'insert slowness into modernity', not as a desire to withdraw from modernity, as Agger charges (2004: 147–9).

15. We would also distinguish the concept of authenticity mobilized by Slow Food from that proposed by Curtin's notion of 'authentic presence to food' (1992: 129). For Curtin, there is a kind of unmediated experience of food which, if approached with the right awareness, will lead to ethical consequences, notably vegetarianism (1992: 130). While Curtin observes that some indigenous cultures carry out respectful slaughtering of animals, he asks the 'moral question': 'What do we become – bodily, politically, spiritually – by killing sentient life for food?' (1992: 130). Curtin calls his position 'contextual moral vegetarianism' but the implication of his 'moral question' is that there is no context in which vegetarianism would not be the better moral

choice. This is a much more essentialist notion of authenticity than is found in Slow Food where authenticity is contextual, rather than tied to given moral responses.

16. Following Nabhan's distinction between 'local' and 'organic' foods, we therefore disagree with Guthman's (2003) conflation of slow food with organic food because it fails to acknowledge the centrality of the local to Slow Food and the specific connotations of 'slow' in relation to food.

17. The negative connotations of plastic in relation to food may also have an Italian historic specificity. As Arvidsson has recounted, when plastic materials became a sign of modernity in Italy in the early 1960s, there was a profound and widespread mistrust of plastic in relation to food: in extensive market research, plastics were thought to be 'poisonous or unhygienic, and hence unfit as food containers' (Arvidsson 2000: 252).

18. *Osterie* listed in *Osterie d'Italia* are initially nominated for inclusion by local *condotte* members, which are then vetted and endorsed by staff at Slow Food head office. So while the profile of this Slow Food guide has influenced the success and standards of *osterie* as Gho suggests, local knowledge of food cultures is integral to the process of recognition and promotion.

19. Miele and Murdoch describe the food practices of the *osteria* kitchen as a 'practical aesthetic', meaning 'one that is rooted in the tacit knowledge, craft skills, creative energies, and socio-natural relationships that comprise typical cuisines' (2002: 313) but this term could also be applied to the situated pleasures of the diner, where taste and presentation of food are enjoyed within an awareness of the specificities of their context.

20. On the cross-class implications of alternative food projects, see Hendrickson and Heffernan (2002). On the ethical consequences of privilege, see also Young who argues: 'Where there are structural injustices, these usually produce not only victims of injustice but also privileged beneficiaries. Persons who benefit from structural inequalities have a special moral responsibility to join in correcting them – not because they are to blame, but because they are able to adapt to changed circumstances without suffering serious deprivation' (2003: 43).

21. Welsch's definition of a provincial is relevant here: 'one is a provincial not in the sense that one is at home in a particular province, but in that one holds this province as unique and mistakes it for the world' (1996: 21).

22. In his consideration of the importance of reflection and attention in food practices, for instance, Curtin proposes 'mindful eating', as distinct from both aesthetic appreciation and moral responses to food (1992:126–7) while, in the same volume, Heldke describes an approach to cooking and eating as 'thoughtful practice', grounded in an everyday awareness of temporality (1992: 227). The 'mindfulness' which Curtin and Heldke advocate, in which food practices become almost a form of meditation, has also recently found a parallel in a method successful in the psychological treatment of Binge Eating Disorder, where patients are taught mindfulness meditation techniques in order to increase their awareness of satiety and reasons for eating (Kristeller and Hallett 1999).

23. In a study of the cultural similarities and differences in the discourse of taste among twenty similarly-classed families in the US and Italy, Ochs et al. found that 'The American families gave priority to food as nutrition, food as a material good, and

food as reward over food as pleasure. The Italian families gave priority to food as pleasure over any other theme' (1996: 9). The Italian families were observed discussing a broad range of the pleasures of food, 'including the pleasures of planning, procuring, preparing, serving, and eating particular food items', leading Ochs et al. to conclude that this perspective on pleasure was 'the heart of socialization of taste in the Italian households in this study' (1996: 25).

24. The implementation of such programmes is clearly influenced by the French taste education programme, *Semaine du goût* (see Petrini 2001; Terrio 2000).

25. Such an overemphasis on the nutrition education aspect is behind Chrzan's (2004) scathing attack on Slow Food USA taste education initiatives, illustrating the pressure such projects may feel from traditional nutrition education, in the process running the risk of losing what is distinctive about the pleasure-based approach Methfessel (2002), for instance, describes.

26. Hollows particularly analyses the work and representation of Nigella Lawson which she argues illustrates the differing significations of cooking in the home and signals shifts in contemporary feminine identity. Lawson's cooking 'starts from the importance of satisfying and caring for the self rather than others and in this way offers an alternative mode of representing the pleasures of domestic femininity' (2003: 184). See also, however, Jones and Taylor (2001) who make a similar argument about the cookery writing of an earlier generation of British women preceding Lawson, namely Elizabeth David and Jane Grigson. In David and Grigson's writings, cooking was represented both as a pleasure and a serious occupation to explore 'beyond the confines of domesticity'(Jones and Taylor 2001: 178).

27. Figures from the Italian National Institute of Statistics in 1993–4 showed that one third of married Italian men still saw their mothers every day, while another 27.5 per cent saw them more than once a week; and seven out of ten unmarried Italian men over the age of thirty-five lived with their parents (quoted in Ginsborg 2001: 79).

28. Counihan has argued, however, that despite family meals being primarily the responsibility of women, they were also full participants at the table in the Florentine families she studied. Such participation was achieved through a variety of means which involved carefully managing both the cooking and serving of food, such as preparing all the courses prior to the family being seated or sharing the tasks among generations of women in extended-family meals (2004: 118–9).

29. While there is no conclusive data on the gender breakdown of Slow Food members and leaders worldwide, based on available figures over half of *convivia* in the USA are led or co-led by women, with a similar or slightly higher ratio of women leaders in Australian *convivia*.

Chapter 6 The Politics of Slow Living

1. While Starr recognizes that a valuation of tradition is not an escape from contemporary political dynamics but a form of engagement with them, the force of the binary she constructs fails to fully consider the reflexive use of tradition.

2. The www.slowfood.com and www.slowfood.it sites had a combined average daily hit total of about 3,500 with visitors from 131 countries, based on the period from

October 2002 to April 2003 (Irving 2003).

3. It also generates new membership: over 1,800 new members signed up during the 2004 *Salone* (http://www.slowfood.com/eng/sf_stampa/sf_stampa_dett_comu. lasso?idstampa=US_00366).

4. In 2005, Petrini floated the idea that Slow Food might now be defined as 'neo-gastronomic', by which he means 'a heterogeneous group of people from every nation in the world committed to the study, promotion and implementation of a new idea of gastronomy, that demands attention to production, consumption, sustainability, quality and social justice' (2005: 7). It is too early to tell if this neologism will be more widely adopted to describe the movement's emphasis but, in any case, Petrini's definition does not differ substantially from earlier definitions of 'eco-gastronomy'.

5. The April 2004 edition of *The Ecologist* magazine devoted to Slow Food is one sign, however, that the traditional differences between the environmental movement and a movement like Slow Food may be diminishing.

6. Other forms of agricultural activism and politics include, for example, the Confédération Paysanne (see Bové 2001) and Via Campesina (http://www.viacam-pesina.org).

7. McMahon notes that 'globalized agriculture does not help poor countries develop and escape poverty'. She cites a United Nations report on the world's forty-eight poorest countries that revealed that poverty actually increased as the countries became more open to international trade (2002: 204).

8. In this respect, eco-gastronomy tourism shares many of the dilemmas and ideals of the ecotourism movement (see Hjalager and G. Richards 2002).

9. We are influenced here by Humphery's concept of 'everyday outsidedness' (1998: 13) to describe an aspect of consumption which avoids the often-polarized positions in cultural studies on consumption as either compliance or resistance. 'In concentrating on people's critical participation in consumption cultures,' Humphery argues, 'such work has tended to ignore or downplay an equally important aspect of everyday life in which people stand back from the market, feel anger at its presence, refuse to participate or, at the very least, question its relevance to other aspects of their lives' (1998: 11). We also share Humphery's view that the concentration on consumption in cultural studies has also often been accompanied by a 'timidity' to 'enter the terrain of political value' (1998: 14) and we have therefore been unapologetic here about advocating the values of slowness.

10. And in the context of cultural studies. See Seigworth and Gardiner on how a new emphasis on everyday life in cultural studies directs attention to the 'immanence of "life"' itself (2004: 152).

11. According to Maniates, the individualization of responsibility has arisen not only because of the 'core tenets of liberalism' but also due to other factors such as 'the historical baggage of mainstream environmentalism, ... the dynamic ability of capitalism to commodify dissent, and the relatively recent rise of *global* environmental threats to human prosperity' (2002a: 46, original emphasis).

12. In this sense, we note the different understandings of the term 'individualization' that are deployed in Maniates' chapter (titled, 'Individualization: Plant a Tree, Buy a Bike, Save the World?') and in Beck and Beck-Gernsheim (2002) that we outlined

in Chapter 1. Beck and Beck-Gernsheim's concept of 'individualization' differs from the neo-liberal individual in the free market, instead refering to the required processes of 'biography formation' and life management practices rather than the autonomous and voluntarist subject.

13. For a related argument, see Young's (2003) account of 'political responsibility' in anti-sweatshop campaigns.

14. We are not, however, confining, the everyday to these categories. As Burkitt contends: 'the term everyday life is often taken to mean the life we all lead when the official forms of relations and activities are taken away, leaving behind the residual relations of family and friendship – the more unofficial relations of social life. Yet, this definition cannot be correct for, as Lefebvre points out ..., everyday life is related to all activities and is the sum total of relations that constitute the human – and every human being – in terms of our collective as well as our individual experience' (2004: 212).

Bibliography

Abbona, A. (2003), personal interview, Bra, Italy, 3 April.

—— and Nano, P. (2003), 'Letter from President. An interview with Stefano Cimicchi, president of the Italian Città Slow movement and mayor of Orvieto', www. cittaslow.net/world/citta_slow.asp?sez=3, accessed 12 April 2004.

Adam, B. (1995), *Timewatch: The Social Analysis of Time*, Cambridge: Polity Press.

—— (2003), 'Reflexive Modernization Temporalized', *Theory, Culture and Society*, 20 (2): 59–78.

Agger, B. (2004), *Speeding Up Fast Capitalism: Cultures, Jobs, Families, Schools, Bodies*, Boulder: Paradigm Publishers.

Ahmed, S. (2002), 'This other and other others', *Economy and Society*, 31 (4): 558–72.

Alexander, S. (2003), 'Beyond the Pilot: The Kitchen Garden at Collingwood College', *Snail Pace*, 2: 1–2.

Ambroise, S. (1997), 'Fast but Slow', *Slow*, 4: 83–5.

Appadurai, A. (1991), 'Disjuncture and Difference in the Global Cultural Economy', in M. Featherstone (ed.), *Global Culture: Nationalism, Globalization and Modernity*, London: Sage.

—— (1993), 'Consumption, Duration, and History', *Stanford Literature Review*, 10: 11–33.

—— (1996), *Modernity at Large: Cultural Dimensions of Globalization*, Minneapolis: University of Minnesota Press.

Apollonio, U. (ed.) (1973), *Futurist Manifestos*, London: Thames and Hudson.

Aronowitz, S. and Cutler, J. (eds) (1998), *Post-Work: The Wages of Cybernation*, New York: Routledge.

Arvidsson, A. (2000), 'The Therapy of Consumption Motivation Research and the New Italian Housewife, 1958–62', *Journal of Material Culture*, 5 (3): 251–74.

Augé, M. (1995), *Non-Places: Introduction to an Anthropology of Supermodernity*, trans. J. Howe, London: Verso.

Bachelard, G. (1994), *The Poetics of Space*, trans. M. Jolas, Boston: Beacon Press.

Bagguley, P. (1992), 'Social change, the middle class and the emergence of "new social movements": a critical analysis', *Sociological Review* 40 (1): 26–48.

Barbero, S. (2003), personal interview, trans. S. Herron, Bra, Italy, 3 April.

Barkham, P. (2004), 'Waking up to the joys of life in the slow lane', *Guardian Unlimited*, 13 September, www.guardian.co.uk/uk_news/story/0,3604,1303109.00.html, accessed 6 October, 2004.

Barndt, D. (2002), *Tangled Routes: Women, Work, and Globalization on the Tomato Trail*, Lanham, MD: Rowman & Littlefield.

Barthes, R. (1985), 'Dare to be Lazy' in *The Grain of the Voice: Interviews 1962–1980*, trans. L. Coverdale, Berkeley: University of California Press.

Bartram, R. (2004), 'Visuality, Dromology and Time Compression: Paul Virilio's New Ocularcentrism', *Time and Society*, 13 (2/3): 285–300.

Baudrillard, J. (1987), 'Modernity,' *Canadian Journal of Political and Social Theory,* 11(3): 63–72.

Bauman, Z. (1998), *Globalization*, Cambridge: Polity.

—— (2001), *Community: Seeking Safety in an Insecure World*, Cambridge: Polity Press.

—— (2002), 'Foreword', in U. Beck and E. Beck-Gernsheim, *Individualization: Institutionalized Individualism and Its Social and Political Consequences*, trans. P. Camiller, London: Sage.

Beck, U. (1992), *Risk Society : Towards a New Modernity*, trans. M. Ritter, London: Sage.

—— (1997), *The Reinvention of Politics: Rethinking Modernity in the Global Social Order*, trans. M. Ritter, Cambridge: Polity.

—— (2000), 'The cosmopolitan perspective: sociology of the second age of modernity', *British Journal of Sociology*, 51 (1): 79–105.

—— (2002), 'The Cosmopolitan Society and its Enemies', *Theory, Culture and Society*, 19 (1–2): 17–44.

—— and Beck-Gernsheim, E. (2002), *Individualization: Institutionalized Individualism and Its Social and Political Consequences*, trans. P. Camiller, London: Sage.

——, Bonss, W. and Lau, B. (2003), 'The Theory of Reflexive Modernization: Problematic, Hypotheses and Research Programme', *Theory, Culture and Society*, 20 (2): 1–33.

——, Giddens, A. and Lash, S. (eds) (1994), *Reflexive Modernization: Politics, Tradition and Aesthetics in the Modern Social Order*, Cambridge: Polity Press.

Bell, V. (2001), 'On ethics and feminism: Reflecting on Levinas' ethics of non-(in)difference', *Feminist Theory* 2 (2): 159–171.

Bender, C. and Poggi, G. (1999), 'Golden Arches and Iron Cages: McDonaldization and the Poverty of Cultural Pessimism at the End of the Twentieth Century', in B. Smart (ed.), *Resisting McDonaldization*, London: Sage.

Bennett, J. (2001), *The Enchantment of Modern Life: Attachments, Crossings, and Ethics*, Princeton: Princeton University Press.

Bennetts, S. (2003), '"Berlusconi hasn't arrived here yet": The contemporary Italian folk revival as a response to modernity', (forthcoming in *Alchemies: Community exChanges, Refereed Proceedings of the Curtin Humanities Postgraduate Research Conference 2003*, Perth: Black Swan Press).

Berlant, L. (2004), 'Critical Inquiry, Affirmative Culture', *Critical Inquiry*, 30 (2): 445–51.

Berman, M. (1983), *All That is Solid Melts into Air: The Experience of Modernity*, London: Verso.

Berry, W. (1992), 'The Pleasures of Eating', in D. W. Curtin and L. M. Heldke (eds), *Cooking, Eating, Thinking: Transformative Philosophies of Food*, Bloomington: Indiana University Press.

—— (2002), *The Art of the Commonplace: The Agrarian Essays of Wendell Berry*, Washington: Shoemaker and Hoard.

—— (2004), 'We have begun', *Slow,* 2: 98–9.

Bessière, J. (1998), 'Local Development and Heritage: Traditional Food and Cuisine as Tourist Attractions in Rural Areas', *Sociologia Ruralis*, 38(1): 21–34.

Bianchino, R. (2004), personal interview, Barossa Valley, Australia, 4 April.

Biel, R. (2000), *The New Imperialism: Crisis and Contradiction on North-South Relations*, London: Zed Books.

Blim, M. (2000), 'What is Still Left for the Left in Italy? Piecing Together a Post-Communist Position on Labour and Employment', *Journal of Modern Italian Studies*, 5 (2): 169–185.

Bloch, E. (1977), 'Nonsynchronism and the Obligation to Its Dialectics (1932)', *New German Critique*, 11: 22–38.

Blumer, H. (1969), 'Collective behaviour', in A. McClung-Lee (ed.) *Principles of Sociology*, New York: Barnes and Noble.

Bogliotti, C. (2002), 'The innocents who made it work', *Slow*, 5: 117–18.

—— (2003), 'Raúl Hernández Garciadiego', *Slow Ark*, 1: 47–51.

Bolt Rasmussen, M. (2002), 'Art and Politics after September 11: Exodus, Intervention or Hospitality?' *Third Text*, 16 (4): 345–55.

Boreham, T., Ellicott, J. and Jimenez, C. (2001), 'Right family-work balance makes a father's day', *The Australian*, 3 September: 5.

Bourdieu, P. (1984), *Distinction: A Social Critique of the Judgement of Taste*, trans. R. Nice, London: Routledge.

—— (2000), *Pascalian Meditations*, trans. R. Nice, Stanford: Stanford University Press.

Bové, J. (2001), 'A Farmers' International?' *New Left Review* 12: 89–101.

Brann, E. (1999), *What Then is Time?* Oxford: Rowman & Littlefield.

Breakspear, C. and Hamilton, C. (2004), *Getting a Life: Understanding the downshifting phenomenon in Australia*, Discussion Paper No. 62, Canberra: The Australia Institute.

Brodie, J. (2000), 'Imagining democratic urban citizenship', in E. F. Isin (ed.), *Democracy, Citizenship and the Global City*, London: Routledge.

Burkitt, I. (2004), 'The Time and Space of Everyday Life', *Cultural Studies*, 18 (2/3): 211–27.

Capatti, A. (1996), 'In Praise of Rest', *Slow*, 2: 5–7.

—— (2001), 'Food Planet', *Slow*, 24: 4–6.

—— (2002a), 'Bad blood?' *Slow*, 2: 4–7.

—— (2002b) 'Fusion cooking', *Slow*, 5: 4–5.

—— (2002c), 'No, I won't eat my soup!' *Slow*, 7: 4–5.

—— and Montanari, M. (2003), *Italian Cuisine: A Cultural History*, trans. A. O'Healy, New York: Columbia University Press.

Capo, E. (1995), 'Transformation and development in Italian rural society', *Sociologia Ruralis*, 35 (3/4): 297–308.

Castells, M. (1996), *The Rise of Network Society (The Information Age: Economy, Society and Culture, Vol. 1)*, Malden, MA: Blackwell.

Ceccarelli, D. (1996), 'The Art of Coming Last', *Slow*, 1: 42–5.

Chaney, D. (1996), *Lifestyles*. London: Routledge.

—— (2002), *Cultural Change and Everyday Life*, Basingstoke: Palgrave.

Chapman, T. (2001), 'There's No Place Like Home', *Theory, Culture and Society*, 18 (6): 135–146.

Charles, N. and M. Kerr (1988), *Women, Food and Families*, Manchester: Manchester University Press.

Chrzan, J. (2002), 'Nutrition education in the US', *Slow*, 7: 22– 7.

—— (2004), 'Slow Food: What, Why, and to Where?' *Food, Culture and Society*, 7 (2): 117–32.

Cimicchi, S. (2003), personal interview, trans. M. Borri, Orvieto, Italy.

Cleveland, J. W. (2003), 'Does the New Middle Class Lead Today's Social Movements?' *Critical Sociology*, 29 (2): 163–88.

Cohen, R. and Rai, S. (2000), *Global Social Movements*, London: Athlone Press.

Connolly, W. E. (1999), *Why I Am Not a Secularist*, Minneapolis: University of Minnesota Press.

Counihan, C. M. (1999), *The Anthropology of Food and Body: Gender, Meaning, and Power*, New York: Routledge.

—— (2004), *Around the Tuscan Table: Food, Family, and Gender in Twentieth-Century Florence*, New York: Routledge.

Craib, I. (1992), *Anthony Giddens*. London: Routledge.

Craig, G. (2002), 'The Spectacle of the Street: an analysis of media coverage of protests at the 2000 Melbourne World Economic Forum (WEF)', *Australian Journal of Communication*, 29 (1): 39–52.

—— (2003), 'New Media Technologies and the making of the new global journalist', *Transformations*, 7, http://transformations.cqu.edu.au/journal/issue_07/article_04.shtml

—— (2004), *The Media, Politics and Public Life*, Crows Nest, NSW: Allen & Unwin.

Crang, M. (2001), 'Rhythms of the city; temporalized space and motion', in J. May and N. Thrift (eds), *Timespace: Geographies of Temporality*, London: Routledge.

Crossley, N. (2003), 'Even Newer Social Movements? Anti-Corporate Protests, Capitalist Crises and the Remoralization of Society', *Organization*, 10 (2): 287–305.

Crouch, M. and O'Neill, G. (2000), 'Sustaining Identities? Prolegomena for inquiry into contemporary foodways', *Social Science Information*, 39 (1): 181–92.

Cullens, C. (1999), 'Gimme Shelter: At Home with the Millennium', *Differences*, 11 (2): 204–27.

Curtin, D. W. (1992), 'Recipes for Values', in D. W. Curtin and L. M. Heldke (eds), *Cooking, Eating, Thinking: Transformative Philosophies of Food*, Bloomington: Indiana University Press.

Curtis, K. (1999), *Our Sense of the Real: Aesthetic Experience and Arendtian Politics*, Ithaca: Cornell University Press.

Davies, K. (2001), 'Responsibility and daily life: reflections over timespace', in J. May and N. Thrift (eds), *Timespace: Geographies of Temporality*, London: Routledge.

Day, S. (2003), 'Rip! Zap! Ding! It's a Classic 6–Minute Pot Roast', *New York Times*, 19/4/03: C.1.

de Certeau, M. (1984), *The Practice of Everyday Life*, trans. S. Rendall, Berkeley: University of California Press.

Deem, R. (1996), 'No Time for a Rest? An exploration of women's work, engendered leisure and holidays', *Time and Society*, 5 (1): 5–25.

Der Hovanesian, M. (2003), 'Zen and the Art of Corporate Productivity: More companies are battling employee stress with meditation', *Business Week*, 28/7/03, Issue 3843: 56.

Derrida, J. (1999), *Adieu to Emmanuel Levinas*, Palo Alto: Stanford University Press.

DeVault, M (1991), *Feeding the Family: The Social Organization of Caring as Gendered Work*, Chicago: University of Chicago Press.

Dickie, J. (1996), 'Imagined Italies', in D. Forgacs and R. Lumley (eds), *Italian Cultural Studies*, Oxford: Oxford University Press.

di Croce, P. and LaValva, R. (2003), 'Slow Food in Brazil,' *The Snail: Slow Food USA Newsletter*, Issue 3: 50–1.

Dimock, M. (2003), 'Why a Slow Constitution Anyway?' *The Snail: Slow Food USA Newsletter*, Issue 3: 12–13.

Dirlik, A. (1996), 'Global in the Local', in R. Wilson and W. Dissanayake (eds), *Global/Local: Cultural Production and the Transnational Imaginary*, Durham, NC: Duke University Press.

—— (1997), *The Postcolonial Aura: Third World Criticism in the Age of Global Capitalism*, Boulder, CO: Westview.

Donati, K. (2004), 'Ethics and Activism: An Analysis of Diversity and Pleasure in the Philosophy of the Slow Food Movement', unpublished dissertation.

Ducasse, A. (2004), 'The Slow Revolutionary', *Time*, 164 (14), www.time.com/time/europe/hero2004/petrini.html, accessed 11 October, 2004.

Dumm, T. L. (1999), *A Politics of the Ordinary*, New York: New York University Press.

Dusi, I. (2001), *Vanilla Beans and Brodo: Real Life in the Hills of Tuscany*, London: Simon & Schuster.

Edible Schoolyard (2004), 'Mission statement', http://www.edibleschoolyard.org, accessed 15 May.

Edwards, G. (2004), 'Habermas and social movements: what's new?' *Sociological Review*, 52 (1): 113–31.

Emmison, M. (1983), '"The economy": its emergence in media discourse', in H. David and P. Watson (eds), *Language, Image, Media*, London: Basil Blackwell.

Eriksen, T. H. (2001), *Tyranny of the Moment: Fast and Slow Time in the Information Age*, London: Pluto Press.

Escobar, A. (2001), 'Culture sits in places: reflections on globalism and subaltern strategies of localization', *Political Geography*, 20 (2): 149–74.

Etzioni, A. (1998), 'Voluntary Simplicity: Characterization, select psychological implications, and societal consequences', *Journal of Economic Psychology*, 19: 619–43.

'Europe finds work ethic' (2004), *The West Australian*, July 17: 22.

'Evaluating the Economic Impact of the Slow Food Presidia in Italy' (2004), accessed 15 May.

Falasca-Zamponi, S. (2002), 'Peeking Under the Black Shirt: Italian Fascism's Disembodied Bodies', in W. Parkins (ed.), *Fashioning the Body Politic: Dress, Gender, Citizenship*, Oxford: Berg.

Falk, P. (1994), *The Consuming Body*, London: Sage.

Falk, R. (1993), 'The Making of Global Citizenship', in J. Brecher, J. B. Childs and J. Cutler (eds), *Global Visions: Beyond the New World Order*, Boston: South End Press.

Featherstone, M. (1992), 'Postmodernism and the Aestheticization of Everyday Life,' in S. Lash and J. Friedman (eds), *Modernity and Identity*, Oxford: Blackwell.

—— (2002), 'Cosmopolis: An Introduction', *Theory, Culture and Society*, 19 (1–2): 1–16.

Felski, R. (1999–2000), 'The Invention of Everyday Life', *New Formations*, 39: 15–31.

—— (2002), 'Introduction', Special Issue on Everyday Life, *New Literary History*, 33: 607–22.

Fernald, A. (2003), personal interview, Bra, Italy, 3 April.

Finkelstein, J. (1999), 'Rich Food: McDonald's and Modern Life,' in B. Smart (ed.), *Resisting McDonaldization*, London: Sage.

Fischler, C. (1980), 'Food habits, social change and the nature/culture dilemma', *Social Science Information*, 19 (6): 937–53.

Fisher, P. (1998), *Wonder, the Rainbow and the Aesthetics of Rare Experiences*, Harvard: Harvard University Press.

Fitzpatrick, T. (2004), 'Social Policy and Time', *Time and Society*, 13 (2/3): 197–219.

Florida, R. (2003), *The Rise of the Creative Class: And How It's Transforming Work, Leisure, Community and Everyday Life*, North Melbourne: Pluto Press.

Foroohar, R. (2001), 'Eat, Drink and Go Slow', *Newsweek*, July 2: 20–4.

Foucault, M. (1985), *The Use of Pleasure. The History of Sexuality: Volume 2*, trans. R. Hurley, London: Penguin.

Freud, S. (1999/1905), 'Infantile Sexuality,' in P. Gay (ed.), *The Freud Reader*, London: Vintage.

Gardiner, M. (2000), *Critiques of Everyday Life*, London: Routledge.

Gaytán, M. S. (2004), 'Globalizing Resistance: Slow Food and New Local Imaginaries', *Food, Culture and Society*, 7 (2): 97–116.

Gervais, P. (2000), *A Garden in Lucca*, Harmondsworth: Penguin.

Gho, P. (2002), 'Presidium Inflation', *Slow,* 5: 32–5.

Giard, L. (1998), 'Doing-Cooking', in M. de Certeau, L. Giard and P. Mayol, *The Practice of Everyday Life. Volume 2: Living and Cooking*, trans. T. J. Tomasik, Minneapolis: University of Minnesota Press.

Giddens, A. (1990), *The Consequences of Modernity*, Cambridge: Polity.

—— (1991), *Modernity and Self-Identity: Self and Society in the Late Modern Age*, Stanford: Stanford University Press.

—— (1994), 'Living in a Post-Traditional Society', in U. Beck, A. Giddens and S. Lash, *Reflexive Modernization: Politics, Tradition and Aesthetics in the Modern Social Order*, Cambridge: Polity.

—— (2000), *The Third Way and its Critics*, Cambridge: Polity.

Ginsborg, P. (2001), *Italy and Its Discontents: Family, Civil Society, State 1980–2001*, London: Penguin.

Gleick, J. (1999), *Faster: The Acceleration of Just About Everything*, New York: Pantheon Books.

Goodman, J. (ed.) (2002), *Protest and Globalization: Prospects for Transnational Solidarity*, Sydney: Pluto.

Gottschalk, S. (1999), 'Speed Culture: Fast Strategies in Televised Commercial Ads', *Qualitative Sociology*, 22 (4): 311–29.

Graham, L. D. (1999), 'Domesticating Efficiency: Lillian Gilbreth's Scientific Management of Homemakers, 1924–1930', *Signs*, 24 (3): 633–75.

Greg. W. R. (1877), *Literary and Social Judgments*, London: Trubner.

Green, F. (2001), 'It's Been A Hard Day's Night: The Concentration and Intensification of Work in Late Twentieth-Century Britain', *British Journal of Industrial Relations*, 39 (1): 53–80.

Griffith, R. M. (2001), 'Don't Eat That: The Erotics of Abstinence in American Christianity', *Gastronomica*, 1 (4): 36–47.

—— (2004), *Born Again Bodies: Flesh and Spirit in American Christianity*, Berkeley: University of California Press.

Grossberg, L. (2000), '(Re)con-figuring Space: Defining a Project', *Space and Culture*, 4–5: 13–22.

Guthman, J. (2003), 'Fast food/organic food: reflexive tastes and the making of "yuppie chow",' *Social and Cultural Geography*, 4 (1): 45–58.

Habermas, J. (1987), *The Theory of Communicative Action. Volume 2. Lifeworld and System: A Critique of Functionalist Reason*, trans. T. McCarthy, Cambridge: Polity Press.

Hale, J. (2004), personal interview, Barossa Valley, Australia, 4 April.

Hall, S. (1996), 'The Question of Cultural Identity', in S. Hall et al. (eds), *Modernity*, London: Blackwell.

Hamilton, C. (2003), *Downshifting in Britain: A sea-change in the pursuit of happiness*, Discussion Paper No. 58, Canberra: The Australia Institute.

—— and Mail, E. (2003), *Downshifting in Australia: A sea-change in the pursuit of happiness*, Discussion Paper No. 50, Canberra: The Australia Institute.

Hannerz, U. (1990), 'Cosmopolitans and Locals in World Culture', *Theory, Culture and Society*, 7: 237–51.

Haraway, D. J. (1991), *Simians, Cyborgs, and Women: The Reinvention of Nature*, London: Free Association Books.

Harris, D. (2000), *Cute, Quaint, Hungry and Romantic: The Aesthetics of Consumerism*, New York: Basic Books.

Harris, L. (2003), 'The Seductions of Food', *Wilson Quarterly*, 27 (3): 52–60.

Harvey, D. (1989), *The Condition of Postmodernity: An Enquiry into the Origins of Cultural Change*, Oxford: Blackwell.

—— (2000), *Spaces of Hope*, Edinburgh: Edinburgh University Press.

Hawes, A. (2001), *Extra Virgin*, London: Penguin.

Hay, D. (1999), *Marie Claire Food Fast*, Sydney: Murdoch Books.

Heiman, R. J. (2001), 'The ironic contradictions in the discourse on Generation X, or how "slacker" are saving capitalism', *Childhood*, 8 (2): 274–292.

Heldke, L. M. (1992,) 'Foodmaking as a Thoughtful Practice', in D. W. Curtin and L. M. Heldke (eds), *Cooking, Eating, Thinking: Transformative Philosophies of Food*, Bloomington: Indiana University Press.

—— (2003), *Exotic Appetites: Ruminations of a Food Adventurer*, New York: Routledge.

Heller, A. (1984), *Everyday Life*, trans. G. L. Campbell, London: Routledge and Kegan Paul.

Helstosky, C. (2004), *Garlic and Oil: Politics and Food in Italy*, Oxford: Berg.

Hendrickson, M. K. and Heffernan, W. D. (2002), 'Opening Spaces through Relocalization: Locating Potential Resistance in the Weaknesses of the Global Food System', *Sociologia Ruralis*, 42 (4): 347–69.

Hermsen, J. J. (1999), 'The Impersonal and the Other', *European Journal of Women's Studies*, 6 (2): 183–200.

Highmore, B. (2002), *Everyday Life and Cultural Theory: An Introduction*, London: Routledge.

—— (2004), 'Homework: Routine, social aesthetics and the ambiguity of everyday life', *Cultural Studies*, 18 (2/3): 306–27.

Hines, C., Lucas, C. and Shiva, V. (2002), 'Local Food, Global Solution', *The Ecologist*, 32 (5): 38–40.

Hirschman, A. O. (1982), *Shifting Involvements: Private Interest and Public Action*, Princeton: Princeton University Press.

Hjalager, A.-M. and Richards, G. (eds) (2002), *Tourism and Gastronomy*, London: Routledge.

Hochschild, A. R. (1997), *The Time Bind: When Work Becomes Home and Home Becomes Work*, New York: Metropolitan Books.

—— (2003), *The Commercialization of Intimate Life: Notes from Home and Work*, Berkeley: University of California Press.

Hoggett, P. (2001), 'Agency, Rationality and Social Policy', *Journal of Social Policy*, 30 (1): 37–56.

Hollows, J. (2003), 'Feeling like a domestic goddess: Postfeminism and cooking', *European Journal of Cultural Studies*, 6 (2): 179–202.

Honig, B. (1996), 'Differences, Dilemmas, and the Politics of Home', in S. Benhabib (ed.), *Democracy and Difference: Contesting the Boundaries of the Political*, Princeton: Princeton University Press.

Honoré, C. (2004), *In Praise of Slow: How a Worldwide Movement is Challenging the Cult of Speed*, London: Orion.

hooks, b. (1992), 'Eating the Other: Desire and Resistance', *Black Looks: Race and Representation*, Boston: South End Press.

Horkheimer, M. and Adorno, T. W. (1982/1944), *Dialectic of Enlightenment*, trans. J. Cumming, New York: Continuum.

Hornby, N. (1998), *About a Boy*, London: Penguin.

Howes, D. (2005), 'Hyperesthesia, or, The Sensual Logic of Late Capitalism', in D. Howes (ed.), *Empire of the Senses: The Sensual Culture Reader*, Oxford: Berg.

Humphery, K. (1998), *Shelf Life: Supermarkets and the Changing Cultures of Consumption*, Cambridge: Cambridge University Press.

Inda, J. X. and Rosaldo, R. (2002), 'Introduction: A World in Motion', in J. X. Inda and R. Rosaldo (eds), *The Anthropology of Globalization: A Reader*, Malden, MA: Blackwell.

'Interview: Carlo Petrini', (2004) *The Ecologist*, April, 34 (3): 50–3.

Irigaray, L. (1993), *An Ethics of Sexual Difference*, trans. C. Burke and G. C. Gill, Ithaca: Cornell University Press.

Irving, J. (2003), personal interview, Bra, Italy, 3 April.

Jackson, P., Crang, P. and Dwyer, C. (2004), 'Introduction: the spaces of transnationality', in P. Jackson, P. Crang and C. Dwyer (eds), *Transnational Spaces*, London: Routledge.

James, A. (1996), 'Cooking the Books: Global or local identities in contemporary British food cultures?' in D. Howes (ed.), *Cross-Cultural Consumption: Global markets, local realities*, London: Routledge.

Jarvis, R. (1997), *Romantic Writing and Pedestrian Travel*, Basingstoke: Houndsmills.

Jennings, J. and Haughton, L. (2002), *It's Not the Big that Eat the Small, But the Fast that Eat the Slow: How to Use Speed as a Competitive Tool in Business*, New York: HarperCollins.

Jones, S. and Taylor, B. (2001), 'Food writing and food cultures: The case of Elizabeth David and Jane Grigson', *European Journal of Cultural Studies*, 4 (2): 171–88.

Keane, A. and Willetts, A. (1995), *Concepts of Healthy Eating: An Anthropological Investigation in South East London*, London: Goldsmiths' College.

Kearney, M. (1995), 'The Local and the Global: The Anthropology of Globalization and Transnationalism', *Annual Review of Anthropology*, 24: 547–65.

Keith, M. and Pile, S. (eds) (1993), *Place and the Politics of Identity*, London: Routledge.

Kern, S. (1983), *The Culture of Time and Space 1880–1930*, Cambridge: Harvard University Press.

Kidd, G. (2004), 'Cittaslow for Ludlow', *Snail Mail*, 4: 4–5.

Kloppenburg, J., Hendrickson, J. and Stevenson, G. W. (1996), 'Coming into the Foodshed', in W. Vitek and W. Jackson (eds), *Rooted in the Land: Essays on Community and Place*, New Haven: Yale University Press.

Knox, P. L. (2005), 'Creating Ordinary Places: Slow Cities in a Fast World', *Journal of Urban Design*, 10 (1): 1–11.

Kriener, M. (2002), 'No more sandwiches!' *Slow*, 5: 82–5.

Kristeller, J. L. and Hallett, C. B. (1999), 'An Exploratory Study of a Meditation-based Intervention for Binge Eating Disorder', *Journal of Health Psychology*, 4 (3): 35–63.

Kummer, C. (2002), *The Pleasures of Slow Food: Celebrating Authentic Traditions, Flavours, and Recipes*, San Francisco: Chronicle Books.

Künast, R. (2004), 'Enjoying life', *Slow*, 1: 78–9.

Labelle, J. (2004), 'A Recipe for Connectedness: Bridging Production and Consumption with Slow Food', *Food, Culture and Society*, 7 (2): 81–96.

La Caze, M. (2002), 'The Encounter Between Wonder and Generosity', *Hypatia*, 17 (3): 1–19.

Langbauer, L. (1992), 'Cultural Studies and the Politics of the Everyday', *Diacritics*, 22 (1): 47–65.

Lappe, M. and Bailey, B. (1999), *Against the Grain: The Genetic Transformation of Global Agriculture*, London: Earthscan Publications.

Laudan, R. (2001), 'A Plea for Culinary Modernism: Why We Should Love New, Fast, Processed Food', *Gastronomica*, 1 (1): 36–44.

—— (2004), 'Slow Food: The French Terroir Strategy, and Culinary Modernism', *Food, Culture and Society*, 7 (2): 133–43.

Lawson, N. (1999), 'Gastroporn', *Talk*, October: 153–4.

Leavis, F. R. and Thompson, D. (1942/1932), *Culture and Environment: The Training of Critical Awareness*, London: Chatto and Windus.

Lefebvre, H. (1991/1958), *Critique of Everyday Life*, trans. J. Moore, New York: Verso.

—— (2000/1971), *Everyday Life in the Modern World*, trans. S. Rabinovitch, London: Athlone Press.

—— (2004), *Rhythmanalysis: Space, Time and Everyday Life*, trans. S. Elden and G. Moore, London: Continuum.

Leitch, A. (2003), 'Slow Food and the Politics of Pork Fat: Italian Food and European Identity', *Ethnos*, 68 (4): 437–62.

Levinas, E. (1986), 'Dialogue with Emmanuel Levinas', in R. Cohen (ed.), *Face to Face with Levinas*, New York: SUNY Press: 13–34.

—— (1989), 'Time and the Other', in S. Hand (ed.), *The Levinas Reader*, Oxford: Blackwell: 37–58.

—— (1998), *Entre Nous: On Thinking of the Other*, trans. M. Smith and B. Harshav, New York: Columbia University Press.

Levine, R. (1997), *A Geography of Time*, New York: Basic Books.

—— and Bartlett K. (1984), 'Pace of life, punctuality and coronary heart disease in six countries', *Journal of Cross-Cultural Psychology*, 15: 233–55.

—— and Norenzayan, A. (1999), 'The Pace of Life in 31 Countries', *Journal of Cross-Cultural Psychology*, 30 (2) : 178–205.

Levy, C. (ed.) (1996), *Italian Regionalism: History, Identity and Politics*, Oxford: Berg.

Lupton, D. (1999), *Risk*, London: Routledge.

Lyon, J. (1999), *Manifestoes: Provocations of the Modern*, Ithaca: Cornell University Press.

McBride, S. (2003), 'Slow Food: Eating well and doing it right', *International Herald Tribune*, November 18, www.slowfood.com/eng, accessed 17 March 2004.

McCarthy, J. and Zald, M. (1977), 'Resource mobilization and social movements', *American Journal of Sociology*, 82 (6): 1212–41.

McCarthy, M. and Kirby, T. (2004), 'Slow Food: More taste, less speed,' *The Independent*, 1 April, http://news.independent.co.uk/uk/environment/story.jsp?story=507154

McLaughlin, L. (2004), 'Feminism and the political economy of transnational public space', *Sociological Review* 52 (1): 156–75.

McMahon, M. (2002), 'Resisting Globalization: Women Organic Farmers and Local Food Systems', *Canadian Women's Studies*, 21 (4): 203–6.

Madison, D. (2001), 'Foreword', in C. Petrini, B. Watson and Slow Food Editore (eds), *Slow Food: Collected Thoughts on Taste, Tradition, and the Honest Pleasures of Food*, White River Junction, Vermont: Chelsea Green Publishing Company.

Maffesoli, M. (1989), 'The Sociology of Everyday Life (Epistemological Elements)', *Current Sociology*, 37 (1): 1–16.

Maniates, M. (2002a), 'Individualization: Plant a Tree, Buy a Bike, Save the World?' in T. Princen, M. Maniates and K. Conca (eds), *Confronting Consumption*, Cambridge, Mass.: MIT Press.

—— (2002b), 'In Search of Consumptive Resistance: The Voluntary Simplicity Movement', in T. Princen, M. Maniates and K. Conca (eds), *Confronting Consumption*, Cambridge, Mass.: MIT Press.

Marinetti, F. T. (1989/1932), *The Futurist Cookbook*, trans. S. Brill, San Francisco: Bedford Arts.

Marx, K. (1993/1939–41), *Grundrisse*, trans. M. Nicolaus, London: Penguin/New Left Review.

Massey, D. (1994a), 'Double Articulation: A Place in the World,' in A. Bammer (ed.), *Displacements: Cultural Identities in Question*, Bloomington: Indiana University Press.

—— (1994b), *Space, Place and Gender*, Cambridge: Polity.

—— (1995), 'Places and Their Pasts', *History Workshop Journal*, 39: 182–192.

Matè, F. (1998), *The Hills of Tuscany: A New Life in an Old Land*, New York: Delta.

May, J. and Thrift, N. (eds) (2001), *Timespace: Geographies of temporality*, New York: Routledge.

Mayes, F. (1996), *Under the Tuscan Sun: At Home in Italy*, New York: Broadway Books.

Mayle, P. (1989), *A Year in Provence*, London: Penguin.

Mayo, C. (2003) 'Riker's Island Garden Project', *The Snail: Slow Food USA Newsletter*,

Issue 3: 79.

Melucci, A. (1988), 'Social Movements and the Democratization of Everyday Life', in J. Keane (ed.), *Civil Society and the State: New European Perspectives*, London: Verso.

—— (1989), N*omads of the Present: Social Movements and Individual Needs in Contemporary Society*, ed. J. Keane and P. Mier, London: Hutchinson Radius.

—— (1996a), 'Individual experience and global issues in a planetary society', *Social Science Information*, 35 (3): 485–509.

—— (1996b), *The Playing Self: Person and meaning in the planetary society*, Cambridge: Cambridge University Press.

—— (1998), 'Inner Time and Social Time in a World of Uncertainty', *Time and Society*, 7 (2): 179–191.

Methfessel, B. (2002), 'Learn to know yourself', *Slow,* 7: 14–21.

Meyer, A. (2004), personal interview, Perth, Australia, 7 October.

Miele, M. and Murdoch, J. (2002), 'The Practical Aesthetics of Traditional Cuisines: Slow Food in Tuscany', *Sociologia Ruralis,* 42 (4): 312–328.

Miller, D. (1995), 'Consumption as the Vanguard of History', in D. Miller (ed.), *Acknowledging Consumption*, London: Routledge.

Miller, J. and Schwarz, M. (1998), *Speed: Visions of an Accelerated Age*, London: Photographers' Gallery.

Mintz, S. (1996), *Tasting Food, Tasting Freedom: Excursions into Eating, Culture, and the Past*, Boston: Beacon Press.

Mohanty, C. T. (2002), '"Under Western Eyes" Revisited: Feminist Solidarity through Anticapitalist Struggles', *Signs*, 28 (2): 499–535.

Montanari, M. (1996a), 'Unnatural cooking', *Slow,* 1: 68–71.

—— (1996b), 'Beware!' *Slow,* 2: 56–9.

Montgomery, J. (1997), 'Café Culture and the City: The role of pavement cafes in urban public social life', *Journal of Urban Design*, 2 (1): 83–102.

Morris, M. (1988), 'Banality in Cultural Studies', *Discourse*, 10: 3–29.

Murcott, A. (1997), 'Family meals – a thing of the past?' in P. Caplan (ed.), *Food, Health and Identity*, London: Routledge.

Murdock, D. (2003), 'That Stubborn "Doing Good?" Question: Ethical/Epistemological Concerns in the Study of NGOs', *Ethnos*, 68 (4): 507–32.

Murray Berzok, L. (2002), 'US women, fat and sex', *Slow,* 4: 22–31.

Nabhan, G. (2002), *Coming Home to Eat. The Pleasures and Politics of Local Foods*, New York: W.W. Norton and Co.

Nash, K. (2000), *Contemporary Political Sociology: Globalization, Politics and Power*, Malden, MA: Blackwell.

Needham, P. (2004), 'Give and Take', *The Weekend Australian*, Weekend Travel and Indulgence, May 15–16: 9.

Nemeroff, C. J. and Graham, C. C. (2002), 'From guele to guilt', *Slow,* 4: 14–21.

Neocleous, M. (1999), 'Radical conservatism, or, the conservatism of radicals: Giddens, Blair and the politics of reaction', *Radical Philosophy*, 93 (Jan/Feb): 24–34.

Nowotny, H. (1994), *Time: The Modern and Postmodern Experience*, trans. N. Plaice, Cambridge: Polity Press.

Ochs, E., Pontecorvo, C. and Fasulo, A. (1996), 'Socializing Taste', *Ethnos,* 61 (1–2): 7–46.

Offe, C. (1985), 'New Social Movements: Challenging the Boundaries of Institutional Politics', *Social Research*, 52 (4): 817–68.

O'Neill, P. and Whatmore, S. (2000), 'The business of place: networks of property, partnership and produce', *Geoforum*, 31: 121–36.

Osborne, P. (1992), 'Modernity is a Qualitative, Not a Chronological Category', *New Left Review*, 192: 65–84.

Ostrow, R. (2003), 'In fitness and in health', *Weekend Australian Magazine*, Nov. 8–9: 32–3.

Parasecoli, F. (2003), 'Postrevolutionary Chowhounds: Food, Globalization, and the Italian Left', *Gastronomica*, 3 (3): 29–39.

Parker, A. (2001), *Seasons in Tuscany: A Tale of Two Loves*, Auckland: Penguin.

Parkins, W. (2004a), 'At Home in Tuscany: Slow Living and the Cosmopolitan Subject', *Home Cultures*, 1 (3): 257–74.

—— (2004b), 'Celebrity Knitting and the Temporality of Postmodernity', *Fashion Theory*, 8 (1): 1–18.

Passerini, L. (1996), 'Gender Relations,' in D. Forgacs and R. Lumley (eds), *Italian Cultural Studies: An Introduction*, Oxford: Oxford University Press.

Paul, C. (2003), 'Farmers' Markets', *Practical Hydroponics and Greenhouses*, 68, http://www.hydroponics.com.au/back_issues/issue68.html, accessed 6 October, 2004.

Pearson, A. (2002), *I Don't Know How She Does It*, London: Chatto and Windus.

Perullo, N. (2003), 'Total education,' *Slow*, 2: 98–101.

Petrini, C. (1996), 'In Praise of Slowness', *Slow*, 1 (1): 7–8.

—— (1997) 'Building the Ark,' *Slow*, 5: 8–11.

—— (2001), *Slow Food: The Case for Taste*, trans. W. McCuaig, New York: Columbia University Press.

—— (2004a), 'The Slow Dreamers', *Slow*, 1: 10–13.

—— (2004b), 'The Gourmet's Return', *Slow*, 2: 6–9.

—— (2005), 'Three Ideas, One Project', *Slow*, 1: 6–7.

Phillips, A. (1998), *The Beast in the Nursery*, London: Faber & Faber.

—— (2000), 'Being Alive: Interview with Adam Phillips', in J. Rutherford (ed.) *The Art of Life: On Living, Loving and Death*, London: Lawrence and Wishart.

Pine, J. and Gilmore, J. H. (1999), *The Experience Economy: Work is Theatre and Every Business a Stage*, Boston: Harvard Business School Press.

Portinari, F. (1996), 'The Labour of the Seventh Day', *Slow*, 2: 8–11.

—— (1997), 'Numbered Thoughts', *Slow*, 5: 22–3.

Pretty, J. (1998), *The Living Land: Agriculture, Food and Community Regeneration in Rural Europe*, London: Earthscan Publications.

—— (2002), *Agri-Culture: Reconnecting People, Land and Nature*, London: Earthscan Publications.

Probyn, E. (1998), 'McIdentities: Food and the Familial Citizen', *Theory, Culture and Society*, 15 (2): 155–73.

—— (2000), *Carnal Appetites: Food Sex Identities*, London: Routledge.

Purdue, D. A. (2000), *Anti-GenetiX: The emergence of the anti-GM movement*, Aldershot: Ashgate.

—— Dürrschmidt, J., Jowers, P. and O'Doherty, R. (1997), 'DIY culture and extended milieux: LETS, veggie boxes and festivals', *The Sociological Review*, 45 (4): 645–67.

Raffoul, F. (1998), 'On Hospitality, between Ethics and Politics', *Research in Phenomenology*, 28: 274–83.

Ranald, P. (2000), *The Case For Fair Trade: A citizen's guide to the World Trade Organization*, Sydney: Australian Fair Trade and Investment Network.

'Reduce Work', (2002), *New Internationalist*, March: 25.

Reisch, L. A. (2001), 'Time and Wealth: The role of time and temporalities for sustainable patterns of consumption', *Time & Society*, 10 (2/3): 367–85.

Revel, J.-F. (1992), 'From *Culture and Cuisine*,' in D. W. Curtin and L. M. Heldke (eds), *Cooking, Eating, Thinking: Transformative Philosophies of Food*, Bloomington: Indiana University Press.

Riley, D. (2002), 'The Right to Be Lonely', *Differences,* 13 (1): 1–13.

Ripe, C. (2001), 'Slow Food marches on', *The Australian*, 4/1/01: 13.

Robertson, R. (1995), 'Glocalization: Time-Space and Homogeneity-Heterogeneity', in M. Featherstone, S. Lash and R. Robertson (eds), *Global Modernities*, London: Sage.

Robinson, J. P. and Godbey, G. (1997), *Time for Life: The surprising ways Americans use their time*, University Park: Pennsylvania State University Press.

Rojek, C. (2001), 'Leisure and Life Politics', *Leisure Sciences*, 23: 115–25.

Rose, N. (2000), 'Governing cities, governing citizens', in E. F. Isin (ed.), *Democracy, Citizenship and the Global City*, London: Routledge.

Ross, K. (1995), *Fast Cars, Clean Bodies: Decolonization and Reordering of French Culture,* Cambridge: MIT Press.

Rozin, P. (1999), 'Food is Fundamental, Fun, Frightening, and Far-Reaching', *Social Research,* 66 (1): 9–30.

Rucht, D. and Neidhardt, F. (2002), 'Towards a "Movement Society"? On the possibilities of institutionalizing social movements', *Social Movement Studies* 1 (1): 7–30.

Ruffa, G. (2002), 'Solid coffee', *Slow,* 7: 112–15.

Runté, M. and Mills, A. J. (2004), 'Paying the Toll: A Feminist Post-structural Critique of the Discourse Bridging Work and Family', *Culture and Organization* 10 (3): 237–49.

Rutherford, J. (ed.) (2000), *The Art of Life: On Living, Loving and Dying*, London: Lawrence and Wishart.

Salone del Gusto (2002), Official Program, Bra: Slow Food Editore.

'Salone del Gusto, 24–28th October 2002, Turin, Italy,' (2003), *Snail Mail: Slow Food UK*, 1: 3–4.

Sandilands, C. (1999), *The Good-Natured Feminist: Ecofeminism and the Quest for Democracy*, Minneapolis: University of Minnesota Press.

Santich, B. (1996), 'Introduction to sustaining gastronomy', in B. Santich et al. (eds), *Proceedings of the Eighth Symposium of Australian Gastronomy,* Adelaide: University of Adelaide.

—— (2002), 'Inevitable, yes, but desirable?' *Slow,* 7: 88–90.

Saraceno, C. (1991), 'Changes in Life-Course Patterns and Behaviour of Three Cohorts of Italian Women', *Signs,* 16 (3): 502–21.

Saraceno, E. (1994), 'Alternative readings of spatial differentiation: The rural versus the local economy approach in Italy', *European Review of Agricultural Economics*, 21: 451–74.

Sardo, P. (2003), 'A Difficult Challenge,' *Slow Ark*, 3: 140–1.

Sardo, R. (2003), personal interview, Bra, Italy, 3 April.

Sardo, S. (2003), personal interview, Bra, Italy, 2 April.

Saturnini, P. (2003), personal interview, Greve-in-Chianti, Italy.

Scaffidi, C. (2003a), personal interview, Bra, Italy, 3 April.

—— (2003b), '¿Y vos?' *Slow Ark*, 1: 117.

—— (2003c), 'Ethio-Organic Seed Action (EOSA)', PremioSlowFood 2003, Bra: Slow Food Editore, http://www.slowfood.com/img_sito/PREMIO/vincitori2003/pagine_en/Etiopia_03.html (accessed 20 August, 2004).

—— and Kummer, C. (2000), *Slow Food Award Bologna 2000: For the Defence of Biodiversity*, Bra: Slow Food Editore.

Scarpato, R. (2002), 'Sustainable gastronomy as a tourist product', in A.-M. Hjalager and G. Richards (eds), *Tourism and Gastronomy*, London: Routledge.

Schivelbusch, W. (1986), *The Railway Journey: The Industrialization of Time and Space in the Nineteenth Century*, Leamington Spa: Berg.

Schlosser, E. (2001), *Fast Food Nation: What the All-American Meal is Doing to the World*, London: Penguin.

Schneider, M. (1997), 'Tempo Diet: A consideration of food and the quality of life', *Time and Society*, 6 (1): 85–98.

Scholte, J. A. (1997), 'Global Capital and the State', *International Affairs*, 73 (3): 427–52.

Schor, J. (1991), *The Overworked American*, New York: Basic Books.

—— (1998), *The Overspent American: Why we want what we don't need*, New York: Harper Perennial.

Segal, J. M. (1999), *Graceful Simplicity: Toward a Philosophy and Politics of Simple Living*, New York: Henry Holt.

Seigworth, G. J. and Gardiner, M. E. (2004), 'Rethinking Everyday Life: And then nothing turns itself inside out', *Cultural Studies* 19 (2/3): 139–59.

Seremetakis, C. N. (1994), 'The Memory of the Senses, Part I: Marks of the Transitory', in C. N. Seremetakis (ed.), *The Senses Still: Perception and Memory as Material Culture in Modernity*, Chicago: University of Chicago Press.

Shaw, J. (2001), '"Winning territory": changing place to change pace', in J. May and N. Thrift (eds), *Timespace: Geographies of Temporality*, London: Routledge.

Shi, D. E. (1985), *The Simple Life: Plain Living and High Thinking in American Culture*, Oxford: Oxford University Press.

Shiva, V. (1997), *Biopiracy: The plunder of nature and knowledge*, Boston, MA: South End Press.

—— (2000), 'A Global Perspective', *The Ecologist*, 30 (4): 37.

Simonsen, K. (1996), 'What kind of space in what kind of social theory?' *Progress in Human Geography*, 20 (4): 494–512.

Simpson, T. A. (2000), 'Streets, Sidewalks, Stores, and Stories: Narratives and Uses of Urban Space', *Journal of Contemporary Ethnography*, 29 (6): 682–716.

Sinsheimer, P. (2002), 'It depends what you mean', *Slow*, 5: 24–31.

Slow Food (2002a), Press Release, *Salone del Gusto: The Città Slow Award 2002*, 26 October, www.slowfood.com/eng, accessed 10 April 2004.

—— (2002b), Press Release, *Salone del Gusto: Official Presentation of Osterie d'Italia 2003*, 28 October, www.slowfood.com/eng, accessed 10 April 2004.

—— (2003), Press Release, *Down to Business at the International Congress*, 11 November, www.slowfood.com/eng, accessed 30 November 2003.

Sonnenfeld, A. (2001), 'Series Editor's Introduction' in C. Petrini, *Slow Food: The case for taste*, trans. W. McCuaig, New York: Columbia University Press.

Spigel, L. (1998), 'Seducing the Innocent: Childhood and Television in Postwar America', in H. Jenkins (ed.), *The Children's Culture Reader*, New York: New York University Press.

Starr, A. (2000), *Naming the Enemy: Anti-corporate movements confront globalization*, Sydney: Pluto.

'Starting a New Convivium: The "how to" guide for new convivium leaders', http://www.slowfood.com/eng/sf_ita_mondo/vadeecum.html, accessed 28/4/05.

Stein, J. (2003), 'Just Say Om', *Time*, August 4: 48.

Stevenson, N. (2002), 'Cosmopolitanism and the Future of Democracy: Politics, Culture and the Self', *New Political Economy*, 7 (2): 215–67.

Stewart, S. (2005), 'Remembering the Senses' in D. Howes (ed.), *Empire of the Senses: The Sensual Culture Reader*, Oxford: Berg.

Tabboni, S. (2001), 'The Idea of Social Time in Norbert Elias', *Time and Society*, 10 (1): 5–27.

Tanner, L. (2003), *Crowded Lives*, North Melbourne: Pluto Press.

Taylor, W. (2004), personal interview, Barossa Valley, Australia, 4 April.

'*Terra Madre*: World Meeting of Food Communities' (2004), brochure, Bra: Slow Food Editore.

Terrio, S. J. (2000), *Crafting the Culture and History of French Chocolate*, Berkeley: University of California Press.

Tester, K. (ed.) (2004), *The Flaneur*, London: Routledge.

Thompson, E. P. (1968), *The Making of the English Working Class*, London: Penguin.

Thrift, N. (2000), 'Still Life in Nearly Present Time: The Object of Nature', *Body and Society*, 6 (3/4): 34–57.

—— and Olds, K. (1996), 'Refiguring the economic in economic geography', *Progress in Human Geography*, 20 (3): 311–37.

Time Out (L'emploi du temps), (2001), dir. Laurent Cantet, Miramax.

Tomasik, T. J. (2001), 'Certeau à la Carte: Translating Discursive *Terroir* in *The Practice of Everyday Life: Living and Cooking*', *The South Atlantic Quarterly*, 100 (2): 519–42.

Tomlinson, J. (1999), *Globalization and Culture*, Cambridge: Polity.

Touraine, A. (1981), *The Voice and the Eye: An Analysis of Social Movements*, Cambridge: Cambridge University Press.

—— (2002), 'The Importance of Social Movements', *Social Movement Studies*, 1 (1): 89–95.

Urry, J. (2000), *Sociology beyond Societies: Mobilities for the twenty-first century*, London: Routledge.

Vannini, P. (2002), 'Waiting Dynamics: Bergson, Virilio, Deleuze, and the Experience of Global Times', *Journal of Mundane Behaviour*, 3 (2): 193–208.

Ventura, M. (2002), 'Daring to Eat', *Slow*, 4: 32–7.

Venturi, A. (2002), 'Learn when you're young!' *Slow*, 7: 54–9.

Vercelloni, L. (2002), 'Searching for lost tastes', *Slow*, 5: 6–15.

Virilio, P. (1986a), *Pure War*, New York: Semiotext(e).

—— (1986b), *Speed and Politics*, trans. M. Polizzoti, New York: Semiotext(e).

—— (1991), *The Lost Dimension*, New York: Semiotext(e).

Walker Bynum, C. (1987), *Holy Feast and Holy Fast: The Religious Significance of Food to Medieval Women*, Berkeley: University of California Press.

Warde, A. (1997), *Consumption, Food and Taste: Cultural Antinomies and Commodity Culture*, London: Sage.

—— and Martens, L. (2000), *Eating Out: Social Differentiation, Consumption and Pleasure*, Cambridge: Cambridge University Press.

Weigert, A. (1981) *The Sociology of Everyday Life*, London: Longman.

Weil, S. (1951), *Waiting for God*, trans. E. Craufurd, New York: E.P. Putnam's Sons.

Welsch, W. (1996), 'Aestheticization Processes: Phenomena, Distinctions and Prospects', *Theory, Culture and Society*, 13 (1): 1–24.

Werner, C. M., Altman, I. and Oxley, D. (1985), 'Temporal aspects of homes: A transactional perspective', in I. Altman and C. M. Werner (eds), *Home Environments: Vol. 8 Human Behaviour and Environment: Advances in Theory and Research*, New York: Plenum: 1–32.

Whatmore, S. and Thorne, L. (1997), 'Nourishing Networks: Alternative geographies of food', in D. Goodman and D. Watt (eds), *Globalizing Food*, London: Routledge.

Williams, R. (1973), *The Country and the City*, Oxford: Oxford University Press.

Wilson, E. (1999), 'The Bohemianization of Mass Culture', *International Journal of Cultural Studies*, 2 (1): 11–32.

Yeomans, M. (2002), 'Italy's Slow Cities', *Travel + Leisure*, Sept.: 180–5, 218–20.

Young, I. M. (1990), 'The Ideal of Community and the Politics of Difference', in L. J. Nicholson (ed.), *Feminism/Postmodernism*, New York: Routledge.

—— (1997a), 'Asymmetrical Reciprocity: On Moral Respect, Wonder, and Enlarged Thought', in *Intersecting Voices: Dilemmas of Gender, Political Philosophy and Policy*, Princeton: Princeton University Press.

—— (1997b), 'House and Home: Feminist Variations on a Theme', in *Intersecting Voices: Dilemmas of Gender, Political Philosophy and Policy*, Princeton: Princeton University Press.

—— (2003), 'From Guilt to Solidarity: Sweatshops and Political Responsibility', *Dissent* (Spring): 39–44.

Zerubavel, E. (1981), *Hidden Rhythms: Schedules and Calendars in Social Life*, Chicago: University of Chicago Press.

Websites

http://www.cittaslow.net
http://www.unisg.it/eng
http://www.mindful.canada.com
http://www.simpleliving.net/timeday
http://www.simpleliving.org
http://www.seedsofsimplicity.org
http://www.slowfood.com
http://www.slowfoodfoundation.com
http://www.slowfoodusa.org
http://www.takebackyourtime.org

http://www.viacampesina.org
http://zeitverein.uni-klu.ac.at

Index